SOUP MANUFACTURE

SOUP MANUFACTURE

CANNING, DEHYDRATION
& QUICK-FREEZING

by

Raymond Binsted, F.I.F.S.T., M. Inst M., M. Inst Pkg., L.M.R.S.H., M.R.I.P.H.H.

&

James D. Devey, B.Sc.. A.R.I.C., F.I.F.S.T.

Third Edition
Revised and Enlarged

©

LONDON
FOOD TRADE PRESS LTD
7 Garrick Street, W.C.2

First Edition, 1940
Reprinted 1947
Reprinted 1955
Second Edition, June 1960
Third Edition, May 1970

This book has been set in Baskerville, printed in Great Britain
on White Art paper by Anchor Press, and
bound by Wm. Brendon, both of Tiptree, Essex

AUTHORS' PREFACE

SINCE publication of the second edition of this book much new technical information has become available and has been incorporated in this new edition together with new formulae and illustrations of the latest equipment and machinery for the manufacture, canning and dehydration of all kinds of soups.

In the United Kingdom production of canned soup in 1968 was 273,000 tons, which was an increase over 1966 and 1967 production. The figures for canned soup include condensed soups and all have been calculated on a ready-to-serve basis. Production of soup mixes in 1968 was 25,219 tons. In 1965 production of soup mixes was only 19,687 tons. About 60 per cent of the production of soup mixes is sold to the catering trade, whereas the major part of the canned soup manufactured is used in the home. Imports of canned soups and soup mixes together, which fluctuate from year to year, amount to about 3,500 tons annually. Imports are clearly insignificant compared to total UK production.

In the United Kingdom over 90 per cent of the total production of canned soups is made by three firms and 10 firms make the remainder, some concentrating on 'specialist' soups. Production of soup mixes is confined to 5 large and 10 small firms. Some firms make both types.

The six most popular types of liquid soup (over 80 per cent of production) are: tomato, vegetable, chicken, oxtail, mushroom and Scotch broth. The order of importance of retail soup mix sales is: minestrone and thick vegetable, oxtail, chicken noodle, mushroom, pea and tomato. For the catering trade: tomato, mushroom, minestrone, oxtail, asparagus and leek. In each case the varieties account for more than 60 per cent of the total sales.

Of the annual *per capita* consumption of soup figures, those of Canada lead (in 1964) with 22 lb., USA is second with 18 lb. and the United Kingdom trails far behind with only 11 lb.

The Authors take this opportunity of thanking the many engineers, machinery manufacturers and suppliers for the loan of photographs to illustrate this book and the descriptions and details of their equipment and products they provided, also many thanks to the Editor of *Food Trade Review* for his advice on the manuscript and arrangement of the illustrations.

RAYMOND BINSTED
JAMES D. DEVEY

May 1970

CONTENTS

LIST OF ILLUSTRATIONS

CHAPTER I

HISTORICAL ASPECTS

THIS chapter is not intended as a complete history of soup nor of soup making, but since the information which has been painstakingly gathered is pertinent it was felt that it could well be included.

Archaeologists suggest that broth or soup was the very first form of cookery. Certainly soup is probably one of man's oldest foods, since it must have developed about the time that boiling was found to be a way of cooking food.

Since the previous edition of this book was published the senior author has had a unique opportunity of looking through a collection of very old cookery books in an endeavour to learn something about soups of yesteryear. Some of these books examined dated back to 1672. At that time there were practically no technical books on food but there were quite a number of cookery books. Some of these early cookery books contained recipes and working instructions on the making of broths or soups. The term 'broth' was used more often than 'soup' in these early books and from a study of the recipes some of these were obviously 'thick' and others 'clear'. Some of the authors of early times used the words 'broth' or 'soup' almost interchangeably.

Incidentally, the distinction of being the author of the first cookery book to be printed in Europe is contested for by Coelius Apicius and Johannes-Baptista Platina, both of whom had their books published at the end of the 15th century. Platina's book is mainly a treatise on gastronomy whereas Apicius' work is a true cookery book, which incidentally includes a recipe for Barley Soup.

The first cookery book published in England c 1535 is aptly entitled *This is the Boke of Cokery*. The author is unknown and the only recorded copy is in the possession of the Marquess of Bath.

Another, published in 1545, was entitled *A proper Newe Book of Cookery*. By Stuart times there were quite a number of good cookery books available. In 1638 *Two books of Cookery and Carving* by John Murrell were published.

In 1651 the first of the modern cookery books with recipes in sequence was published; it was written in French by Monsieur de la Varenne. The book was translated into English and published in 1654 as *The French Cook*. Another 17th-century book was *The Accomplist Cook* by Master Cook Robert May. In 1670 a book written by a lady was published, namely *The Queenlike Closet* by Hannah Wolley, 'stored with all manner of rare recipes for preserving, candying and cookery—very pleasant and beneficial to all ingenious of the female sex'. We believe this was the first cookery book by a lady and was the forerunner of later authoress-inspired cookery books, culminating in Mrs. Beeton's opus.

From a survey of the early cookery books it appears that before about 1653 generally it was not known as soup but usually as broth, or sometimes as pottage, brewis, gruel and other names.

The 'mess of pottage' for which Esau sold his birthright was probably what we would to-day call lentil soup, for the flour of dried peas, beans and lentils flavoured with herbs, but not with meat, was for centuries the ordinary daily food of countless labourers and slaves of the ancient empires of Egypt, Greece and Rome.

Later, meat was added, usually in very small amounts. Medieval stock pots were stewed up daily again and again, for weeks, even months, with fresh beef, veal, mutton and marrow bones being added constantly. Such soups were often highly flavoured with various herbs available locally. By modern standards they contained few vegetables. It may come as a surprise to some readers that these soups were often vividly coloured, e.g. with cinnamon or saffron and sometimes thickened, before eating, with crumbled dry bread.

Centuries ago broth was not eaten as it is today. Mostly it was ladled on to a wooden platter or pewter trencher or flat plate as we would call it today, on which one would have put a thick slice of bread. These pieces of bread known as 'soppes' were used to sop up the broth, to facilitate eating it. A number of people have put forward the suggestion that the word soup emanates from the soppes used at that time.

Broth was always served first in ancient times, as it still is, and if you were lucky or rich enough to have meat or poultry to follow, the slices were cut off and added to your broth or pottage as you ate it—no doubt with your fingers or a bifurcated dagger because table cutlery had not yet been introduced.

Later soups were produced from meat, poultry or fish as ingredients in their own right and no doubt different blends of flavouring herbs, etc., were developed to go with them. Wine also was added to improve the flavour.

Eventually, the national soups evolved, based on materials available in that country or area, flavoured with herbs, spices and wines available locally. Only in the present century have these different national soups emigrated around the world so that they are now available in many different countries.

The 18th century provided more than a trickle of cookery books followed by a stream in the 19th century and a torrent of such books in the present century.

Probably the first technical book on food was *The Art of Preserving* by M. Appert, translated from the French and published in London in 1812. This book contained instructions for the production and preservation of all kinds of foods including broth and vegetable soups. One of these descriptions would appear to be the original 'Condensed Soup':

'I compose and prepare a vegetable soup in the usual way; I make the soup so rich, that a bottle of the size of a litre can supply a dish for twelve persons, by adding two litres of water to it, before it is made use of. When it has grown cool I put it in bottles, to give it half-an-hour's boiling in the water bath.'

Later in the book the author claimed that his soups in bottles would keep for two years.

A 'portable soup', made by evaporating meat broth to the consistency of thick glue, was used by the Captain Cook world voyage in 1772. This was probably the same product known as 'traveller's soup' in the 18th century and possibly earlier. The earliest manufactured canned soups were made between 1800 and 1812 by Nicolas Appert in France and by Donkin and Hall in England.

Davidson and Symington took out British Patent 11,947 in 1847 covering the manufacture of dried soup.

From one of the early books we reproduce an interesting description of how to make what could well be described as a 'preserved soup'.

TO MAKE PORTABLE SOUP

Take two legs of beef, about fifty pounds weight, take off all the skin and fat as well as you can, then take all the meat and sinews clean from the bones, which meat put into a large pot, and put to it eight or nine gallons of soft water; first make it boil, then put in twelve anchovies, an ounce of mace, a quarter of an ounce of cloves, an ounce of whole pepper black and white together, six large onions peeled and cut in two, a little bundle of thyme, sweet marjoram, and winter-savoury, the dry hard crust of a two-penny loaf, stir it all together and cover it close, lay a weight on the cover to keep it close down, and let it boil softly for eight or nine hours, then uncover it, and stir together; cover it close again, and let it boil till it is a very rich good jelly, which you will know by taking a little out now and then, and letting it cool. When you think it is a thick jelly, take if off, strain it through a coarse hair bag, and press it hard; then strain it through a hair sieve into a large earthen pan; when it is quite cold, take off the skum and fat, and take the fine jelly clear from the settlings at bottom, and then put the jelly into a large deep well-tinned stew pan. Set it over a stove with a slow fire, keep stirring it often, and take great care it neither sticks to the pan or burns.

When you find the jelly very stiff and thick, as it will be in lumps about the pan, take it out, and put it into large deep china cups, or well-glazed earthen-ware. Fill the pan two thirds full of water, and when the water boils, set in your cups. Be sure no water gets into the cups, and keep the water boiling softly all the time till you find the jelly is like a stiff glue; take out the cups and when they are cool, turn out the glue into a coarse new flannel. Let it lay eight or nine hours, keeping it in a dry warm place, and turn it on fresh flannel till it is quite dry, and the glue will be quite hard; put it into clean new stone pots, keep it close covered from dust and dirt, in a dry place, and where no damp can come to it.

When you use it, pour boiling water on it, and stir it all the time till it is melted. Season it with salt to your palate. A piece as big as a large walnut will make a pint of water very rich; but as to that you are to make it as good as you please: if for soup, fry a French roll and lay it in the middle of the dish, and when the glue is dissolved in the water, give it a boil and pour it into a dish. If you chuse it for a change, you may boil either rice or barley, vermicelli, celery cut small, of truffles or morels; but let them be very tenderly boiled in the water before you stir in the glue, and then give it a boil all together. You may, when you would have it very fine, add force-meat balls, cocks-combs, or a palate boiled very tender and cut into little bits, but it will be very rich and good without any of these ingredients.

If for gravy, pour the boiling water on to what quantity you think proper; and when it is dissolved, add what ingredients you please, as in other sauces. This is only in the room of a rich good gravy. You may make your sauce either weak or strong by adding more or less.

Among the provisions Parry took with him on his voyage in 1824 to the Arctic in H.M.S. *Fury* was canned pea soup. Some of this was opened 113 years later in 1937 and was found still to be in good edible condition; laboratory examination disclosed bacterial spores that had been in a state of suspended animation all that time.

In 1829 Admiral Sir James Ross included canned soups in the provisions for his voyage and Sir John Franklin for his voyage of 1845 in search of the North West Passage. Some of his stores were found by Admiral McClintock in 1857 and were then perfectly edible.

The word 'Chowder' is probably derived from the chaudières or kettles used by Breton fishermen to prepare cooked fish dishes. In the New World the word was changed and came to mean the soup instead of the kettle.

Cold soups are said to have originated as a result of the time taken by the food tasters of King Louis XIV, since this monarch employed a large number of food tasters to protect him against poisoned food. Another French king is credited with the invention of clear soups when his chef added meat stock to consommé so that the King could have meat on days of religious abstinence.

B

To come to more recent times, it may be of interest to some to read an extract from regulations of the 1939–45 World War.

The Meat Products, Canned Soup and Canned Meat (Control and Maximum Prices) Order, 1941, laid down the wartime standards for canned soups; this fixed the minimum standards:

Type of Soup	Solids per cent	Protein per cent	Fat per cent
Meat	12	2·5	–
Mulligatawny	13	2	2
Cream	10	–	3·5
Vegetable	10	1	–
Clear	7	6	–

These figures were based on fair commercial practice and they were laid down to provide standards for the nutritional value of soups which would form an increasing part of the civilian wartime dietary.

CHAPTER II

SOUP STOCK

G ENERALLY it is agreed that, first and foremost, the basis of a good soup is a good stock. In the hotel or restaurant kitchen, a stock-pot is always on the range, day and night, and into this goes every available raw material in the shape of bones, chicken carcases and the like. According to the size of the establishment, there is one general purpose stock-pot in which a basic stock is made, or there are several stock-pots to hold different types of stock. However, whether there is one general stock-pot or several pots for specialized purposes, the thickness, flavour and general character of the stock will vary from day to day. Thus, partly because of varying stock and partly because of the variation in the other ingredients used, each soup will vary slightly when it is finally served. For example, the chef may make Cream Aurore or Minestrone by much the same method and with much the same ingredients one hundred times, but each brew will vary ever so slightly in character and if he is a good chef, each will be a superb creation in itself—one fine day may be fine like another, but no two days are the same.

Whilst the chef in the hotel kitchen may be allowed to work as he wishes and create his own interpretation of each kind of soup, just as a piano player may vary the interpretation of the written music each time he plays it, such fine arts cannot be allowed rein in the soup kitchen of a big factory. It is of course true that the chef's oxtail soup may be as good on Wednesday as it was on Monday, but if it is different, the trouble will start. When soup is put into cans with the same label on Wednesday as on Monday, nobody can tell for sure that a lady will not buy two tins, in the grocer's shop, one of which was made on Monday and one of which was made on Wednesday. Thus, if the lady opens both cans and finds one a little different from the other, even though they are both very good to taste, she will begin to ask questions—why is this one

darker in colour than the other, is it bad I wonder—and so on.
Thus it will be seen that whilst the good methods of an hotel
or restaurant kitchen may be applied in a factory, these
methods must be subject to rigid control as to quality and
sameness. Once the chef has devised a recipe for a given soup,
nothing must be allowed to alter this, and the whole chain of
manufacturing processes must be arranged on this basis.

Taking the various steps in the process of soup making
one by one, it will be seen at once that the production of
standardized stock is in itself a tremendous task. Indeed, the
problem of controlling stock strength and flavour is such that
many manufacturers of mass-produced soups do not attempt it
at all, but add meat extract or other materials of standard
quality and flavour, to water down to make their base. Such
an operation is of course simple, but nevertheless the results
are not always as good. Also, many large meat packing works
have large quantities of bone and tough meat which they like
to use to make stock for soup making before turning the waste
into animal feeding-stuffs or fertilizer.

In some factories where basic bone stock is used selected
mixtures of bones and meat, chicken carcases or whatever may
be required are simmered in large boilers holding from 500 to
1,000 gallons, as required. These pots are usually made of
stainless steel with a steam heating coil of the same material.
The bones and meat are usually suspended in such pots in
wire mesh baskets or net bags. This method of operation,
however, has several serious snags from the production control
point of view. Firstly, it is very difficult to construct a stock-
pot which is both easy to fill and clean, and yet which allows
of a reasonable ratio of bones and meat to water. Secondly,
and arising partly from the first objection, the resulting stock
is not very strong, i.e. the solids are low. It is of course possible
to dilute the stock with plain water to a uniform strength, but
this means diluting to an undesirably low average standard.
Various methods of stock making are applied with the object
of overcoming the objections to the conventional stock-pot,
including the retorting of the bones under steam pressure. This
method is very good indeed, but unless it is done very carefully the stock may taste gluey. Undoubtedly, the best system
devised for stock making is that in which the bones are sub-

jected to elevated temperatures and pressure in a special double retort in which the bones are kept constantly under water. By this method it is possible to produce a stock with a high average solids content and yet which has an excellent flavour. This high-solids stock can then be diluted with hot water, to a solids content just below the average figure, so that quality can be maintained day after day.

Of course it must be understood that good soup stock requires other ingredients beside meat or meat and bones. In most cases some sort of vegetable is added to the stock, together with a few herbs and spices. Further, some stocks are made from vegetables only, and as vegetables cannot be handled easily by the pressure cooking method described above, it is always really advisable to have large stock-pots, even when the pressure method is used.

Where the ordinary stock-pot method of making stock is used, most stock recipes call for the addition of vegetables or herbs towards the end of the simmering period, so that in the one case these are added to the stock which is already in the pot, whilst in the other case, the standardized stock from the pressure cooker is run into the stock-pot for further cooking with the vegetables. Thus, even where the special stock-making system is used, it is not possible to do away with the conventional stock-pot.

At this stage, it is perhaps as well to divert from the theme of factory production and machinery, to deal for a moment with the more culinary aspects of stock making. There are four main types of stock, at any rate so far as commercial soup making goes. These are brown meat stock, white meat stock, vegetable stock and fish stock, the last of which is not very important, at any rate for canning. These basic stock types can be sub-divided into various kinds, e.g. you can have white or brown game stock and so on. There is also a special stock, which is really a soup from the beginning, not a stock, and this is of course the clear base for consommé.

General brown meat stock is usually made from bones and lean beef meat, the more meat the better the stock. The bones should be well cracked up and some high-class cookery books will tell you to remove the marrow. Obviously, however, this cannot be done in commercial soup making on a large scale.

The best machine for cracking the bones is a bone crusher of the waste disposal plant type. This machine consists of two rollers with spikes in them, between which the bones are fed from a chute. In small factories, the bones may be broken up by hitting them with the back of a chopper.

For some brown soups, e.g. oxtail, which require to be tasty and to have that roast meat flavour, the bones may be lightly roasted in a large oven. This has the advantage of rendering out some of the fat, but great care has to be taken to prevent burning as this leads to black flecks in the soup.

It is very difficult to give any exact recipe for the stock as so much depends upon the availability of raw material, the costing basis and so on, but as a starting point it can be said that one pound of meat or bone to the pound of water is good. In the same way one can say that, for ordinary brown meat stock, you should add about 25 lb. each of carrot, turnip and onion and 12 lb. of celery, per 100 gallons of stock. Herbs and spices are added to taste. Of course, the water to meat ratio will alter when the pressure stock making method is used, but the amount of vegetables will not, because these are added after the stock has been put into the stock-pot.

White stock is usually made from veal or calves' heads or, where certain special soups are being made, poultry or rabbit may be used. White stock is not so easy to make by the pressure method, although with care it can be done. About the same quantities of vegetables are used for this type of stock.

Vegetable stock cannot be made in the pressure cooker unless it is to be used for making the thick purée type of soup. In this case, certain soups, e.g. carrot soup, are improved by this method of treatment.

The best vegetable soup stock recipes, especially those designed for use in soups in which the vegetables are left in whole pieces as in ordinary vegetable soups, suggest that the vegetables should be fried in butter until golden brown, before putting in the stock. Unless butter is very cheap, however, this is not an economical procedure, and in any case it is not easy to use the stock vegetables in the final soup. This is because it is almost impossible on a large scale to remove the diced vegetables from the stock-pot and place these evenly in the cans or other package. On a commercial scale, vegetable soup

stocks are best made from diced vegetables, which are afterwards thrown away or used for some other purpose.

Fish stock is not very generally used, but has some considerable possibilities for freezing. This will therefore be dealt
with under the heading of Quick-Freezing.

Whatever the type of stock being made, the general
procedure is as follows:

1. Prepare the raw materials, meat or vegetable.

2. Convert the meat part of the raw materials into stock
by simmering, never boiling, in the stock-pot, or by the pressure
method. When the stock-pot method is used, the scum should
be skimmed off the top of the pot from time to time—a hand-
bowl on a broom handle is very useful for this. Once the basic
stock is made, it should be standardized and in the case of the
pressure method, run into the large stock-pot. The vegetables
and salt, if any, are then added and simmering continued until
the desired stage is reached.

At this point, most cookery books will tell you that the
stock should be cooled to allow the fat to come to the top, and
also that all but vegetable stocks can be kept from day to day
by means of leaving the hard fat crust on the top. This
definitely does not hold good for commercial soup stocks which
are to be used for canning or especially freezing. However
hard you may try, soup stocks cannot be kept cold in a big
factory soup kitchen. Unless refrigeration is used, and the
stock is in fact kept very cold (below 40° F.), the bacteria count
will increase and cause trouble in the final retorting process
where the cans are sterilized. The question then is, is it worth
while cooling off the stock at all, merely to get the fat out? The
answer to this is that it depends upon the type of soup to be
made. If it is a thick soup, then the fat is useful and will blend
into the thickener used. If on the other hand the soup is to be
of the clear type, then the fat has to be got rid of or it will
settle on the garnish and look very bad.

Quite a lot of fat can be got rid of in the hot stage by
skimming, but if soup requiring an absence of fat is to be made
on a commercial scale, then there is no doubt that it pays to
put in a machine separator.

Where soup has to be made very clear, the stock has to be
clarified, and this again may be done by machine, in fact one

machine can be obtained to take out both fat and small solids. That is to say, after the bones, meat, vegetables and bags of spices, if any, have been removed from the stock, it is run out into another vessel, through a centrifugal separator.

Where only small-scale operations are undertaken, the stock can be clarified in a settling tank by means of eggs or isinglass, and some chefs use coffee grounds for this purpose. Where eggs are used, it will take the whites and shells of three or four eggs to clear each gallon of stock and this is obviously expensive. Where isinglass is used, the clarifying agent must be prepared beforehand, by covering about 5 oz. of best isinglass with cold water and allowing this to stand for 7 or 8 hours. At the end of this time, the water is drained off and the swollen isinglass put into about a gallon of cold water into which 3¾ oz. of tartaric acid has been dissolved. Stir well, adding more and more cold water until three gallons has been produced. No heat should be used in this process and the resulting liquor will be a smooth and rather heavy syrup, entirely free from lumps.

If the actual stock-pot is to be used for clearing the stock, then it should be fitted either with a floating draw-off pipe or a series of pet cocks down the side, so that the clear liquor between the top scum and the bottom mud may be drawn off easily. Alternately, a special vessel may be used.

At this stage, it should perhaps be emphasized that the validity of many of the points made heretofore depends very largely upon the scale of operations undertaken. For example, whilst we have said that it is difficult to use the diced vegetables which have been used for stock to garnish finished cans of soup, this does depend upon the scale. If only a very limited production is being handled and small pans are used with hand filling, then such things are possible. As a general rule, it is possible to do almost anything where the scale is very small or again where it is very large, because in the one case hand methods are used and in the other all sorts of pumps, pipes and other apparatus can be installed, just to make one particular kind of soup. It is always where semi-large-scale operations are undertaken that difficulties arise with the volume of raw material which has to be handled in many differing ways without large capital expenditure on plant.

CHAPTER III

SOUP MAKING PLANT

PREVIOUS editions of this book have contained illustrations and descriptions of the more traditional items of machinery and equipment used in the manufacture of soups. The Authors felt that it was unnecessary to repeat all these illustrations in the new edition, but rather devote the space to illustrations of the latest machinery and equipment available and the most recent installations.

Whilst for small-scale operations, all the various phases of soup making and canning may be carried out in one room on one floor level, there is no doubt at all that for large-scale operations, one or two floors are most desirable. Stock-pots are of necessity rather large and high and if these are standing on the floor with sufficient clearance for drainage cocks underneath, then they are very awkward to charge with raw materials. It is therefore desirable to have them let into an upper floor with a discharge pipe in the room below. Actual soup making can then be carried out below, together with the canning, or this last operation can be put on a lower floor still. In view of the fact that soup making is almost always carried out in a factory which makes other foods as well, the layout must really depend upon how soup production fits in with the other foods being made.

Stainless steel is the best material for soup stock-pots, but there is no need to have a heavy material, because the pots may be heated by steam coils and do not therefore need to withstand the pressure of a steam jacket.

Stock for soup making may be drawn off from the stock-pots by means of a bottom draw-off valve and filled into stainless steel buckets or transporters for transfer to the soup-making pans, or it may be piped by gravity or pumped. There is much to be said for manhandling as pipes are difficult to keep clean in soup-making plants and block very easily with small pieces of bone and meat. Certainly, if pipes are used, the greatest care has to be taken to provide an easy-to-get-at strainer or filter on the outlet of the stock-pot, and the pipes must be arranged in such a manner that they can be taken down for cleaning every day. The set-up in this respect should be on the same lines as an ice-cream factory and indeed ice-cream pipes and pumps are ideal for this work. It is also a good idea to have both fresh water and live steam inlets in the pipe system at various points so that the lines can be sterilized and flushed during working hours.

Stainless steel steam-jacketed pans are usually used for the actual blending of soup. These should be as large as possible to save labour by increasing batch sizes, but not so large as to make the finishing of batches too intermittent. The size must therefore be reasonably balanced with the production rate.

Besides steam pans, the following items of equipment are required for anything other than very small production:

A horizontal or vertical steam pressure cooker or retort, fitted with deep stainless steel trays, which should have loose-fitting lids. This item is most useful and is used for pressure cooking items such as ox tails, chickens and so on. The foods are placed into the trays with a little stock and covered so that steam does not condense into them.

One or more gas, electric or coke-fired baking ovens and a supply of deep stainless baking or roasting trays. These ovens are used for browning flour, roasting meats or vegetables, cooking rice and so on.

A motor-driven pulping or sieving machine, fitted with inter-changeable stainless steel sieves of various mesh sizes and with an oversized motor. This machine is used for sieving vegetables for purée, and also for removing meat from small bones. If, for example, cut-up cooked rabbit, chicken or ox tail is fed slowly to such a machine, all the meat will be removed from the bones in the form of a fine purée. For this operation, however, it is desirable to have an oversized motor.

The soup may be given its final 'gloss' before canning, by running it through a fine-mesh pulper, but these machines are not entirely suitable for this work. It has been found much better to use a very rapidly vibrating screen for many soups, or alternatively an 'in-vat' type emulsifier. For a small factory, an ice-cream type in-vat emulsifier is most useful as it may be removed from one pot to the next, but in a larger establishment it is desirable to have both an emulsifier and a final vibrating screen, which acts as an inspection table, before the soup is passed to the fillers.

(By courtesy Varley-FMC Ltd.)

Urschel model O.V. transverse slicer. The product delivered into the feed hopper at a uniform rate is fed by high-speed belts into the slicing wheel. The knives serve as spokes and are spaced according to the thickness of slice or cut required by the Canner.

A vertical whisk or cake mixer is usually used to make up batter for thickening purposes, and an ordinary baker's type mixing machine is quite suitable. It is, however, desirable to have a warm-water feed to the machine, with a device for measuring standard quantities into the bowl, as most cereals mix much more freely if the water used is slightly warmed.

Besides the above-mentioned main items of equipment, the kitchen should have an ample supply of stainless steel buckets, transporters, bogies, scales, knives, spoons, paddles and so on. Also, in an ancillary department, it is necessary to have vegetable washing and cleaning plant, vegetable dicers and so on.

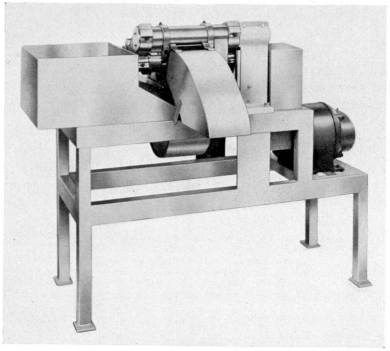

(By courtesy Varley-FMC Ltd.)

Urschel model GK. This machine is used for dicing, strip cutting and slicing. Especially suitable for producing crinkle cuts. Mounted on a stainless steel frame it has a capacity of up to 3,000 lb. per hour.

The plant required for the actual canning operations is dealt with in another chapter, but the main requirements are a can feed conveyor for filling in solid garnish; a soup filling machine; a can sealer; followed by a can washer; a number of steam retorts and crates to go in them; means of cooling the cans, although this is often completed in the retorts, a labeller, and possibly a can caser and sealer.

For large-scale production of canned soups hydrostatic sterilizers may be used.

Machinery and equipment for the cleaning and preparation of vegetables, processing, canning, can seaming and retorting is described in considerable detail and profusely illustrated in *Practical Canning* by Arthur Lock, 1969, Food Trade Press Ltd., London.

(*By courtesy Mather & Platt Ltd.*)

Steam Peeler. This machine will handle all root vegetables and is fully automatic in operation. The steam consumption is very low, 1 lb. steam for every 7 lb. of product.

Steam vapour removal and floor drainage are two major problems in the soup kitchen and the cost of the latter is often overlooked when calculating installation costs. Stock-pots and pans should all be fitted with overhead steam removal cowls as the amount of steam given off is considerable. These cowls may

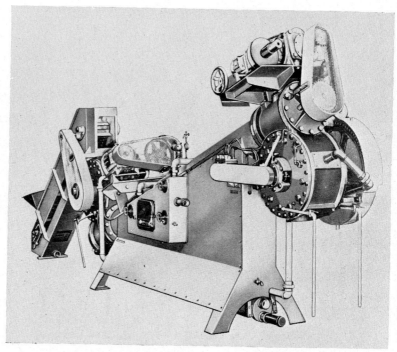

(By courtesy Varley-FMC Ltd.)

The F.M.C. Steam peeler. This machine is fully automatic in operation and will handle a large amount of vegetable with a low steam consumption.

be of the natural draft type or connected to ducting and fans. There are one or two exceptionally good natural draft ventilator hoods available, although these are usually made of wood which is difficult to keep clean. Where ducting and fans are used, a problem does arise from corrosion arising from vinegar fumes, especially if the same plant is used to make sauce or spiced vinegars, etc.

There is no doubt that floors are best constructed of special tiles which last longer than straight concrete, but they do of course cost a lot more. Most newcomers to the food manufacturing trade make the grave error of planning drainage points in the floor, from which the water is removed by underground

(By courtesy S. A. Bertuzzi)

Can Opener. Semi-automatic machine for opening No. 10 cans, containing tomato paste for soup making.

pipes. This is a serious mistake and inside any meat works the drains should be in the form of open channels cut in the floor, about 9 in. to 12 in. wide and varying in depth according to the fall. These channels should fall to a common exit from the room and should then feed into a grease trap in the form of a series of separation tanks. The channels themselves should be covered with perforated steel covers set in steel angle iron let into the floor, so that they can be taken up every night and

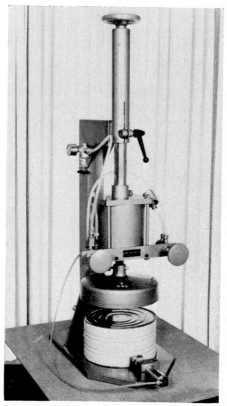

(By courtesy Peter Holland (Food Machinery) Ltd.)

Pneumatic can opener. Simple but very useful for opening cans of materials, tomato paste, etc.

brushed clean. It is best to use perforated steel plates, rather than fabricated bar grid gratings, as although these cost less in the first place, they do cause a lot of trouble with trolley wheels. If proper grease traps are installed, a lot of waste fat can be recovered and rendered for sale as technical grease.

Where there is an excessive amount of spillage in any one area of a department, it is wise to have the floor specially drained in this area, and surrounded with a little tiled kerb, to prevent the water spreading. In certain cases where no one walks on the area in question, fat wastes can be removed by separation and used for food purposes.

The use of colloid mills for the production of soups is a well-

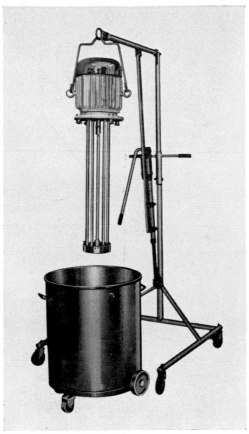

(*By courtesy Silverson Machines Ltd.*)

A Silverson batch-type high-speed multi purpose mixer emulsifier on mobile hydraulic floor stand. These machines are manufactured to handle capacities from a few to several thousand gallons of low, intermediate and high viscosities.

C

established process. Generally, in the manufacture of cream soups, it is necessary to carry out two operations with a high speed mill—one is the smoothing out of thickening agents such as flour, and the other the emulsification into the soup of the

(*By courtesy Silverson Machines Ltd.*)

A Silverson 5 h.p. in-line multi purpose mixer emulsifier shown for use on a recirculating basis. The machine pumps under its own pressure. Silverson in-line machines are made from ¾ to 100 h.p.

fats which have a tendency to separate in certain cases in storage. While in actual fact these are the two ▪perations which are carried out by high speed milling, the end effect is to produce a product which is smoother to the tongue.

In certain cases it may be necessary at the same time to grind into certain soups vegetables or meats, and in these cases

(By courtesy The APV Co. Ltd.)

The APV type HX Plate Heat Exchange, with plate pack open to show plate formation. Plants of this type are used for heating and cooking duties in the soup industry and particularly for continuous cooling of soups prior to canning.

(*By courtesy The APV Co. Ltd.*)

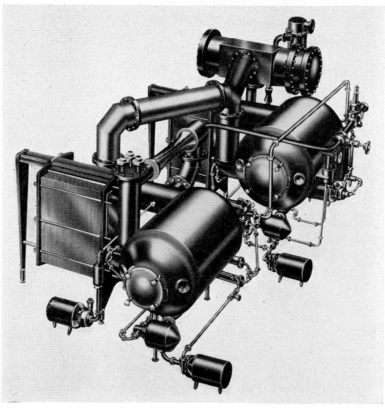

(*By courtesy The APV Co. Ltd.*

Opposite. Top: The APV Clarke-Built Rota-pro scraped surface heat exchanger used in the soup industry for heating and cooling duties on viscous materials. *Below:* The APV Plate Evaporator, used for concentration of soup stocks. Its short heat contact time gives this plant special advantages with regard to flavour preservation, while its low height and flexible layout can greatly reduce installation costs.

(By courtesy The APV Co. Ltd.)

APV Manton-Gaulin K type homogenizers installed for cream and fat dispersion duties in a soup factory.

(By courtesy The APV Co. Ltd.)

Soup processing plant comprising 12 APV steam-jacketed pans of 50 and 100 gallon capacities in which starch, fats and other ingredients are prepared.

An impressive installation of soup boiling pans installed at the Kitt Green factory of H. J. Heinz Co. Ltd.

(By courtesy Food Trade Review, London)

colloid mills which have abrasive type working surfaces are better suited to this type of work since they will grind solid particles to a smooth cream and at the same time homogenize and disperse other products in the soup.

Showing high-pressure-jet washing down of stainless steel soup processing equipment at the Kitt Green factory of H. J. Heinz Co. Ltd.

CHAPTER IV

SOUPS FOR CANNING

THE conversion of basic stock into good soups for canning is not nearly so simple as it sounds and before embarking upon actual operations the following fundamentals must be understood.

1. After the soup has been made in the kitchen, it has to be filled into the can and sterilized at a high temperature. This high temperature sterilization definitely alters the flavour and texture of the soup and allowance must be made for this when planning the recipe and method of production.

2. Through the years, the public seems to have been educated to, or at any rate to have developed, a liking for a somewhat tastier soup from a can than one normally expects to find in a high-class restaurant. That is to say, the most popular canned soups today are more like very mild sauces than soups, they are piquant and appetizing rather than fine and delicate.

3. Quite apart from the necessity to make a soup according to public taste and according to the requirements of high temperature sterilization, the time-honoured methods of the kitchen have to be modified again and again to allow for quality control—to achieve a standard 'sameness' in each batch. This is a most important aspect of commercial soup making and leads to countless modifications of standard kitchen procedure.

For a start, whatever type of soup is to be made, it is essential to have a standardized stock. This has already been dealt with in a previous chapter, but the user of the stock produced in the chapter, i.e. the soup kitchen proper, should keep a constant check upon the sameness of the stock supplied. Most certainly a solids content test should be carried out on each main batch of stock made up for use. At the same time, it is most advisable to check the salt content. This can vary a great deal and upset the recipe used for the making of the actual soup. Salt contents may be checked very quickly by an electrical device.

There are two main methods used for the conversion of stock into finished soup, irrespective of the type of soup involved. These are the method by which the extra ingredients, e.g. oxtail, are simmered in the stock in very large batches, and the whole lot then finished afterwards, and the method by which the extra ingredients are processed separately and then added to the soup at the last minute before canning. On the whole the former method leads to a better soup, whereas the latter enables closer quality control to be exercised. In either case, the various ingredients to be used must be subjected to various cooking processes to make them suitable for conversion into soup.

It is obviously impossible to deal in detail with the methods which may be applied to making soup from each and every possible recipe, because the method of making on a factory scale will vary with each recipe, and again the use of a different recipe will perhaps require an altogether different arrangement and usage of plant. A selection of possible recipes is given at the end of this chapter, but it is now proposed to deal with some of the salient points which arise in the making of certain different types of soup and more especially the special adaptations which have to be made in order to subject the processes to absolute quality control.

1. Soup Fillers or Thickeners

Soup fillers are the most important because upon them depends the thickness of the soup and it is by the thickness or ability to absorb additional water, as well as upon flavour, that the thrifty housewife judges quality.

Perhaps it is wrong to state that the thickness of the soup depends upon the amount of filler, because obviously filler is only a second-class thickener and meat solids, vegetable solids etc., are the best. However, most commercial soup makers could not afford to use all meat solids so that fillers are essential.

In general, the thickness of a soup should not be judged by its physical appearance of being thick. That is to say, some soups which are quite 'runny' looking will stand more dilution than very 'porridgy' soups. This is because the best form of thickness in canned soups takes the shape of what are known as soluble solids. That is to say, the solid material is dissolved or dispersed in liquid, like sugar in water. If all the solids are in the form of jelly-like material such as cooked starch, the soup will look and taste thick. Further, the amount of cereal needed to produce such thickness might kill the natural flavours of the meat or vegetable constituents of the soup.

It is generally agreed that a good commercial soup should have about 12 to 16 per cent total solids and of these solids a good proportion should be in the form of soluble solids.

It is reasonable to say that in a soup made from stock, about 2 per cent of the solids will be derived from this stock, with perhaps a further 5 per cent from meat or some other added pulp substance. The rest must be filler of some sort.

Where possible, the filler used should be of a type which gives the maximum actual solids with the minimum actual thickening. Some manufacturers treat their starchy cereal fillers specially to make them suitable for this purpose. This is done by warming a water and cereal mixture gently in the presence of a starch splitting enzyme. By this means, part of the starch in the cereal is converted into sugar and the mix is made thinner, but with very nearly the same total solids. An advantage of this process is that the mix is made sweet and this may contribute quite a lot to the flavour of the soup, especially in times when sugar is expensive. Perhaps it may also be noted at this point that the viscosity of starch thickeners is reduced quite a lot when the mix is made acid and thus the use of vinegar in soup does help to reduce physical thickness.

Quite a range of cereal thickeners may be used for soup, such as ordinary wheat flour, cornflour, arrowroot, oatmeal and so on, but the most common is of course ordinary wheat flour, because it is cheap. Generally speaking, wheat flour is the best filler for brown thick soups, but also there is no doubt that cornflour or arrowroot makes a better cream soup, especially arrowroot. Rice flour and similar products are not widely used in canned soup manufacture.

Where cornflour is used, it is best made up as a smooth paste and then added to the boiling soup, but when wheat flour is used, it may be added in the same manner as cornflour, or it may be browned in fat first and the hot soup added afterwards. Again, either type of filler may be subjected to enzyme conversion before use.

Where wheat flour is to be browned, this may be done in either of two ways. Firstly, the flour may be mixed with fat, rather like shortbread, and then baked very, very slowly in a cool oven in trays. Secondly, it may be mixed with fat and browned in the bottom of the pan to which the hot soup will be added. From a production point of view the oven method has many attractions, as it is easier to manipulate than a small quantity of flour in the bottom of a large pan. In either case, great care has to be taken with the low extraction flours, as these tend to develop off-flavours very easily during browning.

Whatever type of cereal thickener is added to canned soups, the very greatest care must be taken to boil the soup enough really to thicken the flour before canning, and preferably the mix should be emulsified first. If the filler is not properly boiled out, it will tend to thicken as a sort of pudding in the can. That is to say, it will not be properly dispersed in the mix and will make the soup look thicker and rougher in texture than it should.

In the United States, there are a number of specially prepared cereal thickeners for soup and other food products, which give the maximum solids with just the right amount of physical thickening, but no such products are made in this country to the Authors' knowledge.

Besides cereal thickeners, there are a number of other substances which can be used to thicken soups, but most of them are rather too costly. For example, gelatine or gums may be used, as in sauces, and also pectin has its uses, especially in the jelly type of soup. Some of these special soups will be dealt with later. One interesting U.S. Patent 2,142,093, deals with a method of rendering casein suitable as a thickener for soups. The resulting product is free from lactose and disperses easily in soup mixes.

No notes on soup thickeners would be complete without a solemn warning to the user of such products to be very careful about quality control. Cereals especially can vary enormously from lot to lot and where a control laboratory is available, steps should be taken to ensure that purchases are made to given standards. Otherwise it is all too easy to find that one day the soup is totally different because the flour is of quite a different type from the previous delivery.

Use of Soya

It may be said that the two most important qualities in soups to the consumer are body and flavour. In all but clear soups body is a combination of viscosity and thickness. Viscosity alone can be provided by colloidal materials such as starches and gums but these cannot provide thickness. Their effect if they are used in too great a proportion is to give a very viscous soup with a quality of sliminess on the palate very different from the thickness that is not due to viscosity. This desirable thickness can only be achieved with a sufficient proportion of protein and fat dispersed in the aqueous medium made just sufficiently viscous with starch. Because soya consists to the extent of 60 per cent of protein and fat it is an ideal ingredient for providing the desirable thickness which gives good body to the soup.

It is important that soya should be properly processed to be free from objectionable flavour and from residual enzyme activity which might lead to deterioration of the soup during processing or storage. Standards of quality for soya in these respects have been proposed.

In canned cream soups agreed standards of fat content have been established which are more easily achieved if soya is used to contribute a substantial proportion, if not all, of the total fat content. The advantages of soya lie in the fact that its fat content is completely stable and is already in a finely dispersed form. The difficulties of emulsifying added fats and of ensuring that the emulsion remains stable during freezing, canning or storage are thereby avoided. Breakdown of fat emulsions and the consequent appearance of unattractive pools or globules of fat in the soup when served greatly diminish the eye appeal of the product.

The fact that soya presents the fat in a stable form is even more important in the preparation of dry soups. The difficulty of incorporating added fats in such preparations is considerable and their stability towards oxidative or lipolytic rancidity is uncertain. Not only is their surface area greatly increased when they are thoroughly dispersed throughout the non-fatty solids of the formula, so that the risk of oxidation is increased, but they are intimately in contact with the cereal components and the lipolytic enzymes which these contain. The fat of a properly processed full-fat soya on the other hand is well protected by the natural antioxidants of soya and, being included in the soya particles, need never come into contact with the lipolytic enzymes of the cereal components.

Soya, by virtue of its protein and lecithin content, is a powerful emulsifying agent and it is an advantage, if additional fat is required, to mix this thoroughly with soya before combining with the other ingredients. Such added fats will then be well dispersed and protected by the natural antioxidants of soya against the risk of oxidative rancidity.

Where soups are produced for canning or freezing it has been found that soya flour is best incorporated in the roux.

In this case, soya flour can be used principally in two ways. Where a roux is of a high fat content, soya flour may be used as a stabilizer, so that the tendency to separate or curdle on pre-heating is eliminated or minimized. The rate of addition can be in the order of 5–10 per cent of the fat content.

The stability of the roux will probably necessitate a reduction of the amount used for stock, this being controlled by the requirements of the manufacturers.

A typical recipe would be as follows:

Clarified Margarine	40 lb.
Processed Soya Flour ('Trusoy')* .	4 ,,
Flour	68 ,,

The margarine is heated to 240° F. in a steam-jacketed boiler with stirring blades. Soya is blended with the flour and incorporated by stirring for 10 minutes. The stirring is then stopped and the roux cooked for 10 minutes. A further 10 minutes' stirring is then given, the steam turned off and the roux removed from the boiler.

The roux can be made in bulk for chilling and used when required at the rate of 1 lb. per gallon of stock.

The second principle is to use soya flour to reduce the

* British Soya Products Ltd.

quantity of fat in a rich roux or to supplement the fat content
of a lean roux.

In the first instance, soya could replace fat, weight for
weight, up to 10 per cent of the fat content of the roux. In the
second instance the flour would be adjusted proportionately to
maintain the jelling factor of the roux.

The use of soya flour in the roux used for soups of an acid
nature, such as tomato, would reduce the precipitation of the
proteins, this being a common fault with low-fat soups of this type.

Soya flour is also used extensively in pre-mixed powdered
soups and ranges from 10 to 25 per cent of the total mixture
according to the degree of richness required and the type of
soup being made. Again soya would be used as the fat factor
and would be adjusted to suit the manufacturer's requirements,
taking into consideration the protein content with the added
soya.

A full fat soya flour such as 'Soyolk' can be satisfactorily
incorporated in soup manufacture, especially in connection
with cream soups.

The analysis of 'Soyolk'* is as follows:

Moisture	7·0 per cent	
Protein (N × 6·25) . .	40·0 ,, ,,	
Fat	18·0 ,, ,,	
Phosphatides . . .	2·0 ,, ,,	(as lecithin)
Ash	4·6 ,, ,,	
Fibre	1·81 ,, ,,	
Calcium	0·2 ,, ,,	
Phosphorus . . .	0·6 ,, ,,	
Sugars	8·0 ,, ,,	
Other Carbohydrates .	18·0 ,, ,,	(no Starch)

Overtails on 100 mesh sieve   1–2 ,,   ,,

Calorific value per 100 grams = 413
Calorific value per lb.   = 1,870

The analysis shows clearly that soya flour is constituted to
act as an emulsifier and stabilizer in a wide range of foods. The
phosphatide fraction (known commercially as lecithin) acts as

* Soya Foods Ltd.

an emulsifying agent in the formation of both oil-in-water
(e.g. salad cream) and water-in-oil (e.g. margarine) emulsions.
The large amount of protein serves to stabilize the emulsion.
In this manner, soya flour has a beneficial effect on the texture
of cream soups in which a smooth, stable creamy emulsion is
required.

In connection with dry mixes, the inclusion of 'Soyolk' at
between 10 and 15 per cent is suitable. The reasons are exactly
the same as for canned soups. In addition, 'Soyolk', being a
natural antioxidant, has a very long shelf-life, and would
certainly keep fresh longer than most other ingredients included
in a prepared dry mix.

2. *Soup flavours*

The question of the actual flavours to use in any given soup
is largely a matter of opinion, between one manufacturer and
another, and the blends so varied that it is almost impossible
to deal with all the possibilities. It is therefore proposed to deal
with general principles here.

Probably the first and most important question which any
would-be soup manufacturer will ask is: Shall I use real spices
or shall I use the standardized liquid and powdered spices? This
is a very difficult question to answer, because whilst there is little
doubt that the best flavours are obtained by the use of whole
spices and herbs, these are very, very difficult to standardize and
control. One may hang a bag of this or that in the stock or in
the soup and one may use the same amount each time, but so
much depends upon the age and quality of the spices that the
results can vary enormously. On the other hand, liquid and
powdered spices can be measured and used to a fine degree of
accuracy each time.

Probably the answer to this question is that for most commercial purposes it is easier to use the standardized products,
but that if the factory is very large and can afford to buy spices
in big quantities and employ an expert to handle them, then
whole spices are best. There are, however, certain techniques
which may be employed by the smaller manufacturer which
may enable him to make more standardized products with
whole spices than is possible by other means, which are described below.

In general, it is not enough just to hang a bag of spices or herbs in the stock-pot or soup-making pot, or to add liquid spices to the brew for canning. This method is all very well for the household or restaurant soup and it will of course produce quite a good article for canning, but it must be remembered that the household soup usually has more high-class contents, such as meat, than a commercial soup maker can afford, and it does not therefore need either such a lot or as careful spicing as the cheaper commercial mix. Further, it must be remembered that the public taste for a commercial canned soup is for something tasty. If sufficient whole spices or oils are added to a commercial soup to give it that excitement which is called for, then there is a danger that it will taste like Christmas pudding! If these extra spices and other flavours are to be added, then some means must be found of blending the flavours more deeply into the mix and of producing a matured flavour. Indeed, it may be noted in passing that very few manufacturers seem to realize the staggering difference between a product which is just mixed up and one containing the same ingredients but precisely blended in such a manner that the flavours produced are 'rounder'.

At this stage, it may perhaps be noted that both sugar and wine are more than useful in producing that smooth, natural effect in spiced or flavoured foods. Where it can be afforded, there is no doubt that a little wine added to the recipe will work wonders, but a very little sugar or, as has been mentioned, sweetened cereal, will go a long way. Many famous chefs have stated in their cookery books that they always add a very little sugar to all dishes, 'last of all', to round off and mature the flavour. However, in commercial soup making, it is through the use of vinegar or sauce that the best maturing effects can be obtained.

In almost all soups a little vinegar is required and the skilful manufacturer can use this vinegar content to 'carry' the spices and flavours. That is to say, apart from just ordinary malt vinegar, there are a host of special vinegars which can be bought or made up for soup making. There are for example the various spirit vinegars, there is cyder vinegar—a most useful ingredient in soup—and there are the flavoured vinegars such as tarragon vinegar. In addition to these, the soup manufacturer can make up his own special brews for adding to soups, and

D

once made these brews can be casked and left to mature for as long as they will keep. Thus, for example, all the spices and even some of the other flavouring ingredients to be used in a given soup, may be added to vinegar and put away until the full flavours are drawn from the spices and the whole effect blended together to form a really savoury and mature flavouring agent for the soup. Apart from cyder vinegar, many pleasing vinegars can be made from fruits, such as pineapple, raspberry and even tropical fruits such as guava.

Along with the straight or spiced vinegars in soup making, go the slightly more complicated vinegar products, which are really sauces, such as Worcester sauce, beefsteak sauce and so on. All these are useful in soup making.

Besides straight spices and herbs, etc., there are a number of important flavouring ingredients for soup, especially where a tasty commercial product is required.

First of all, there is the group of materials of the protein derivative type, including such items as yeast extract, hydrolysed protein, and of course monosodium glutamate (M.S.G.). The yeast extract type of flavouring is much cheaper than M.S.G. but is used in larger quantities to produce a definite piquant meaty flavour, whereas M.S.G. is comparatively expensive and is used in very small quantities of the order of 0·5 per cent to pep up existing flavours. M.S.G. is a very useful product, as it improves many soups out of all recognition, even when only a trace is added. In other products, e.g., tomato soup, it prevents the formation of that slightly metallic flavour often noticed. In passing, it is perhaps worth noting that the paste type of meat or vegetable extract is often very difficult to get out of the can and this may be overcome by having a steam-heated cabinet in which there is a container with a tap and with a wire grid on top. The opened cans of extract may then be inverted on the grid and the contents allowed to drip slowly into the container as heat is applied.

Whilst not properly a flavouring ingredient, but rather a bulk ingredient in soup, tomato paste plays a very important part in almost all commercial soup flavouring. It is difficult to describe just what it is that tomato gives to the soup, but undoubtedly a little tomato in almost any recipe adds 'life' to the flavour not provided by anything else.

Again, whilst not properly a flavouring ingredient, it is surprising what effect upon flavour the use of extruded dough products of the right type may have upon certain soups. In soups in which vegetables and extruded dough products are used as garnish also, the use of cheese or cheese oil has been found to be advantageous.

In view of the great importance of proper control over the amount of each type of flavouring ingredient which is added to each batch of soup, as it is made, it is good practice to have a small room set aside apart from the rest of the soup kitchen, in which the spices, flavours and colours, if any, are weighed up. If such a room is conveniently arranged, all the necessary flavour or colour ingredients for one batch may be weighed out and placed into standard-sized containers assembled on one tray. These trays are then issued to the chef in charge and the entire contents of that one tray put into one batch. This system reduces risk of double lots being added to the soup or of one or another ingredient being missed. Further, as spices and flavours are very costly, it is important to keep these ingredients where they will be carefully handled, away from the rest of the factory production line.

SOUP IMPROVERS

A range of soup improvers for incorporation in soup made commercially has been developed by Bush Boake Allen Ltd., which is available with suggested usage per ten gallons of soup:

		Per 10 *gallons Soup*
Soup Flavour Improver C.3600 ⎫	for Tomato	$\frac{1}{4}$ fl. oz.
Soup Flavour Improver C.4982 ⎬	Soups	$\frac{3}{4}$–1 ,, ,,
Soup Flavour Improver C.5298 ⎭		$\frac{1}{4}$,, ,,
Soup Flavour Improver C.6472	for Julienne Soups	$\frac{1}{4}$,, ,,
Soup Flavour Improver C.7080	for Pea Soups	$\frac{3}{4}$,, ,,
Soup Flavour Improver C.7081	for Mulligatawny Soups	$\frac{1}{3}$,, ,,
Soup Flavour Improver C.7082	for Mock Turtle Soups	$\frac{3}{8}$,, ,,
Soup Flavour Improver C.7083	for Celery Soups	$\frac{1}{3}$,, ..
		Per 100 *lb. base*
Soup Flavour Improver H.5685	for Chicken Soups	10 oz.
Soup Flavour Improver Powder H.7391	for Chicken Soups	3 lb.

The following range of Emulsion Flavours is also available in the Bush 'Flavor-Mist' series of Improvers for Soups.

	Per 100 *gallons Soup*
'FLAVOR-MIST' CELERY SOUP IMPROVER	3½ fl. oz.
'FLAVOR-MIST' KIDNEY SOUP IMPROVER	3 ,, ,,
'FLAVOR-MIST' MEAT EXTRACT IMPROVER	4–5 ,, ,,
'FLAVOR-MIST' MIXED VEGETABLE SOUP IMPROVER	3½–4 ,, ,,
'FLAVOR-MIST' MOCK TURTLE SOUP IMPROVER	4½ ,, ,,
'FLAVOR-MIST' OXTAIL SOUP IMPROVER	4–5 ,, ,,
'FLAVOR-MIST' PEA SOUP IMPROVER	8 ,, ,,
'FLAVOR-MIST' TOMATO SOUP IMPROVER	2½ ,, ,,

3. *Thick Meat Soups*

Probably the most important canned soup in this category is oxtail soup. In this case, the most important point is to get the maximum flavour out of the oxtails. As has been stated, the oxtails must be cut up into small pieces before use. In most cases, the small sections at the end of the tail are saved to garnish the cans, whilst the larger sections are used to make the actual soup. If the sections of tail are first given a light roast in the oven and then subjected to a steam pressure cooking in the retort, it will be found that the meat develops a full flavour and a considerable quantity of golden oil is released. The next stage must of course be to get all the meat possible off the bones and into the soup, together with the maximum flavour.

This may be done in either of two ways. In the first method, a measured quantity of cooked oxtail is put into the steam pan along with vegetables and stock and the whole lot cooked for several hours. At the end of this time the entire batch is run through the pulper to finish it off and to remove the meat from the bones. This method is very good and results in a good soup, however there is absolutely no way of telling just what quantity of oil and meat will result from a given weight of tails and thus the soup may be thicker at one time than another. It is indeed surprising by just how much such soup can vary. The second method of operation is to cook the tails sufficiently in the retort stage to allow of the easy removal of the meat before passing it to the pulping machine or colloid mill. Thus all tails are put through the machine together with a quantity of stock to wash out the machine. The resulting pulp is then measured out into standard quantities and added to the batches of soup in the finishing kettles. The same applies to the golden oil.

When the smaller pieces of tail are used to garnish the cans, great care must be taken to see that no extra large pieces are allowed to be used, as if the retorting time is exactly calculated for small pieces of tail, one or two cans with large pieces in them may be incompletely sterilized.

Some manufacturers make a straightforward meat soup, or of course try to use the meat solids of the meat they have used for making up the stock. This is always rather a problem as meat varies enormously in texture and sometimes the yield from the pulper is very poor and hardly ever is it possible to get all the meat through in the form of pulp suitable to put into the soup. One method of getting over this, is to stew the meat up with B.P. standard hydrochloric acid and then to neutralize the whole brew with sodium hydroxide. The result is of course to produce very tender meat and a certain amount of salty water from the neutralization processes. This process is the subject of several patents, and in any case should not be under-taken unless stringent laboratory control is available. As an alternative to the acid hydrolysis method, there are certain enzymes which can be used to soften meats, but care has to be taken to avoid the formation of off-flavours.

In the handling of all meats for meat soups, great care has to be exercised to avoid either cooking the meats too much, or more especially, keeping them lying about in the cooked state too long. This is partly because the bacterial count can go up very quickly, but also because meats which are either over-cooked or held too long seem to develop a peculiar gluey, almost dirty, taste when sterilized in the final soup product in the can.

Mulligatawny is quite a popular thick soup and in its original form was a very highly spiced thick soup, of which the essential spice character was curry powder. The actual name 'mulliga-tawny' is derived from two native words meaning 'pepper-water'. This soup, in a slightly milder form can be most attractive and a very good starting base is rabbit, as this flesh seems to blend very well with curry powder. It is most impor-tant to use a really good curry powder, as otherwise it is very easy to produce a musty flavour. This soup can be very much

improved by the incorporation of mango chutney of the sweet
type and also coconut meat and rice. The coconut meat, and
milk if it is available, makes a great deal of difference as it
smooths off the taste of the curry. When rice is used as a garnish
in the can, for this or any other soup, it cannot be put into the
can raw, but must be cooked first, as otherwise it merely sticks
together in a lump in the bottom of the can. The best way to
treat rice in order to make it float through the soup evenly
when it is served, is to roast it first in trays in the oven. In this
method, the rice grains are first coated with hot fat or oil and
then given a gentle roast in the oven. Not enough to make the
mix brown, but enough to start to soften the rice and to drive
the fat or oil into the grain. The trays are then topped up with
hot water or stock and the rice cooked until it is firm and free
running. It is then placed into the cans, preferably whilst still
hot.

Thick mock turtle soup is usually made from calves' heads
and should have at least some bacon in it. One of the most
important flavouring ingredients is lemon. Some manufacturers
have found it an advantage to use sieved lemon marmalade, as
this is a standard product available at all times and at the same
time the peel is then used and imparts a rather pleasant bitter
element.

4. *Vegetable Soups*

There are of course both thick purée type vegetable soups,
the most important of which is tomato (notwithstanding the
fact that the tomato is a fruit), and also the diced vegetable type
of soup, which often has a meat base.

There is no doubt at all that in the soups where the main
flavour is that of vegetables, the real secret lies in using really
fresh vegetables which have been freshly prepared. Whilst the
purchase of fresh vegetables does not present an enormous
problem to the manufacturer, at any rate in the autumn of the
year, the actual production of cleaned and diced vegetables in
big quantities is quite a problem. In many cases, it is found
most convenient to prepare diced vegetables well in advance of
actual soup making, often in fact the day before. These vegetables are usually then stored in half-barrels in water. There is
no doubt, however, that this is quite wrong if a quality product

is required, as stored vegetables definitely develop a strong flavour. Wherever possible then, the vegetables should be cleaned and prepared at a rate equalling that of consumption in the soup kitchen, even if this does raise some management problems.

Diced vegetables for garnishing the cans may be greatly improved by pre-browning in hot fat, but in any case they should be pre-blanched and cooled in cold water. They should never be added to the can raw.

Soups of the diced vegetable type really need other ingredients as well as the diced vegetables themselves and as has already been pointed out in another section of this chapter, extruded dough products, rice, and such items as cheese oil make a world of difference to the flavour.

Extruded dough products, or pasta, are now available in the United Kingdom in a great variety of shapes and sizes, as may be seen from the colour inset incorporated in this edition.

Some of these pasta products have already been incorporated in canned soups and soup mixes. Other shapes illustrated give an idea of the wide range of pasta products available as standard. Special shapes and different sizes may be produced if required.

Pea soup is particularly popular and this may be made from either fresh peas or dried peas. Where fresh peas are used, the pods may be utilized to make stock with good results, and mint oil should be used for flavouring. Pea soup in particular should be well emulsified before canning as it tends to go 'grainy' very easily.

Tomato soup is really a subject all on its own, as it is probably the most popular soup of all and one of the most difficult to make, especially the creamed variety. In the United Kingdom, nearly all tomato soup is made from canned imported tomato paste,* which can of course be bought in various degrees of concentration. In this respect, it may be said that the best soups result from paste of higher concentration, although this paste is usually relatively dearer.

* Ref.: *Tomato Paste, Purée, Juice and Powder* by Peter G. Goose and Raymond Binsted, 1964, Food Trade Press Ltd., London; or in Italian language: *Derivati Di Pomodoro Concentuati, Succhi E Polvere* Di Peter G. Goose and Raymond Binsted, 1967, Food Trade Press Ltd., London.

There are of course innumerable recipes for making tomato soup, but there are three points of special interest. Firstly, arrowroot has been found to be the best thickener for this type of soup. Secondly, this soup should be emulsified and if it is to be sieved to give it a final gloss this should be done over a vibrating screen rather than through a pulper. Thirdly, if milk is to be added this should be done last. In this case, the milk should be heated to at least 200° F. before it is added to the soup, or it will curdle. Where a laboratory is available, a constant check should be kept upon the acidity of the milk purchased to obviate souring and curdling troubles even during the initial heating-up period.

A final note on the problem of curdling in creamed soups is of interest. The following points should be observed in this connection:

1. The starch or flour ingredient should be pre-gelatinized beforehand. With wheat flour, this should be cooked for $2\frac{1}{2}$ minutes at 210° F.

2. Fat should be homogenized before this is mixed with the pre-cooked starch. If the pre-cooked starch fraction is homogenized breakdown is experienced.

3. Salt tends to accelerate curdling and clotting in cream soups but this effect is minimized in the presence of emulsified fat.

4. When the pH is reduced to 5·0 or lower heavy clotting is experienced but this does not happen with cream of tomato soups where the pH is usually 4·6 or so.

5. Time and temperature of retorting, sieving, sugar and milk condition do not appear to affect curdling.

Some interesting facts about British eating habits were compiled by a marketing firm for the year 1955–6 and published as 'The Foods We Eat' in 1958. It was disclosed that in the country as a whole 6 per cent of men and women have soup at the midday meal in summer whereas this rises to 18 per cent for men and 19 per cent for women in winter. For Scotland the comparable figures are, men 30 per cent and women 3 per cent in summer, and men 48 per cent and women 56 per cent in winter.

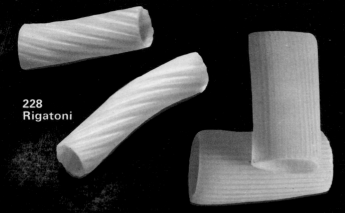

228 Rigatoni

bow Tubetti

229 Large Rigatoni

ow Macaroni

230 Canneloni

Ibow Macaroni

232 Small Wheels

**231 Waggon
Wheels**

Cornetti

234 Miniature Stars

235 Stars

SHORT PASTA

239 Soup Noodles

244 Lumache

250 Miniature Sh

240 Fideli

246 Spirals

251 Medium Sh

**241 Spaghettini
(Short Cut Spaghetti)**

247 Twistetti

252 Shells

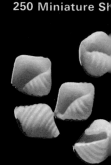

243 Lumachine

248 Spiral Macaroni

253 Corrugated

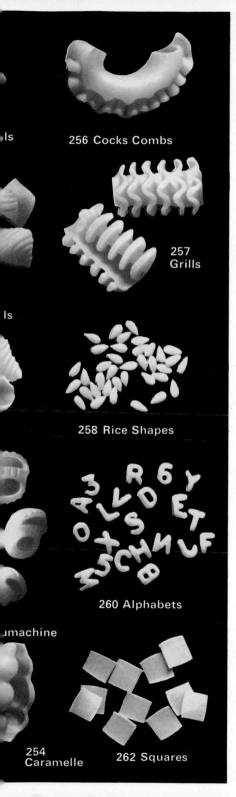

256 Cocks Combs

257 Grills

258 Rice Shapes

260 Alphabets

254 Caramelle

262 Squares

machine

FOLDED PAST

402
Fine
Folded
Noodles

405 Folded
Broad Noodles

By courtesy of Pasta Foods Ltd. w
of their Pasta Shapes Guide recent

In recent years an increasing variety
become available and a number of these
in canned soups and packet soups. I†
that other shapes illustrated or shapes y
be included in soups in the future.

Every shape in this Guide is manufacture
Semolina under strict quality control, to t
The latest production plant enables alr
produced and packed to customers ow
The research and development facilities
are available to food manufacturers con
sion of pasta in their soups or other foo

For further information please contact:
**PASTA FOODS LTD., 224 LON
ST. ALBANS, HERTS.   Te
*Designed and produced by Richmond Tov
Printed in England.*

401
Folded
Vermicelli

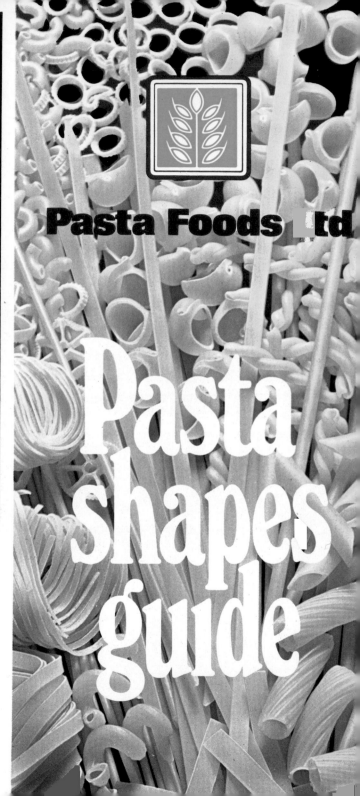

Pasta Foods Ltd

Pasta shapes guide

e include a copy
y issued by them.

of pasta shapes has
are already included
is more than likely
et to be evolved will

d from 100% Durum
he highest standards.
ost any shape to be
specifications.
of Pasta Foods Ltd.
emplating the inclu-
products.

DON ROAD,
. ST. ALBANS 60461
ers Limited, London, W.C.1.

Again, in the whole country, 3 per cent of men and women take soup at the principal evening meal in summer whereas the figures are 8 per cent for men and 7 per cent for women in winter. For Scotland the figures are: *Summer,* men 9 per cent and women 7 per cent; *Winter,* men 23 per cent and women 16 per cent. The London figures are only a very small proportion of the Scottish ones, as may be imagined.

The annual consumption of canned soups in the United Kingdom has been calculated at about 170,000 tons per annum, and, no doubt, this figure is increasing.

CANNED SOUPS AVAILABLE IN U.K.

The following partial list of commercially canned ready-to-serve and condensed soups shows the wide range available in the United Kingdom:

Asparagus
Asparagus, Creamed
Barley
Bean with Bacon
Beef
Beef Bouillon
Beef Broth
Beef Consommé
Beef, Curried
Beef Noodle
Beetroot Borsht
Bird's Nest
Bouillabaisse
Cabbage Borsht
Celery
Celery, Creamed
Chicken Broth
Chicken Broth with Rice
Chicken Consommé
Chicken, Creamed
Chicken Gumbo
Chicken Gumbo, Clear
Chicken Mulligatawny
Chicken Noodle
Chicken and Ham, Creamed

Chicken and Mushroom,
   Creamed
Chicken with Rice
Chicken Tomato
Chicken Vegetable
Clam Chowder
Cock-a-Leekie
Consommé
Cornish Crab
Cornish Scallop
Cottage Broth
Cottage Style Potato
Country Vegetable with Beef
Dietetic Soups
Duck with Orange
Farmhouse
Fish
Fish Pottage
Golden Vegetable
Green Pea
Green Pea, Creamed
Green Turtle
Harvest Cream
Julienne Consommé
Kangaroo Tail

Kidney
Kidney Lentil
Kneidlach
Kreplach
Lentil
Lobster Bisque
Lobster, Creamed
Minestrone
Mock Turtle
Mulligatawny
Mushroom
Mushroom, Creamed
Onion
Onion, Creamed
Onion, French Style
Oxtail
Oxtail, Clear
Oxtail, Thick
Oyster
Paprika Goulash
Pea and Ham
Pheasant Consommé
Pheasant, Creamed
Royal Game
Scampi, Creamed
Scampi Bisque
Scotch Beef

Scotch Broth
Scottish Vegetable with
    Lentils
Shark's Fin
Soups for Babies
Stock Pot
Thick Vegetable and Beef
    Broth
Tomato
Tomato, American
Tomato, Creamed
Tomato, Hawaiian
Tomato Rice
Turkey
Turtle
Turtle Consommé
Turtle, Green
Turtle, Thick
Vegetable
Vegetable Beef
Vegetable with Beef Stock
Vegetable and Chicken
Vegetable, Creamed
Vegetable Oxtail
Venison with Vegetables
Vichyssoise
Wild Duck Consommé

Canned Soups Available in U.S.A.

The following soups are part of the wide range canned commercially in the United States, in addition to some of those already listed on the previous pages:

Almond, Creamed
Artichoke, Creamed
Avocado, Creamed
Bean
Bean, Black
Bean 'n Franks
Bean, Lima
Bean with Ham
Bean with Smoked Pork
Beef Bouillon

Beef Consommé, Jellied
Beef, Vegetables and Barley
Cheddar Cheese
Chicken, Country Style
Chicken Consommé, Jellied
Chicken Curry
Chicken 'n Dumplings
Chicken Noodle with
    Dumplings
Chicken Rice with Mushrooms

Chicken and Stars
Chicken with Stars and Stripes
Chicken with Wild Rice
Chili Beef
Clam Broth
Clam Chowder, Manhattan
Style
Clam Chowder, New England
Style
Clam Consommé
Clam Madrilène
Claret Consommé
Consommé Madrilène
Consommé Printanier
Corn Chowder
Corn, Creamed
Crab Bisque
Cucumber, Creamed
Fish Chowder
Green Turtle and Pea
Gumbo Creole
Hot Dog Bean
Hunter's
Lobster Chowder
Mutton Broth
Navy Bean
Noodle
Noodles and Ground Beef

Okra
Onion, Bretonne Style
Oyster, Creamed
Oyster Stew
Pea with Smoked Ham
Pepper Pot
Petite Marmite
Potato, Creamed
Purée Mongole
Quahaug Chowder
Seafood Style
Shrimp, Creamed
Soup Stock
Spinach
Tomato, Bretonne Bean
Tomato Bisque
Tomato Okra
Tomato Rice, Old Fashioned
Tomato Vegetable
Turkey Noodle
Turtle Vegetable
Vegetable Bean
Vegetable and Beef Stockpot
Vegetables with Ground Beef
Vegetable, Old Fashioned
Vegetable, Vegetarian
Vermicelli
Watercress, Creamed

STANDARD FOR TOMATO PURÉE AND PASTE

*Approved and adopted by the C.I.P.C. Sub-Committee for
the regulation and definition of canned tomato products at the
meeting in Brussels in October 1958*

ARTICLE I—DEFINITION

1. The terms 'tomato purée' and 'tomato paste', accompanied by the words 'light', 'medium' or 'heavy' in accordance
with the degrees of concentration as hereafter defined, apply to
the canned products prepared by straining the fresh fruit of the
tomato *Lycopersicum esculentum* L., and concentrating, thereby
removing part of the water, the resulting pulpy liquid.

2. According to the degree of concentration, estimated by

the determination of the refractometer solids (less added salt) as set out in Article IV, the products listed in paragraph 1 above are described as follows:

Minimum percentage of refractometer solids (less added solids)	Description
11	Light tomato purée, minimum solids 11 per cent
15	Medium tomato purée, minimum solids 15 per cent
22	Heavy tomato purée, minimum solids 22 per cent
28	Light tomato paste, minimum solids 28 per cent
36	Medium tomato paste, minimum solids 36 per cent
45	Heavy tomato paste, minimum solids 45 per cent

The minimum percentage of solids, corresponding to the degree of concentration in accordance with the list given above, shall be stated on the label, immediately following the name of the product and given as a single number written in the same type, as follows: 'minimum solids: × %'.[1]

The sale of tomato purées containing less than 11 per cent solids is not permitted. This prohibition does not however apply to tomato juice, nor to tomato soups, sauces, seasonings or pickles.

The percentage of solids shall always be given less added salt, that is to say minus the quantity of salt which has been added to the product, corrected for the natural chlorides present in the tomato, which are arbitrarily rated as amounting to 2 per cent of the solids.[2]

3. The tomato purées and pastes defined above may be sold either without any statement of quality (standard quality) or with the statement 'extra quality'. They should satisfy the requirements set forth in Article III.

No other description is permitted.

ARTICLE II—GENERAL CHARACTERISTICS
A—*Raw Materials*

1. Tomatoes intended for the preparation of the products described above shall be fresh, sound and in good condition, free from rot and generally free from mould, and shall have reached a suitable degree of ripeness.

2. They shall have been graded, washed, and if necessary trimmed.

3. Trimmings shall not be used in the preparation of food for human consumption.

B—*Finished Product*

1. The tomato purées as described above shall have been freed from seeds and skin. They must also satisfy the conditions stated in Article II herein.

2. White cooking salt (sodium chloride) may be added provided that this addition be declared conspicuously on the label by the words 'salt added', and provided that the amount added does not exceed 2 per cent in the finished product for purées of 11, 15 and 22 per cent minimum solids, 3 per cent for purées of 28 and 36 per cent minimum solids and 5 per cent for purées of 45 per cent minimum solids.

The addition of herbs and natural spices or their extracts to tomato purées is permitted provided that such addition be stated on the label by the word 'flavoured' or 'spiced', or both, as the case may be.

The addition of sugars (sucrose, dextrose, dextrose syrup, invert sugar and the like) to tomato purécs and tomato pastes covered by the present specification is not permitted. It shall however be allowed in products shipped to processors and provided it has been expressly asked for by the buyer or his agent; in this case the statements 'sugar (sucrose, dextrose, etc.) added × %' and 'product not intended for direct consumption' shall appear on the label. These statements shall be given in type of the same appearance and not smaller than half the size of the type used for the description prescribed under Article I, paragraph 2 above.

3. It is forbidden to add to products sold commercially under the descriptions given in Article I, paragraph 2 above, or under a description capable of being confused with the former, ingredients other than those described in Article II, B, paragraph 2, especially cereals or thickening agents (e.g., flour, cornflour, starch, dextrin, pectins, alginates) and purées of other vegetables (e.g., carrots, beetroots, apples, pumpkin, paprika).

Tomato products other than those defined above or which will be defined in other special standards, to which addition of one or more of the ingredients covered by this paragraph is permitted, must be described by a name which cannot give rise to any confusion between them and the preparations covered by these standards, and their qualitative composition must be shown on the labels.

4. Tomato purées covered by the present standards should not contain artificial colours, preservatives or artificial sweetening agents.

5. The cans shall be filled as much as practicable without impairment of the appearance, the quality or the good preservation of the product.

ARTICLE III—QUALITY GRADES
A—*Physical Properties*

	Standard quality	Extra quality
Colour	Red colour characteristic of ripe tomatoes.	Equivalent or better, in the sense of an increase in the ratio of red to yellow, to that of the following combination of Munsell colours.[3] Red 5R 2,6/13 brilliant 65 per cent Orange 2,5 YR 5/12 brilliant 8 per cent Black N.1 brilliant ⎫ Grey N.4 dull ⎬ 27 per cent
Texture and consistency	Reasonably homogeneous.	Homogeneous.
Impurities	The presence is allowed of natural vegetable impurities visible only on a careful examination by the naked eye. Microscopic examination according to the Howard method should not show the presence of mould in more than 60 per cent of the fields.	Examination by the naked eye should not reveal any impurity. Microscopic examination according to the Howard method should not show the presence of mould in more than 40 per cent of the fields.
Flavour and smell	Absence of foreign and abnormal tastes and odours.	Absence of foreign and abnormal tastes and colours.

B—*Chemical Properties*

	Standard quality	Extra quality
Minimum content of total reducing sugars, expressed as invert sugar p.100 of solids less added salt	45	50
Maximum titratable acidity, expressed as hydrated citric acid p.100 of solids less added salt	10	9
Maximum volatile acidity, expressed as acetic acid p.100 of solids less added salt	0·50	0·25
Maximum water insoluble inorganic impurities p.100 of solids less added salt	0·1	0·05
Maximum copper content p.100 of solids less added salt	0·01	0·01

ARTICLE IV—METHODS OF EXAMINATION

The sampling and the estimation of the different characteristics described in the present standards shall be carried out by methods approved by the C.I.P.C.

It is specified that the percentage of solids estimated by the refractometric reading at 20° C., according to the method described in the appended note.

Filling of Cans

Solids		11 per cent	15 per cent	22 per cent	28 per cent
Dimensions[4] of cans mm.	Capacity of cans ml.	Minimum net weight in grams			
55 × 68	142	140	140	145	150
100 × 118·5	850	850	860	890	910
153 × 181	3100	3100	3150	3250	3300
153 × 246	4250	4250	4300	4450	4550

APPENDIX I

Filling of Cans

The minimum weight of product to be packed in the can corresponds to the figures given hereafter for certain sizes of cans; for can sizes other than those listed, it shall be calculated in proportion to the volume of the can.

APPENDIX II

Determination of the Refractometer Solids in Tomato Purées

Details are given in an appendix published in the official schedule of the apparatus suitable for such determinations and the method employed.

APPENDIX III

Estimation of Chlorides

Describes the method and the reagents necessary.

[1] This provision concerning labelling does not apply to tomato purées and pastes sold to processors.

[2] The figure represents the approximate average natural chloride content of tomatoes; but under certain circumstances the natural chloride content of tomatoes may reach and even exceed 4 per cent of the solids.

[3] These figures apply essentially to light tomato paste with 28 per cent minimum solids.

[4] Inside diameter and overall height.

Commercial Soup Formulae

CANNED CREAM OF ASPARAGUS SOUP

Milk	12	gals.
Asparagus, (Fresh, Frozen or Canned)	69	lb.
Butter	15	,,
Wheat Flour	11	,,
Salt	3	,,
Monosodium Glutamate (M.S.G.) .	10	oz.
Hydrolysed Vegetable Protein (H.V.P.)	10	,,
Ground White Pepper . . .	1	,,
Ground Bay Leaves	$\frac{1}{2}$	,,

Bulk to 30 gallons with water.

Macerate the asparagus and add to the other ingredients which have been previously mixed to a smooth consistency in a steam-heated jacketed stainless steel pan, fitted with a stirrer. Bulk to 30 gallons with water, bring to the boil, simmer for 5 minutes and then fill hot into No. 1 Tall plain cans. Seal, process at 240° F. for $1\frac{1}{4}$ hours, then water cool.

When canned asparagus is used, the liquor is added to the soup when making up to volume. Asparagus tips may be added as a garnish.

CANNED CLEAR BEEF NOODLE SOUP

STOCK:

Beef Bones .	160	lb.	—Roasted to brown.
Carrots	14	,,	⎫
Leeks .	12	,,	⎪
Turnips	$10\frac{1}{2}$	,,	⎬ Fried to brown.
Parsnips	$18\frac{1}{2}$	,,	⎪
Swedes .	$24\frac{1}{2}$	,,	⎭

When the above is ready, water is added and the mixture boiled 2–3 hours. The stock is strained and the yield is of the order of 30 gallons, but this can be increased by addition of water.

Soup:

Stock	30 gals.
Beef, minced . . .	42 lb.
Leeks	16 ,,
Egg White	10½ ,,
Salt	2 ,, 2 oz.
Hydrolysed Vegetable Protein	14 oz.
Monosodium Glutamate .	6 ,,
Peppercorns . . .	4 ,,
Ground White Pepper . .	1½ ,,
Caramel	As necessary

All the ingredients, except the stock, are thoroughly mixed, added to the stock and well stirred until the soup boils and a crust forms. The soup is gently simmered for ½ hour then it is carefully strained through a fine cloth.

No. 1 Tall cans are garnished with raw beef and ½ oz. of blanched noodles (2–3 minutes in boiling water, drained and rinsed in cold water) then filled with the hot soup. The cans are processed at 240° F. for 75 minutes and finally water cooled.

CANNED BEEF CONSOMMÉ

Stock	30 gals.
Beef	42 lb.
Leeks	16 ,,
Egg White	10½ ,,
Salt	2 ,,
Hydrolysed Vegetable Protein (H.V.P.)	14 oz.
Monosodium Glutamate (M.S.G.)	6 ,,
Peppercorns	1½ ,,
Ground White Pepper . . .	1½ ,,

The leeks are shredded and mixed with the meat, egg whites, peppercorns and seasoning. This mixture is then added

E

to the heated stock, brought to the boil and stirred gently. This is allowed to simmer gently for $\frac{1}{2}$ hour after which the consommé is strained and filled hot into plain No. 1 Tall cans. A small amount of Julienne strips of leek and carrot is placed in each can. The cans are then sealed, processed for 75 minutes at 240° F. and water cooled.

CANNED BROWN WINDSOR SOUP

Carrots	20 lb.
Parsnips	20 ,,
Swedes	20 ,,
Onions	20 ,,
Margarine	$11\frac{1}{2}$,,
Wheat Flour	11 ,,
Beef Extract	6 ,,
Salt	2 ,,
Hydrolysed Vegetable Protein . .	1 ,,
Yeast Extract. . . .	$\frac{1}{2}$,,
Monosodium Glutamate . . .	1 oz.
Ground White Pepper . . .	$\frac{2}{3}$,,
Caramel	As desired

Bulk to 30 gallons with water.

Place the margarine in a steam-jacketed boiling pan, fitted with a stirrer and brown the chopped prepared vegetables in it. Add the flour and allow to brown, then the rest of the ingredients. Stir well during the preparation and simmer the soup until the vegetables are tender. Pass the soup through a sieve so that the vegetables form a purée, then rebulk to 30 gallons with water. Bring to the boil and fill hot into No. 1 Tall plain cans. Seal, process at 240° F. for $1\frac{1}{4}$ hours, then water cool.

CANNED CREAM OF CELERY SOUP

Milk	12	gals.
Celery	75	lb.
Butter	15	,,
Wheat Flour	11	,,
Salt	3	,,
Monosodium Glutamate . . .	10	oz.
Hydrolysed Vegetable Protein . .	10	,,
Ground White Pepper . . .	1	,,
Ground Bay Leaves	$\frac{1}{2}$	,,

Bulk to 30 gallons with water.

Macerate the celery in a suitable machine and mix the other ingredients to a smooth paste. Add the celery, mix and bulk to 30 gallons with water. Bring to the boil, simmer for 5 minutes, then fill hot into plain No. 1 Tall cans. Seal, process at 240° F. for $1\frac{1}{4}$ hours, then water cool.

CANNED CREAM OF CHICKEN SOUP

Chicken Stock	15	gals.
Milk	$11\frac{1}{2}$	,,
Wheat Flour	16	lb.
Butter	9	,,
Salt	$2\frac{1}{2}$	,,
Hydrolysed Vegetable Protein . .	1	,,
Monosodium Glutamate . . .	10	oz.
Onion Powder	10	,,
Sugar	6	,,
SAROMEX Celery (on salt) . .	4	,,
Ground White Pepper . . .	1	,,

Cover dressed chickens and giblets with water and retort until the flesh comes away easily from the bones. Drain off liquor and retain for stock. Remove flesh from bones and use diced as a garnish. Digest the bones, skin and giblets in water for 1 hour at 250° F. in a retort. Drain and add this liquor to the original liquor. This is the chicken stock. Whisk the flour with the milk to a smooth paste and add to the rest of the ingredients which have been brought to the boil in a stainless steel steam-heated jacketed pan, equipped with a stirrer. Homogenize at 1,500–2,000 p.s.i. and hold at 180°–200° F.

prior to filling. Place $\frac{1}{2}$–$\frac{3}{4}$ oz. of diced chicken meat in each plain No. 1 Tall can and fill with soup. Process, after sealing, for 75 minutes at 240° F. and water cool.

Yield: approximately 30 gallons.

CANNED CHICKEN BROTH

Salt	1 lb. 14 oz.
Monosodium Glutamate . .	10 oz.
Onion Powder	5 ,,
Ground Celery Seed . . .	$\frac{1}{2}$,,
Ground Bay Leaves . . .	$\frac{1}{2}$,,
Ground White Pepper . .	$\frac{1}{2}$,,
Caramel	As required

Bulk to 30 gallons with chicken stock.

Chicken stock is prepared by retorting dressed chickens (i.e. defeathered, all entrails and feet removed) until tender. The bones and giblets are processed further with the drained liquor for one hour longer. The fat is then skimmed from the stock and the seasoning added. The broth is brought to the boil and filled hot into No. 1 Tall plain cans, each containing about $\frac{1}{2}$ oz. of diced white chicken and $\frac{1}{2}$ oz. of blanched Patna rice. The cans are sealed, processed for one hour at 240° F., and then water cooled.

CANNED CHICKEN AND GREEN PEA SOUP

Green Peas (Fresh or Frozen) . .	42 lb.
Milk	3 gals.
Butter	9 lb.
Wheat Flour	9 ,,
Salt	5 ,,
Cornflour	$4\frac{1}{2}$,,
Sugar	$1\frac{1}{2}$,,
Monosodium Glutamate . . .	1 ,,
Onion Powder.	$\frac{3}{4}$,,
Hydrolysed Vegetable Protein . .	10 oz.
Ground Bay Leaves . . .	$1\frac{1}{4}$,,
Ground White Pepper . . .	$1\frac{1}{4}$,,

Bulk to 30 gallons with stock.

A good stock is prepared by retorting or boiling 3–4 chickens per gallon of water. When the chickens are tender, the meat is removed and the bones and giblets processed for a further 2 hours. The stock is then strained. All the ingredients, except the peas, are mixed with the milk to a smooth paste. The mixture is bulked to 30 gallons with stock (and water, also, if necessary) and then brought to the boil. After simmering for 2–3 minutes the peas are added and the hot soup is filled into plain No. 1 Tall cans. A garnish of chicken meat is placed in each can before filling and the sealed cans are processed at 240° F. for 75 minutes and then water cooled.

CANNED CLEAR CHICKEN NOODLE SOUP

Salt	2½ lb.
Monosodium Glutamate . . .	10 oz.
Hydrolysed Vegetable Protein . .	10 ,,
Onion Powder	5 ,,
Ground White Pepper . . .	1 ,,
Ground Celery Seed	1 ,,
Bulk to 30 gallons with stock.

A good stock is prepared by retorting or boiling 3–4 chickens per gallon of water. When the chickens are tender, the meat is removed and the bones and giblets processed for a further 2 hours. The stock is then strained. The above ingredients are mixed with stock to a smooth paste, bulked to 30 gallons with stock and brought to the boil. Diced chicken meat and ½ oz. of blanched noodles (2–3 minutes in boiling water, drained and rinsed in cold water) are placed in each No. 1 Tall can which is then filled with hot soup. The cans are processed at 240° F. for 75 minutes then water cooled.

CANNED CREAM OF CORN SOUP

Fresh Milk	6 gals.
Sweet Corn (Fresh, Quick-frozen or Canned)	55 lb.
Butter	7½ ,,
Wheat Flour	6 ,,
Salt	3 ,,
Hydrolysed Vegetable Protein . .	10 oz.
Monosodium Glutamate . . .	10 ,,
Ground White Pepper . . .	⅛ ,,
Bulk to 30 gallons with water.

If fresh or frozen corn is used, it is cooked with water until soft, then passed through a fine sieve. Canned whole kernel corn will require sieving but canned cream-style corn can be used directly. The rest of the ingredients are added and well mixed and then bulked to 30 gallons with water. The soup is brought to the boil and simmered for 5 minutes. It is then filled hot into plain No. 1 Tall cans, sealed and processed for 75 minutes at 240° F., and then water cooled.

CANNED DUTCH PEA SOUP WITH FRANKFURTERS

Dried Split Green Peas .	.	.	$67\frac{1}{2}$ lb.
Sliced Onions	.	.	.	$22\frac{1}{2}$,,
Sliced Potatoes	.	.	.	$18\frac{3}{4}$,,
Wheat Flour	.	.	.	$4\frac{1}{2}$,,
Salt .	.	.	.	.	$2\frac{1}{4}$,,
Hydrolysed Vegetable Protein	.	$1\frac{1}{4}$,,
Monosodium Glutamate	.	.	$\frac{1}{2}$,,
Ground Celery Seed	.	.	$1\frac{1}{4}$ oz.
Ground White Pepper .	.	.	$\frac{1}{3}$,,
Bacon	.	.	.	.	For stock
Frankfurters.	.	.	.	As required

Bulk to 30 gallons with water.

The vegetables and bacon are boiled, and then the bacon is removed and diced for use as a garnish. When the vegetables are soft they are passed through a fine sieve, the other 'pasted' ingredients added, the soup bulked to 30 gallons with water and the whole brought to the boil and simmered for 5 minutes.

Sliced frankfurters and diced bacon are placed in each plain No. 1 Tall can and the cans filled with hot soup. The cans are sealed and processed for 75 minutes at 240° F., and then water cooled.

CANNED GOULASH SOUP

Beef, Diced ($\frac{1}{4}$ inch cube) . . .	34	lb.
Tomato Paste (30 per cent solids) .	18	,,
Onions, Chopped	9	,,
Paprika	5	,,
Wheat Flour	$3\frac{1}{4}$	,,
Salt	$2\frac{3}{4}$	,,
Vegetable Fat	$2\frac{1}{4}$	,,
Hydrolysed Vegetable Protein . .	$1\frac{1}{2}$	,,
Monosodium Glutamate . . .	10	oz.

Bulk to 30 gallons with water.

The meat and onions are browned in the fat. The other ingredients are mixed to a smooth paste with water and the meat and onions added. The whole is bulked to 30 gallons with water, brought to the boil and simmered 2–3 minutes, and then filled hot into No. 1 Tall cans garnished with diced potato. The sealed cans are processed for 75 minutes at 240° F. and water cooled.

CANNED CREAM OF GREEN PEA SOUP

Green Peas (Fresh or Frozen) . .	85	lb.
Milk	$6\frac{1}{2}$	gals.
Wheat Flour	$13\frac{1}{2}$	lb.
Butter	$5\frac{1}{4}$	,,
Salt	$2\frac{1}{4}$	,,
Hydrolysed Vegetable Protein . .	$1\frac{1}{4}$	,,
Sugar	$\frac{3}{4}$	,,
Onion Powder.	$\frac{3}{4}$	,,
Monosodium Glutamate . . .	7	oz.
Ground White Pepper . . .	$\frac{1}{2}$	,,
Ground Bay Leaves	$\frac{1}{4}$	,,

Bulk to 30 gallons with stock.

Prepare stock by processing in a retort bacon bones and bacon pieces with water. Strain off the liquid and skim off fat, if necessary. Purée the cooked green peas and add the other ingredients. Bulk to 30 gallons with stock, bring to the boil and then fill hot into plain No. 1 Tall cans. Seal, process for $1\frac{1}{4}$ hours at 240° F. then water cool.

CANNED KIDNEY SOUP

Chopped Onions.	30	lb.
Chopped Carrots	30	,,
Wheat Flour	15	,,
Salt .	$2\frac{1}{2}$	,,
Yeast Extract	1	,,
Hydrolysed Vegetable Protein	1	,,
Monosodium Glutamate	10	oz.
Ground White Pepper	$\frac{1}{2}$	,,
Caramel .	As required	
Beef Bones (for stock) .		

Bulk to 30 gallons with stock.

Simmer the carrots, onions and beef bones with water for approximately two hours. Remove the bones and purée the vegetables. Place 1 oz. of chopped raw kidney into each No. 1 Tall plain or meat-lacquered can. Mix the remaining ingredients to a smooth paste with cold stock and add to the vegetable purée. Make up to volume with stock, bring to the boil and simmer for 5 minutes. Fill into the cans, seal and process at 240° F. for 75 minutes and water cool.

CANNED CREAM OF LEEK SOUP

Leeks, Chopped	96	lb.
Milk	6	gals.
Butter	18	lb.
Salt	$2\frac{3}{4}$	,,
Cornflour	$2\frac{1}{2}$	,,
Hydrolysed Vegetable Protein	10	oz.
Monosodium Glutamate	10	,,
Thyme, Whole	5	,,
Bay Leaves, Whole	5	,,
Ground White Pepper	$2\frac{1}{2}$	,,

Bulk to 30 gallons with water.

The leeks are sweated in butter without colouring, water is added and the mixture boiled until the leeks are tender. This is then passed through a fine sieve. The dry ingredients are pasted with milk, added to the purée and bulked to 30 gallons with water. The soup is simmered for 2–3 minutes and filled into plain No. 1 Tall cans which have been garnished with chopped leek. The sealed cans are processed at 240° F. for 75 minutes and water cooled.

CANNED LENTIL SOUP

Lentils	61	lb.
Wheat Flour	8	,,
Margarine	$6\frac{1}{2}$	,,
Salt	2	,,
Monosodium Glutamate . . .	$1\frac{1}{4}$	,,
Onion Powder	11	oz.
Hydrolysed Vegetable Protein . .	5	,,
Ground White Pepper . . .	1	,,

Bulk to 30 gallons with stock.

Place the lentils in a fine mesh sieve and boil until soft, in water containing bacon bones and scraps. Remove and sieve the lentils to form a purée and to it add the rest of the ingredients. Bulk to 30 gallons with strained bacon stock, bring to the boil and simmer for 5 minutes. Fill into plain No. 1 Tall cans, seal and process for 75 minutes at 240° F. Water cool.

CANNED MEAT SOUP

Chopped Onions. . . .	30	lb.
Minced Beef	27	,,
Chopped Carrots . . .	21	,,
Wheat Flour	12	,,
Salt	3	,,
Hydrolysed Vegetable Protein .	$1\frac{1}{2}$	,,
Monosodium Glutamate . .	$4\frac{1}{2}$	oz.
Ground White Pepper . .	2	,,
Caramel	As required	
Beef Bones (for stock)		

Bulk to 30 gallons with stock.

Boil the beef bones, carrots and onions in water for approximately two hours. Remove the bones, strain the stock and purée the vegetables. Mix the dry ingredients to a smooth paste with water, add to the vegetable purée and bulk to 30 gallons with stock. Bring the soup to the boil, simmer for a few minutes and fill into No. 1 Tall plain cans. After sealing, process the cans at 240° F. for 75 minutes and water cool.

CANNED MINESTRONE SOUP

STOCK:

Beef Bones	160	lb.
Bacon Trimmings . . .	40	,,
Carrots	16	,,
Onions	16	,,
Beef Dripping	16	,,
Tomato Trimmings . . .	$3\frac{1}{2}$	,,

Bulk to 30 gallons with water.

SEASONING:

Salt	$3\frac{1}{2}$	lb.
Monosodium Glutamate . .	$\frac{1}{2}$	,,
Hydrolysed Vegetable Protein .	$\frac{1}{2}$	,,
Ground White Pepper . .	1	oz.
Parsley	1	,,

TO CLEAR STOCK:

Minced Beef	32 lb.
Egg Whites	150

GARNISH:

	Per cent
Carrots (diced or strips) . .	22
Onions (chopped) . . .	16
Tomato (without seeds) . .	16
Peas	16
Spaghetti	10
Rice	10
Haricot Beans	10
	——
	100
	——

The bones, chopped vegetables and trimmings are fried in the beef dripping. The mixture is bulked to 30 gallons with water and the stock is boiled for at least 2 hours. The strained stock is then allowed to cool, after which the fat is skimmed off. The minced beef and egg whites are mixed and added to the cold stock. This is brought to the boil and simmered for 30 minutes, with occasional stirring. The soup is finally strained, reheated, then filled hot into plain No. 1 Tall cans, into each of which 2 oz. of the prepared garnish has been placed. The sealed cans are processed for $1\frac{1}{4}$ hours at 240° F., then water cooled.

CANNED MOCK TURTLE SOUP

Chopped Beef	24	lb.
Carrots	24	,,
Onions	24	,,
Tomato Paste (30 per cent solids) .	19	,,
Wheat Flour	14	,,
Salt	$3\frac{1}{2}$	,,
Hydrolysed Vegetable Protein . .	2	,,
Yeast Extract	2	,,
Lemon Juice	2	,,
Monosodium Glutamate . . .	$1\frac{1}{2}$	,,
Caramel	$\frac{1}{2}$	,,
Ground Thyme	$1\frac{1}{2}$	oz.
Bay Leaves	1	,,
Ground Coriander	$\frac{1}{2}$	,,
Ground Paprika	$\frac{1}{2}$	,,
Ground White Pepper . . .	$\frac{1}{2}$	,,

Bulk to 40 gallons with beef bone stock.

Boil beef bones in water for 2 hours to prepare a beef bone stock. Strain and remove fat from stock before use. Prepare and chop the vegetables and cook in water with the bay leaves until tender. Remove the bay leaves and sieve the vegetables to form a purée. Mix the rest of the ingredients with stock to form a smooth paste. Add the chopped beef and the vegetable purée and bulk to 40 gallons with stock. Boil the soup, simmer for 5 minutes, then fill hot into plain No. 1 Tall cans. Seal and process for $1\frac{1}{4}$ hours at 240° F., then water cool.

CANNED MULLIGATAWNY SOUP

Wheat Flour	30	lb.
Minced Beef	30	,,
Tomato Paste (30 per cent solids) .	$13\frac{1}{2}$	,,
Apples	$13\frac{1}{2}$	,,
Onions	11	,,
Beef Dripping	$10\frac{1}{2}$	,,
Mango Chutney	$7\frac{1}{2}$	,,
Sugar	6	,,
Curry Powder	$5\frac{1}{2}$	,,
Carrots	$5\frac{1}{2}$	,,
Salt	$5\frac{1}{2}$	,,
Hydrolysed Vegetable Protein . .	13	oz.
Paprika	13	,,
Monosodium Glutamate . . .	13	,,
Turmeric	$6\frac{1}{2}$	,,
Caramel	6	,,
Ground Marjoram	1	,,
Ground Thyme	1	,,
Ground Cloves	1	,,

Bulk to 50 gallons with water.

The prepared and chopped carrots, onions and apples are covered with water and cooked until soft. This mixture with the mango chutney is passed through a fine sieve to make a purée. All the other ingredients are mixed with water to form a smooth paste and the purée added. The mixture is bulked to 50 gallons with water, brought to the boil and simmered for 5 minutes. The hot soup is filled into plain No. 1 Tall cans, to which $\frac{1}{2}$ oz. blanched rice has been added. The sealed cans are processed for $1\frac{1}{2}$ hours at 240° F., then water cooled.

CANNED CREAM OF MUSHROOM SOUP

Milk	$8\frac{1}{2}$ gals.
Mushrooms, chopped . . .	13 lb.
Amioca	7 ,,
Butter	$7\frac{1}{2}$,,
SOYOLK A	$6\frac{1}{2}$,,
Salt	$2\frac{1}{2}$,,
Sugar	$1\frac{3}{4}$,,
Onion Powder.	15 oz.
Monosodium Glutamate . . .	15 ,,
Hydrolysed Vegetable Protein . .	10 ,,
Ground White Pepper . . .	$1\frac{1}{2}$,,

Bulk to 30 gallons with water.

Mix the dry ingredients with sufficient milk to form a smooth paste. Add the chopped mushrooms and the remainder of the milk and bulk to 30 gallons with water. Bring to the boil, simmer for 5 minutes, then fill hot into plain No. 1 Tall cans. Seal and process for $1\frac{1}{4}$ hours at 240° F. Water cool.

CANNED CREAM OF ONION SOUP

Milk	11 gals.
Onions, Chopped	108 lb.
Butter	$13\frac{1}{2}$,,
Wheat Flour	$12\frac{1}{2}$,,
Salt	$2\frac{3}{4}$,,
Monosodium Glutamate . . .	9 oz.
Hydrolysed Vegetable Protein . .	9 ,,
SAROMEX Pepper (on salt) . .	$\frac{3}{4}$,,
SAROMEX Bay (on salt) . .	$\frac{1}{4}$,,

Bulk to 30 gallons with water.

Mix the dry ingredients to a smooth paste with the milk. Add the chopped onions and bulk to 30 gallons with water. Bring to the boil and simmer for 5 minutes. Fill hot into plain No. 1 Tall cans, seal and process for $1\frac{1}{4}$ hours at 240° F. Water cool.

CANNED FRENCH STYLE ONION SOUP

Onions, sliced	90	lb.
Wheat Flour	$11\frac{1}{4}$	,,
Butter	$7\frac{1}{2}$	,,
Salt	3	,,
Sugar	$1\frac{3}{4}$	,,
Hydrolysed Vegetable Protein	$1\frac{3}{4}$	,,
Beef Extract	1	,,
Yeast Extract	1	,,
Monosodium Glutamate	6	oz.
SAROMEX White Pepper (on salt)	$\frac{1}{2}$	,,
SAROMEX Thyme (on salt)	$\frac{1}{2}$	,,
SAROMEX Bay (on salt)	$\frac{1}{4}$	,,

Bulk to 30 gallons with water.

Cook the sliced onions in the butter in a boiling pan until they are golden brown in colour. Whisk the other ingredients with water to form a smooth paste and add this to the onions. Bulk to 30 gallons with water, bring to the boil and simmer for 5 minutes. Fill hot into plain No. 1 Tall cans, seal and process for $1\frac{1}{4}$ hours at 240° F. Water cool.

CANNED OXTAIL SOUP

Oxtail Meat	24	lb.
Onions	18	,,
Carrots	18	,,
Wheat Flour	17	,,
Salt	$3\frac{1}{2}$	,,
Yeast Extract	2	,,
Monosodium Glutamate	$1\frac{1}{2}$	,,
Hydrolysed Vegetable Protein	$1\frac{1}{2}$	,,
Caramel	$\frac{1}{2}$	oz.
Paprika	$\frac{1}{2}$	,,
Ground White Pepper	$\frac{1}{2}$	,,
Bay Leaves (Whole)	$\frac{1}{3}$	,,
Ground Thyme	$\frac{1}{6}$	,,
Ground Coriander	$\frac{1}{6}$	,,

Bulk to 30 gallons with stock.

Prepare bone stock by boiling beef bones at the rate of 40 lb. per 10 gallons of water. Skim off all fat and strain before use.

Bones from the oxtail can be used additionally, if desired. Prepare and chop the vegetables and retort in stock with the bay leaves for 30 minutes at 240° F. Remove the bay leaves and pass the vegetables through a sieve to form a purée. Make a paste with the rest of the ingredients (except oxtail meat) and stock and add to the purée. Bulk to 30 gallons with stock, bring to the boil and simmer for 10 minutes. Place $1\frac{1}{2}$ oz. of oxtail meat (chopped) into each No. 1 Tall plain can and fill with hot soup. Seal, process for $1\frac{1}{4}$ hours at 240° F. and water cool.

CANNED CREAM OF POTATO SOUP (POTAGE PARMENTIER)

Milk	3	gals.
Potato, chopped	67	lb.
Onion, chopped	36	,,
Butter	18	,,
Salt	$2\frac{1}{3}$	,,
Cornflour	$2\frac{1}{2}$	,,
Hydrolysed Vegetable Protein . .	$1\frac{1}{2}$	,,
Monosodium Glutamate . . .	10	oz.
Thyme } in muslin bag .	5	,,
Whole Bay Leaves } in muslin bag .	5	,,
Parsley, dried	$2\frac{1}{2}$	,,
Ground White Pepper . . .	$1\frac{1}{2}$	,,

Bulk to 30 gallons with water.

The potatoes and onions are softened in hot butter without colouring. Water and the herb bag are added and the vegetables boiled until soft. The herb bag is removed and the mixture passed through a sieve. The other dry ingredients are mixed to a smooth paste with the milk, added to the purée and bulked to 30 gallons with water. The soup is brought to the boil, simmered for 2–3 minutes and filled hot into plain No. 1 Tall cans containing a garnish of diced potato.

The sealed cans are processed for $1\frac{1}{4}$ hours at 240° F. and water cooled.

CANNED SCOTCH BROTH NO. 1

Carrots	30	lb.
Mutton	25	,,
Dried Peas (soaked)	20	,,
Onions	13	,,
Flour	9	,,
Barley	8	,,
Potatoes	$6\frac{1}{2}$	,,
Swedes	$6\frac{1}{2}$	,,
Salt	4	,,
Monosodium Glutamate . : .	12	oz.
Hydrolysed Vegetable Protein . .	8	,,
Ground Celery Seed	2	,,
Ground White Pepper . . .	2	,,
Dried Parsley	$\frac{1}{2}$	,,

Bulk to 30 gallons with stock.

Prepare and dice the mutton and vegetables and boil the mutton bones in water for about one hour. Mix the ingredients well and bulk to 30 gallons with the strained mutton stock. Bring to the boil, simmer for a few minutes and fill into No. 1 Tall plain cans. Seal and process for 75 minutes at 240° F., then water cool. This soup is of thick consistency and can be diluted with water or milk before use.

CANNED SCOTCH BROTH NO. 2

Carrots	30	lb.
Mutton	25	,,
Dried Peas (soaked)	20	,,
Barley	16	,,
Onions	13	,,
Wheat Flour	$4\frac{1}{2}$	,,
Salt	4	,,
Monosodium Glutamate . . .	12	oz.
Hydrolysed Vegetable Protein . .	$4\frac{1}{2}$	,,
Ground Celery Seed	2	,,
Ground White Pepper . . .	2	,,
Dried Parsley	$\frac{1}{2}$	,,

Bulk to 40 gallons with stock.

Prepare and dice the mutton and vegetables and boil mutton bones in water for about one hour. Mix the ingredients well and bulk to 40 gallons with the strained mutton stock. Bring to the boil, simmer for a few minutes and fill into No. 1 Tall plain cans. Seal and process for 75 minutes at 240° F., then water cool.

CANNED SCOTCH LENTIL SOUP

Lentils	54	lb.
Bacon, diced	$12\frac{1}{2}$	,,
Carrots, diced	15	,,
Carrots, grated . . .	9	,,
Swedes, diced	9	,,
Salt	1 lb. 13	oz.
Parsley, chopped . . .	5	oz.
Monosodium Glutamate . .	14	oz.
Hydrolysed Vegetable Protein .	5	,,
Ground White Pepper . .	1	,,
Ground Bay Leaves . . .	$\frac{1}{4}$	,,

Bulk to 30 gallons with water.

The lentils are boiled in 20 gallons of water with ham bones, bacon bones, bacon pieces, bacon trimmings, etc. When the lentils are soft the bones are removed and the meat stripped and diced for garnish. The liquor is passed through a fine sieve and the rest of the ingredients added. The soup is then bulked to 30 gallons with water, brought to the boil and then filled hot into plain No. 1 Tall cans. The cans are sealed and processed for 75 minutes at 240° F. and finally water cooled.

CANNED TOMATO SOUP

Tomato Paste (30 per cent solids) .	73	lb.
Sugar	13	,,
Wheat Flour	$4\frac{1}{2}$	,,
Salt	3	,,
Onion Powder	13	oz.
Hydrolysed Vegetable Protein . .	6	,,
Sodium Bicarbonate	6	,,
Ground White Pepper . . .	$\frac{1}{5}$	,,

Bulk to 30 gallons with water.

Mix the dry ingredients into a smooth paste with the water,

F

then add the tomato paste and bring to the boil. Allow to simmer for several minutes. Fill No. 1 Tall plain cans with the hot soup, seal and process for 75 minutes at 225° F. and water cool. The amount of sodium bicarbonate given in the recipe is intended as a guide and the exact amount required should be determined on the tomato paste used and for each batch of soup. The pH of the soup before processing should be 4·6–4·7.

CANNED CREAM OF TOMATO SOUP NO. I

Tomato Paste (30 per cent solids)	50 lb.
Onions, chopped . .	30 ,,
Vegetable Fat . . .	15 ,,
Sugar	12½ ,,
SOYOLK A . . .	7½ ,,
Wheat Flour . . .	5 ,,
Salt	5 ,,
Skim Milk Powder . .	5 ,,
Monosodium Glutamate .	8 oz.
Ground White Pepper .	4 ,,
Ground Mace . . .	½ ,,
Sodium Bicarbonate . .	Sufficient to adjust finished soup to pH 4·6–4·7

Bulk to 50 gallons with water.

The chopped onions can be pre-cooked in water if desired. It is advisable to homogenize the other ingredients separately and then to add to the starch ingredients, to minimize curdling. Otherwise bulk the ingredients to volume with water and mix thoroughly in a steam-heated kettle. Bring to the boil and simmer for 5 minutes, then homogenize at 3,000 p.s.i. while hot. Fill hot into plain No. 1 Tall cans and seal and process at 225° F. for 1¼ hours and finally water cool.

CANNED CREAM OF TOMATO SOUP NO. 2

Tomato Paste (30 per cent solids)	68	lb.
Sugar	18	,,
Skim Milk Powder . .	17	,,
Butter	10	,,
Cornflour . . .	$5\frac{1}{2}$	,,
Salt	4	,,
Hydrolysed Vegetable Protein	10	oz.
Monosodium Glutamate .	10	,,
SAROMEX Onion (on salt)	8	,,
SAROMEX Garlic (on salt)	1	,,
SAROMEX Pepper (on salt)	$\frac{1}{2}$	,,
Sodium Bicarbonate . .	Sufficient to adjust finished soup to pH 4·6–4·7	

Bulk to 30 gallons with water.

Bulk to volume and whisk vigorously in a stainless steel steam-heated pan, fitted with a stirrer. Bring to the boil and simmer for 5 minutes. Homogenize at 1,500–2,000 p.s.i. and 180° F., and fill into plain No. 1 Tall cans at 200° F. Seal and process at 225° F. for $1\frac{1}{4}$ hours and water cool. The pH of the processed soup should be 4·6–4·7.

CANNED TOMATO RICE SOUP

Tomato Paste (30 per cent solids) .	29	lb.	
Wheat Flour	$8\frac{1}{2}$	,,	
Butter	$6\frac{3}{4}$	,,	
Carrots) Prepared & Liquidized .	$6\frac{3}{4}$	,,	
Onions)	$6\frac{3}{4}$	,,	
Sugar	$4\frac{1}{4}$	,,	
Salt	1	,,	4 oz.
Hydrolysed Vegetable Protein .	2	,,	
Monosodium Glutamate . .	1	,,	
Ground White Pepper . . .	1	,,	
Ground Bay Leaves . . .	$\frac{1}{2}$	,,	
Sodium Bicarbonate* . . .	4	,,	

Bulk to 30 gallons with water.

* This quantity will vary according to the acidity of the tomato paste. The pH of the finished soup is 4·9.

The vegetables are prepared and liquidized with a little water. All the ingredients are mixed together and bulked with water to 30 gallons. The mixture is then brought to the boil and simmered for 5 minutes.

Patna rice is boiled in unsalted water then drained and flushed with cold water. The rice is added as a garnish to the cans, about ⅓–½ oz. per can being used.

The soup is then filled hot into plain No. 1 Tall cans containing garnish (the rice may be added to the soup before filling), the cans sealed and processed for 75 minutes at 240° F., and then water cooled.

CANNED VEGETABLE SOUP

Carrots (diced)	36½ lb.
Onions (rings)	26½ ,,
Tomato Paste (30 per cent solids) .	14½ ,,
Dried Peas (soaked)	12½ ,,
Wheat Flour	10 ,,
Potatoes or Swedes (diced) . . .	7½ ,,
Dried Beans (soaked) . . .	7½ ,,
Noodles (alphabet)	6½ ,,
Sugar	3½ ,,
Salt	3¼ ,,
Monosodium Glutamate . . .	1 ,,
Hydrolysed Vegetable Protein . .	13 oz.
SAROMEX Garlic (on salt) . .	1½ ,,
SAROMEX White Pepper (on salt) .	1 ,,

Bulk to 30 gallons with water.

Mix the dry ingredients with water to form a smooth paste, then add the prepared vegetables, etc., and bulk to 30 gallons with water. Bring to the boil and simmer for 5 minutes, with stirring. Fill hot into plain No. 1 Tall cans, seal, and process for 1¼ hours at 240° F. Water cool.

CANNED CREAM OF VEGETABLE SOUP

Fresh Milk	5	gals.
Leeks, chopped	24	lb.
Carrots	18	,,
Turnips	18	,,
Parsnips	18	,,
Swedes	18	,,
Butter	12	,,
Salt	4½	,,
Wheat Flour	4½	,,
Hydrolysed Vegetable Protein . .	1	,,
Monosodium Glutamate . . .	6	oz.
Ground White Pepper . . .	3	,,

Bulk to 30 gallons with water.

The prepared and chopped vegetables are softened in the butter without colouring. Sufficient water is added and the vegetables are boiled until just tender. They are then passed through a fine sieve. The dry ingredients are mixed to a smooth paste with the milk, added to the vegetable purée and bulked to 30 gallons with water. To prevent chances of curdling or separation it is preferable to homogenize the butter with water before adding this to the other pre-cooked ingredients.

The soup is finally brought to the boil and simmered for 2–3 minutes. A garnish is made of ¼ inch diced vegetables and is added to each can or this can be mixed with the liquid soup. The hot soup is filled into plain No. 1 Tall cans which are sealed, processed at 240° F. for 75 minutes and water cooled.

CANNED VICHYSOISSE SOUP

Potatoes (chopped)	108	lb.
Milk (whole, fresh)	4¼	gals.
Leeks (chopped)	36	lb.
Butter	18	,,
Salt	2¾	,,
Cornflour	2½	,,
Hydrolysed Vegetable Protein . .	10	oz.
Monosodium Glutamate . . .	10	,,
Whole Thyme ⎫ in muslin bag .	2½	,,
Whole Bay Leaves ⎭	2½	,,
Ground White Pepper . . .	1½	,,

Bulk to 30 gallons with water.

The prepared potatoes and leeks are sweated in the butter without colouring. Water and the herb bag are added, and the vegetables boiled until soft. They are then passed through a sieve after the herb bag is removed. The dry ingredients are mixed to a paste with the milk, added to the purée and bulked to 30 gallons with water. The soup is brought to the boil and then filled hot into No. 1 Tall plain cans.

Diced potato and leek are used for garnish, if desired, and added to the cans before filling. The sealed cans are processed for 75 minutes at 240° F. and then water cooled.

CANNED CREAM OF WATERCRESS SOUP

Watercress	68 lb.
Potatoes	30 ,,
Milk	3 gals.
Butter	18 lb.
Onions	15 ,,
Leeks	15 ,,
Salt	$2\frac{3}{4}$,,
Cornflour	$2\frac{1}{4}$,,
Hydrolysed Vegetable Protein . .	$1\frac{1}{2}$,,
Monosodium Glutamate . . .	9 oz.
Whole Thyme ⎱ in muslin bag .	$4\frac{1}{2}$,,
Whole Bay Leaves ⎰ .	$4\frac{1}{2}$,,
Ground White Pepper . . .	1 ,,

Bulk to 30 gallons with water.

The vegetables are prepared, roughly chopped and then sweated in the butter until soft but not coloured. A little water is added and also the herb bag. The mixture is boiled, the herb bag removed and the product sieved. The dry ingredients are mixed with milk to a smooth paste, added to the purée and bulked to 30 gallons with water. The soup is brought to the boil and filled hot into No. 1 Tall cans which have been garnished with watercress leaves. The sealed cans are processed for 75 minutes at 240° F. and water cooled.

In 1969 a U.S. company launched 'piggy-back' combination packs consisting of a canned food and a miniature 'jiffy stove', the latter containing lighter fluid. Vegetable beef soup was one

8 oz. pack and a key on the 'jiffy stove' unwound a scored strip half-way round the can. To use, the soup can was opened, the lighter fluid ignited and the soup was then heated ready for eating. This item was obviously intended for specialist markets such as campers, hunters and other sportsmen.

During World War II a self-heating soup can was developed in the U.K. for the Armed Services. This consisted of a composite can, part of which was a conventional soup can whereas the other, smaller section, was a canister containing a quick-burning chemical similar to the propellant used in cartridges. Application of the tip of a burning cigarette was sufficient to ignite the heating element via an aperture. After ignition the can contents were quickly heated by convection and agitation. Cans similar to this are still available to campers in the U.K.

CHAPTER V

CONDENSED SOUPS

CONDENSED soups in cans were manufactured in the
United Kingdom many years before the second world
war and revived in 1959 when a U.S. company
opened a condensed soup plant in England. Other soup manufacturers anticipated this operation and launched their own
condensed soup varieties almost simultaneously. Soup sales
received a stimulus and condensed soups gained a part for
themselves in the growing U.K. domestic market. At the time
of writing, condensed soups probably account for nearly one-
fifth of the total soup market and for a little more than this of
the canned soup market.

It would appear, in this country at least, that many soup
consumers prefer simply to open a can of soup, heat the
contents and serve. Perhaps there is a psychological barrier to
adding water to the contents of a can of condensed soup and
thereby 'diluting the goodness' of the soup?

Condensed soups are attractive for two main reasons:

1. Normally they are packed in A 1 cans containing 10–11
oz. of soup, which gives one pint of soup for the table. The
smaller can size is economical in tinplate, labels and carriage
space and some of these savings are passed on to the consumer
in lower prices.

2. Being in a concentrated form they can be used undiluted
for sauces or as ingredients in many savoury dishes.

Within the past two or three years in the United Kingdom
condensed soups have been retailed also in 6 oz. cans, in No. 1
Tall cans containing $15\frac{1}{4}$ oz. of soup, and in 40 oz. cans.
Condensed soups are also used in some vending machine
systems. The term 'condensed' is something of a misnomer as
the soups are not literally condensed—they are made with less
water so that an equivalent volume of water should be used
when heating for serving.

It should be remembered by the U.K. manufacturer that the Code of Practice for Canned Soups should be followed to allow for double the main ingredients so that the regulation concentrations are present on dilution for serving.

Since condensed soups are much more viscous than ordinary canned soups the processing conditions are more severe. Examples are as follows:

Condensed Cream of Tomato Soup

A 1 cans	60 minutes at 240° F.
No. 1 Tall cans	70 minutes at 240° F.

Other Condensed Soups

A 1 cans	80 minutes at 240° F.
No. 1 Tall cans	90 minutes at 240° F.

The soups should, of course, be filled at a temperature of not less than 160° F. Before serving, an equivalent volume of water should be added to the contents of each can and then heated. The soup can also be used, undiluted, as a sauce or base.

CANNED CONDENSED CREAM OF CHICKEN SOUP

Milk	16	gals.		
Wheat Flour	16	lb.		
Butter	14	,,		
Amioca	$10\frac{1}{2}$	,,		
Salt	3	,,	5	oz.
Hydrolysed Vegetable Protein	1	,,	2	,,
Monosodium Glutamate			13	,,
Onion Powder			13	,,
Sugar			9	,,
SAROMEX Celery (on salt)			$5\frac{1}{2}$	,,
SAROMEX Pepper (on salt)			1	,,

Bulk to 30 gallons with chicken stock.

Cover dressed chickens and giblets with water and retort until the flesh comes away easily from the bones. Drain off liquor and retain for stock. Remove flesh from bones and use diced as a garnish. Digest the bones, skin and giblets in water for 1 hour at 250° F. in a retort. Drain and add the liquor to the original liquor. This is the chicken stock. Whisk the flour and starch with the milk to a smooth paste and add to the rest of the ingredients which have been brought to the boil in a stainless steel steam-heated jacketed pan, equipped with a stirrer. Homogenize at 1,500–2,000 p.s.i. and hold at 180°–200° F. prior to filling. Place 1 oz. of diced chicken meat in each plain A 1 can and fill with soup. Process, after sealing, for 80 minutes at 240° F. and water cool.

CANNED CONDENSED OXTAIL SOUP

Oxtail Meat	.	.	.	36 lb.
OR Beef .	.	.	.	. 29 ,,
Oxtail (with bone)	.	.	7 ,,
Onions	.	.	.	. 22½ ,,
Carrots	.	.	.	. 22½ ,,
Wheat Flour	.	.	.	21 ,,
Salt .	.	.	.	. 4½ ,,
Yeast Extract	.	.	.	2½ ,,
Monosodium Glutamate	.	1 ,, 13 oz.
Hydrolysed Vegetable Protein	1 ,, 13 ,,
Caramel	.	.	.	. ½ ,,
Paprika	.	.	.	. ¾ ,,
Ground White Pepper	.	½ ,,
Whole Bay Leaves	.	.	¼ ,,
Ground Thyme .	.	.	¼ ,,
Ground Coriander	.	.	¼ ,,

Bulk to 30 gallons with beef bone stock.

Cook the prepared chopped vegetables with bay leaves until tender. Remove bay leaves and purée the vegetables. Mix the other ingredients, except meat, with cold water to form a smooth paste. Bulk with purée and beef bone stock to 30 gallons. Remove the oxtail meat from the bones and dice with beef, if used. Use the oxtail bones for stock also. Bring the soup to the boil and simmer for 5 minutes. Fill hot into A 1 plain cans containing raw meat, seal and process for 80 minutes at 240° F. Water cool.

CANNED CONDENSED CREAM OF TOMATO SOUP

Tomato Paste (30 per cent solids)	76 lb.
Sugar	$20\frac{1}{2}$,,
Skim Milk Powder . .	$19\frac{1}{2}$,,
Butter	15 ,,
Cornflour . . .	$6\frac{1}{2}$,,
Salt	$4\frac{1}{2}$,,
Yeast Extract . . .	11 oz.
Monosodium Glutamate .	11 ,,
SAROMEX Onion (on salt)	$8\frac{1}{2}$,,
SAROMEX Garlic (on salt)	$1\frac{1}{2}$,,
SAROMEX Pepper (on salt)	$\frac{3}{4}$,,
Sodium Bicarbonate . .	Sufficient to adjust finished soup to pH 4·6–4·7

Bulk to 30 gallons with water.

Bulk to volume and whisk vigorously in a stainless steel steam-heated pan, fitted with a stirrer. Bring to the boil and simmer for 5 minutes. Homogenize at 1,500–2,000 p.s.i. and 180° F. and fill into plain A 1 cans at 200° F. Seal and process at 240° F. for 1 hour and water cool. The pH of the processed soup should be 4·6–4·7.

CANNED CONDENSED VEGETABLE SOUP

Carrots (diced)	47 lb.
Onions (rings)	$34\frac{1}{2}$,,
Tomato Paste (30 per cent solids) .	18 ,,
Dried Peas (soaked)	$15\frac{1}{2}$,,
Wheat Flour	$12\frac{1}{2}$,,
Potatoes or Swedes (diced) . . .	$9\frac{1}{2}$,,
Dried Beans (soaked) . . .	$9\frac{1}{2}$,,
Noodles (alphabet)	8 ,,
Sugar	$4\frac{1}{2}$,,
Salt	4 ,,
Monosodium Glutamate . . .	$1\frac{1}{4}$,,
Hydrolysed Vegetable Protein . .	1 ,,
SAROMEX Garlic (on salt) . .	2 oz.
SAROMEX Pepper (on salt) . .	$1\frac{1}{4}$,,

Bulk to 30 gallons with water.

Mix the dry ingredients with water to form a smooth paste, then add the prepared vegetables, etc., and bulk to 30 gallons with water. Bring to the boil and simmer for 5 minutes, with stirring. Fill hot into A 1 plain cans, seal, and process for 80 minutes at 240° F. Water cool.

CHAPTER VI

SOUP CANNING AND PROCESSING

THE degree of mechanization and therefore the number of machines used for actual filling and processing canned soups naturally depends upon the scale of production. But however large or small the production may be, the various steps are the same, as is the general technique.

1. *Filling*

The first operation is usually to fill into the empty cans any garnish which is to be used. This may be diced vegetables, oxtail, chicken meat and so on. This operation may be undertaken on an ordinary table, or on a moving conveyor running between table tops or suitable bins. In either case, it is most important that the cans be cleaned before use. This may be done by hand or, where a conveyor feed is used, the cans may be inverted and either blown clean with compressed air or washed with hot water. Considerable trouble can arise at this point of production from two causes.

Firstly, through the use of either too large or badly constructed garnish-holding vessels, leading to bacteriological contamination due either to food being left in the crevices of the containers or just being held too long in too great a bulk. Secondly, through improper checking of the amount of garnish added to each can. This last trouble can be controlled to a degree by use of specially made scoops of the right size for each product handled, but even then, this part of the line needs constant supervision. It is of course possible to buy automatic fillers which will fill standardized quantities of certain items into the cans, but it is not possible to obtain any one machine which will deal with everything, unless the garnish is premixed.

After the filling of solids, the cans pass to the actual soup-filling stage. This again, may be done by hand from a jug or perhaps by means of a trigger valve on a hose connected to an

(By courtesy The Metal Box Co. Ltd.)

Empty cans on pallets being unloaded from a specially designed motor trailer from one of Metal Box can factories. The pallets are delivered by fork lift truck to the de-palletizers.

(By courtesy The Metal Box Co. Ltd.)

Cans being fed to a high-speed canning line from a de-palletizer.

Machine for washing, rinsing and drying empty cans, prior to filling at 120 a minute. The spiral guides on the feed and discharge invert the cans prior to washing and then return them to their upright position after drying in the steam-heated hot air drying unit.

overhead tank. Again, the cans may be fed automatically to a soup filler which will fill the cans accurately at speeds up to 150 or even 300 per minute. Some of these machines will also deal with solids such as diced vegetables.

Quite a good filling machine of comparatively simple design which is not too costly, may be either purchased or made by the user. This consists of a straight conveyor on which the cans run under a number of nozzles from which the soup pours in a continuous stream. The soup supply, either from a tank or from a pump is controlled by a valve, and provided that the cans are fed so that they each touch the one next on the conveyor and, provided that the flow rate is even, cans may be filled quite accurately by this system without serious spillage.

Whatever method of filling is used, it is most essential that the temperature of the soup be maintained at at least 175° F. at the seaming point. This means that the soup must be filled very hot, or else an expensive and in this case rather unnecessary steam exhaust box must be installed. In some of the latest canneries there is an arrangement whereby a small jet of superheated steam is injected into the headspace of the can

(*By courtesy Mather & Platt Ltd.*)

A 12/16 solid and liquid filler arranged for filling liquids only. It will fill to a level controlled by displacement pieces and can be arranged for direct couple to the clincher or seamer to prevent any spill on transfer.

just before the end is put on, thus ensuring that all the air is removed from the headspace and a good final vacuum results. In this respect, it should be noted that cans should never be filled quite full, but a small space allowed for expansion during retorting. This space must be evacuated and this can only be done by having the soup hot enough to fill the headspace with water vapour, or by using the steam-jet method.

(*By courtesy Mather & Platt Ltd.*)

12 × P Type Filler. This machine will fill soup into cans up to 250 c.p.m.

There are many reasons why canned foods must be sealed under vacuum, or at least in such a manner that a vacuum will result when the can is cooled. The technical reasons for this belong more properly to a book on canning technology, but broadly they are as follows:

  1. If air is left in the headspace of a can, this air will expand

G

enormously when the can is heated in the retort and lead to straining or even bursting of the can.

2. Air left in the can, especially if there is no vacuum at all, may lead to apparent blowing of the can on the grocer's shelf in warm weather, due to the expansion of the air. It should perhaps be noted that the rate of expansion of air when heated is many times that of water.

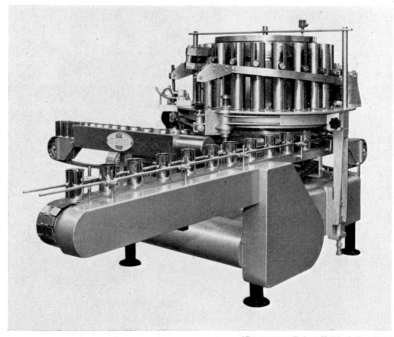

(By courtesy Robert Kellie & Son Ltd.)

Piston type can filler. Ideal for filling soups into cans. Large output.

3. Air in the can will lead to oxidation of the food in the can, and thus to the formation of off-flavours, vitamin loss, loss of colour and flavour and rancidity of fat.

4. Air in the can, in the presence of water also, will lead to an eventual rusting through of the can from the inside. This is known as pinholing. This fact may be explained simply by stating that water alone does not cause rust, it is always water plus air. For example, an iron post driven into a river will always rust at the point where the post enters the water.

The actual seaming of the cans has to be done on a machine of some kind. The only difference here is whether the machine is hand operated and fed, semi-automatic or fully-automatic. In most cases a fully-automatic machine is desirable for soups as they are hot and spill very easily if manhandled.

At this stage, it is most desirable to mark the cans in some way, because as they are not yet labelled it is otherwise difficult to be sure of the contents. The same marking, if it is permanent, may be used to identify the can for years after it has been sent out, should it be sent back for any reason, even without a label.

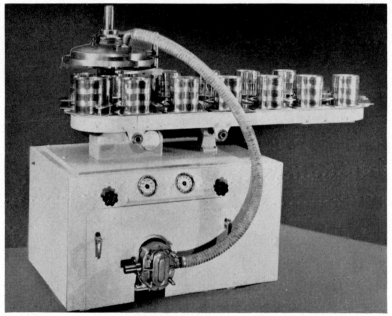

(By courtesy Mather & Platt Ltd.)

Rotary pump filler. The ideal filler for large cans. Easily controlled and maintained.

Code marking, for date and batch number, etc., may be carried out by the use of special inks and stampers, by hand, or automatically, or more simply by making a suitable impression in the lid end which is put on to the can. Most fully-automatic seaming machines have a device for impressing letters and numbers on to the lid ends of the cans, but where

such machines are not used, a small treadle-operated stamper
may be obtained. Whichever type of stamper is used, however,
when the actual can is indented great care must be taken to see
that the impression is not too deeply cut. If the numbers or
letters are too deeply cut into the can end, this may damage
the internal lacquer of the can, or externally the tinplate,

(*By courtesy The Metal Box Co. Ltd.*)

The M.B 6 Vacuum closing machine for all sizes of can up to A 2½.
Available with steam injection.

leading to premature rusting. In extreme cases the can end is sometimes cut right through.

As cans come from the seamer, they are packed into metal crates to be placed into the retorts. The shape of these crates

(*By courtesy The Metal Box Co. Ltd.*)

The M.B. Differential Double Seamer for seaming the lids on to cans at high speed at the canning factory.

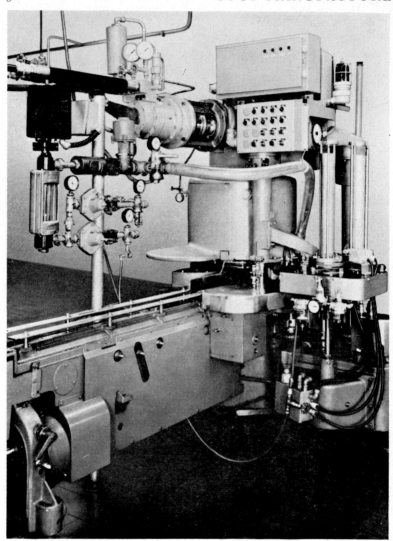

(By courtesy The Metal Box Co. Ltd.)

The M.B.449/C machine introduces a new generation of seamers, built
in the United Kingdom by the machinery building group of The Metal
Box Co. Ltd. It is capable of a line speed of 5,000 dozen cans per hour
(1,000 cans per minute). It is believed that this is the first time that a
seaming machine capable of operating at such speeds has been built in the
U.K.

will of course depend upon the type of retort to be used. However, unless flat trays are used the crates are all fairly deep and
there are several methods of packing the cans. Some canners
place the cans into the crates all jumbled up or 'scrambled',
whilst others place them in in definite layers one on top of the
other. On the whole the layer method is best for canned soups
as if the cans are scrambled or even laid in layers on their sides,
they tend to become dented as the end seam of one can pushes
into the side of another. From a processing point of view, laying
the cans on their sides is the best method.

The handling of cans from the seamer into the retort crates,
and for that matter out again, after sterilization, is one of the
most labour-consuming tasks in the cannery, especially where
production is large, but it is in fact usually done by hand in this
country. In America, three different methods are adopted to
eliminate much of the hand work in this operation. In system
number one, the cans are presented to the retort crate loader
on their ends on a conveyor. The loader has a long bar-like
pipe with handles on the ends, rather like bicycle handlebars,
on which are fitted eight or so nozzles with rubber sucker ends.
The whole apparatus is connected to a vacuum line and
mounted on an overhead pulley with counterweights. The
operator places the bar so that the nozzles descend on to a line
of eight cans and by means of a trigger exerts a vacuum suction
on to the cans, thus lifting them with the bar. The whole eight
cans are then lowered into the crate and the vacuum broken
by a reverse motion of the control trigger. This is a very simple
and labour-saving method which might well be copied in this
country.

System number two, which is more complicated, consists of
a revolving plate the size of the crate, on to which the cans are
fed by a conveyor until it is full. A large electro-magnet then
automatically descends and lifts the whole plateful of cans up
and swings them round so that they can be deposited gently
into the crate by releasing the magnetic force. System three is
even more complicated and calls for special crates with a hole
in the middle which are placed down upon an hydraulic ram
set in the floor. The crate has a solid plate false bottom which is
then raised by the ram so that the cans can be slid on to it by a
conveyor and pusher arm. When this is full, the plate is lowered

(*By courtesy Reads Ltd.*)

Canco syncro-steam closing machine at present the world's fastest can
seamer capable of 1,300 cans per minute.

to allow the second layer to be put on top of the bottom layer of cans. In all cases, emptying is carried out in the same manner.

In very large canneries soups are sometimes sterilized in continuous automatic retorts, into which the cans are fed in a continuous stream. However, production has to be very large to warrant this, although there are undoubtedly many advantages to this system.

(By courtesy John Fraser & Son Ltd.)

A Millwall Vertical Retort and one of the baskets.

In most cases, either vertical or horizontal batch retorts are used and in the case of soup it does not matter much which type is used and probably the odds are in favour of the vertical type. Horizontal retorts are either round or rectangular in cross-section with a door at one end and they are charged by means of small trolleys which carry the crates and run in on rails. There is no doubt that the round horizontal retort gives the best steam circulation with less risk of cold spots or air pockets, but unless very large-scale operations are undertaken, vertical retorts are easiest to charge and work generally.

(By courtesy Mather & Platt Ltd.)

A Retort Crate Loader

The retort loader and unloader can be used on high-speed lines and will
handle all cans without damage.

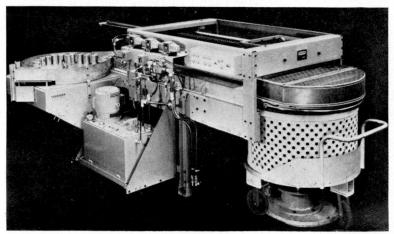

(By courtesy Mather & Platt Ltd.)

A Retort Crate Unloader

The movement of the can contents is important for soups, especially where vegetables or other solids are added.

Vertical retorts are round and are usually set in a row in a pit, so that the tops are at a reasonable level from the floor. In this case, the baskets or crates are charged into them by means of an overhead hoist running along a joist.

Batch retorts vary a good deal in size and when laying out a cannery it is necessary to match the size reasonably with the output required. That is to say, arrangements must be made so that a retort can be filled and put into operation at least every forty minutes or so. It is useless to have a retort so big that it takes an hour or so to produce enough cans to fill it. If hot cans are allowed to lie around waiting for sterilization, bacteria are apt to multiply in the cans and this may lead to souring.

The retorting cycle is fairly simple and consists of a 'coming-up' period, while the retort and the cans are warming up to the actual sterilization temperature; the sterilization time itself and a cooling down period.

When the cans are put into the retort and the lid fastened down, the steam is turned on and the temperature begins to rise. During this period, however, there will be a great deal of condensed water to be got rid of ard also all the air in the retort itself must be displaced by steam. For this reason, the bottom drain is usually left partly open as are the air vent pet-cocks on the top of the retort. It is quite a good idea to have a small permanent hole tapped across the drain-off valve at the bottom so that excess condensate is always allowed to drain away at all periods of the process. Once the air has stopped coming from the pet-cocks and steam is coming out freely, they may be closed and the temperature allowed to rise to the required level. The temperature should, however, be constantly checked against the steam pressure in the retort and if the pressure is in excess of the corresponding temperature, then air must be bled off through the pet-cocks. This could also be due to an air pocket around the thermometer bulb and a pet-cock should be fitted to all retorts to bleed this air.

The actual temperature employed and the duration of the retorting time will depend upon the size of the can and the nature of the contents. Cans with solids in them, such as oxtail garnish, will take longer than those which are all liquid. Again, the higher the temperature, the shorter the period. Temperatures from 230° F. to 260° F. are employed, but obviously the higher the temperature the greater the risk of scorching the contents of the can. In most cases, the higher temperature ranges are only used in the continuous automatic retorts, where the cans are moving and the contents therefore agitated.

The most usual temperature for canned soups in a batch retort is 240° F. and the time for No. 1 Tall cans about 1¼ hours. It should be understood, however, that this is an average figure and actual times must be worked out most carefully.

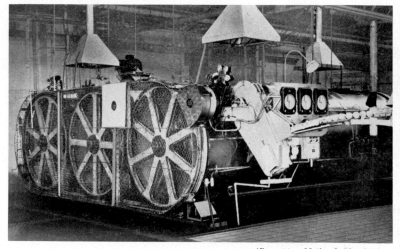

(*By courtesy Mather & Platt Ltd.*)

Automatic Rotary Pressure Cooker Cooler

This machine is in three sections, each connected by pressure valves. The cans are brought up to temperature in the first section, processed in the second and are cooled in the third section.

At the end of the sterilization time, the steam should be turned off and at the same time the compressed air supply eased up, so that the pressure in the retort does not drop. The water valve is then opened slowly, at the same time increasing the air supply again, so that the pressure does not drop. The use of compressed air is continued until it is found that the water pressure is itself enough to maintain pressure, at which time the use of air may be discontinued. The pet-cocks may then be opened and water will eventually spurt out of them.

The main water overflow valve may then be opened and water allowed to pass freely through the retort.

When the cans are reasonably cool (they should not be allowed to become quite cold) the retort may be drained off and the cans removed. If the cans are allowed to get too cold, they will not dry off when they are brought out and may therefore go rusty at the seams.

The above is only a very general description of the operations involved in cooling and the procedure may vary quite a lot according to the retort set-up. The cooling-down operation

(By courtesy Varley–FMC Ltd.)

A four shell rotary pressure cooker/cooler.

is, however, rather critical, as during this stage it is very easy to undo the good work of sterilization or to ruin the cans by what is known as panelling, that is to say, causing the cans to collapse and dent in.

What actually happens inside the retort is this. While the cans are very hot during the actual sterilization process, the pressure inside the can is slightly greater than that in the retort itself and this causes the ends of the cans to bulge out. (It has already been pointed out that if the cans are not properly exhausted, the pressure will be great enough to burst the cans, because of the great expansion factor of air.) When the sterilization period is over the cans begin to cool, the steam inside the can condenses and causes a vacuum in the headspace. This pulls the ends back into their normal form as seen on the grocer's shelf. However, if cold water is suddenly poured into the retort, the steam will condense in the retort itself quicker than it does in the can, and a vacuum will be created in the retort, whilst there is still a pressure in the can. This will of course cause the cans to burst or at least will seriously strain the seams of the can. Thus, compressed air is used to prevent a vacuum forming in the retort when the water is turned on. Again, if the cans are cooled too quickly and too much air pressure is used, then the vacuum formed in the can, combined with the external pressure, may be enough to push in the sides of the can and cause panelling.

From the above, it will be seen that the aim must be to achieve a nice balance between the internal pressure or vacuum in the can and the pressure in the retort, to prevent excessive straining of the can seams. It should also be appreciated that at this stage, the rubber solution in the can seam is still hot and possibly molten and if the seams are unduly strained, especially when the end formation of the can reverts from convex to flat or concave, there is a grave risk that minute drops of water may be sucked into the can. If this water contains even one bacterium, then all the good work of sterilization will be undone. In most canneries, the water used for cooling is fairly heavily chlorinated, to minimize this risk. Too much chlorination may cause rusting of the cans.

In most small canneries, cooling of the cans is completed to the right stage in the retort itself, but in larger establishments, the cans are either passed along some sort of cooling conveyor with water sprays over it, or the complete crates are dipped in or sprayed with water. The cans are then emptied from the crates and stacked up until required for labelling.

In small canneries, and indeed in some very large ones, the entire output of canned foods is held for up to two weeks,

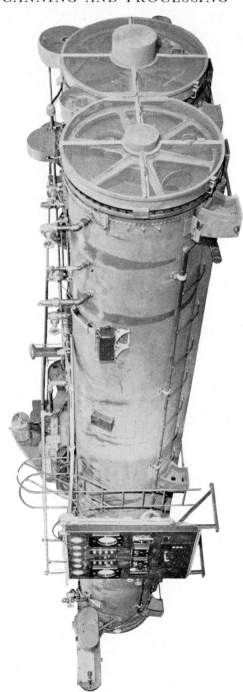

(By courtesy Varley-FMC Ltd.)

Automatic reel type two-shell pressure cooker/cooler.

stacked in a warm room, to ensure that any cans which have been improperly sterilized, or which have sucked in bacteria during cooling, will blow before shipment, but in establishments where there is high-grade laboratory control, the cans are often inspected, labelled and cased right away and then shifted to the warehouse to await final clearance after a laboratory report upon the batch, based upon test cans.

In the general operation of retorting crates of cans, there is one risk which must be guarded against very carefully, either by close supervision or by check methods. This is the possibility of a crate of unsterilized cans slipping through into the finished can line, without even going into the retort. This can happen surprisingly easily and cause a considerable loss. It is comparatively easy for an experienced canner to spot a crate of cans which has not been sterilized, because the cans do lose some of their shine during the process, but still it does happen. Some canners use a tell-tale check system whereby each crate has a small wax disc attached, which melts only when subjected to heat or paper strips which change colour.

There is one matter which has not been mentioned in the course of the above discussion on retorting, and this is the question of cleaning the cans. These often get very dirty during the filling process, from spillage, and they must therefore be washed at some stage. This is sometimes done before retorting and sometimes afterwards, although there is no doubt that it is easier if done while the soup is still soft on the can and has not been baked on. There are a number of good can-washing machines made to couple on to the seamer or it is fairly easy to make a simple device for the smaller canner.

As an alternative, there is a process whereby the cans are actually sterilized under pressure in hot water instead of steam in the retort, and this water can be made to contain a detergent and so clean the cans.

RETORTING BOTTLED SOUPS

Where the soup is bottled instead of being put into cans, the same procedure is used, except that the retorting is somewhat more tricky in that the bottles break more easily. Retorts for bottling should be fitted with top water sprays instead of bottom inlets, as bottles must always be sprayed from above if

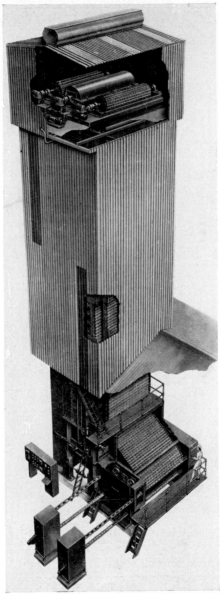

(By courtesy Mather & Platt Ltd.)

Cut out view of hydrostat sterilizer showing the double feed and
discharge at bottom and the small driving gear at the top. Cans are
carried on both sides of the chains and the sterilizer will handle all cans
from 211 dia. to 307 dia. and any height at high speeds. See diagram
on next page.

H

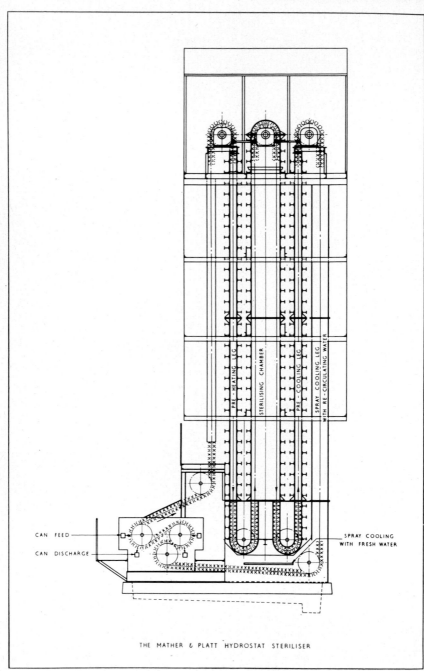

CAN FEED

CAN DISCHARGE

PRE - HEATING LEG

STERILISING CHAMBER

PRE - COOLING LEG

SPRAY COOLING LEG
WITH RE - CIRCULATING WATER

SPRAY COOLING
WITH FRESH WATER

THE MATHER & PLATT HYDROSTAT STERILISER

(By courtesy Mather & Platt Ltd.)

Diagrammatic drawing of the hydrostat sterilizer giving details of process travel and the feed and discharge points.

cracking is to be minimized. Correct air pressure in the retort is essential.

Soups generally fall into the so-called medium acid food group, with a pH value of between 4·5 and 5·0. Foods with pH values greater than 4·5 require fairly severe heat treatments as the lower limit of growth of *Clostridium botulinum* is at pH 4·5. Foods capable of sustaining the growth of this organism are processed on the assumption that the organism is present and must be destroyed.

The following are examples of processing conditions for canned soups:

CREAM OF TOMATO (pH 4·6–4·7)
         No. 1 Tall cans   75 minutes at 225° F.

OTHER SOUPS
         A 1 cans   75 minutes at 240° F.
         No. 1 Tall cans   75 minutes at 240° F.
         A 2 cans   100 minutes at 240° F.
         A 2½ cans   120 minutes at 240° F.

A word should be said here concerning internal lacquers for cans, although many soups can be packed quite safely in plain cans.

When a soup contains a high protein content a small amount of the protein may be broken down during processing to produce sulphur compounds. Unless protective measures are introduced these compounds then react with the iron of the tinplate to produce black iron sulphide. Two types of lacquers have been produced to counteract this. One form has an oleoresinous lining containing finely divided zinc oxide which forms white zinc sulphide with sulphur products. The other type is made with phenol-formaldehyde compounds which are impermeable to sulphur products.

From a corrosion standpoint most soups are relatively non-reactive. As has been partly discussed above, corrosion depends on many factors, including: acidity, pH, trace amounts of copper and sulphur, pigments and air. Internal corrosion may be minimized by taking the following precautions:

1. Avoidance of over- or under-filling of soup.

2. Elimination of the air before closing.

3. Adequate cooling to, say, 95°–105° F., then air cooling, or cool to 90° F. and no air cooling.

4. Storage in a cool atmosphere after processing.

(By courtesy Robert Kellie & Son Ltd.)

A spray-type can washer which has no mechanical parts other than the pump and will deliver the cans out clean.

(*By courtesy Campbell's Soups Ltd.*)

Aerial view of Campbells' Soups canning factory at Kings Lynn, England.

It should be noted that chemical corrosion reactions, in common with others, double their reaction rate with each 18° F. rise in temperature.

To eliminate or cut down external corrosion the following points should be observed:

1. Dry storage of empty cans.
2. High temperature of exhausting or filling.
3. Prevention of injury to can surfaces.
4. Washing of cans after processing.
5. Avoidance of rust in retorts, trucks and crates.
6. Adequate air removal by venting in retorts.
7. Control of chemical composition of water used in processing.
8. Adequate cooling of cans.
9. Avoidance of casing of wet cans.
10. Selection of a non-hygroscopic paste for can labels.
11. Selection of a non-corrosive storage atmosphere.
12. Good air circulation in store.

A new type of canning process in use in the United States is the Martin aseptic canning method. This consists, basically, of sterilization of the food product prior to filling into sterile cans. The following steps are observed:

1. The product is sterilized in a heat exchanger using an HTST (high temperature—short time) process.
2. The cans and ends are sterilized in superheated steam.
3. The relatively cool sterile product is filled into the sterile cans.
4. Sterile ends are applied to the filled cans in an atmosphere of either saturated or superheated steam.

Another relatively new technique for certain food products is the rotation-agitation method. This may be continuous end-over-end, continuous axial rotation or intermittent axial rotation. The rate of heat penetration is increased by these methods. An example of mushroom soup may be quoted whereby a 603 × 700 (U.S.A. No. 10) can required only 19 minutes at a process-agitated temperature of 260° F.

The heating time is reduced and higher temperatures may be used with less danger of over-cooking. Greater retention of certain nutrients is also an advantage and large cans, up to A 10 size, of viscous products may be processed successfully. Colour and texture are improved in certain foods also.

(*By courtesy The Metal Box Co. Ltd.*)

The M.B. top feed can dryer for drying filled cans after processing, by means of cold air at high velocity. The machine is easily and quickly adjusted for different sizes of can and is fitted with controlled in-feed to prevent can damage.

(*By courtesy The Metal Box Co. Ltd.*)

Magnetic Elevator. This machine will handle full or empty cans
without any danger of scratching the lithography.

Just as this edition of *Soup Manufacture* was being closed for press we received photographs and a description of the very latest soup manufacturing and canning plant installed in the U.K. at Cerebos Foods Ltd. in Greatham. The three accompanying illustrations give an impression of the modern hygienic stainless steel plant designed for production of high quality canned soups under the most hygienic conditions.

The soup is finally prepared in batches, in six 100 gallon

(*By courtesy Robert Kellie & Son Ltd.*)

Showing the stainless steel soup manufacturing pans, control panel and mixing vessels. All vessels, pipe work and control gear were supplied by Robert Kellie and Son Ltd., as well as the filling machine and the filled can washer.

stainless steel boiling pans, which are themselves fed from pre-mixing pans using automatic weighing and dispensing equipment. This ensures that the soup is continuously available to be pumped via a metal detector to the Kellie rotary piston filling machine at the required speed. The plant is ventilated to prevent condensation.

The filled cans of soup then pass through a C.R.S. type seaming machine after which they roll through a spray can washer and are then conveyed to a hydrostatic sterilizer by means of a wire rope conveyor system.

(By courtesy Robert Kellie & Son Ltd.)

General view of the soup manufacturing and filling area, showing the Kellie filling machine, which operates at a speed of 250 cans per minute and is linked to the C.R.S. can seamer. Also in the foreground is the Kellie spray can washing machine type 27JJ for washing filled cans.

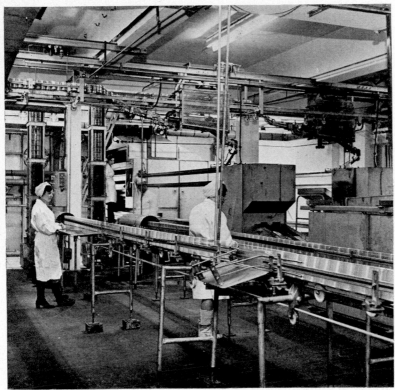

(*By courtesy Robert Kellie & Son Ltd.*)

From the filled can washer, the cans are conveyed to a hydrostatic sterilizer
by means of a wire rope conveyor system.

CHAPTER VII

QUICK-FROZEN SOUPS

Q UICK-FREEZING (Q/F) is the newest of the methods of preservation of processed soups described in this book and it is also the least used in this country. In the United States and Canada Q/F soups form a significant part of the market and, as an example, the following Q/F soups are marketed by just one U.S. company: clam chowder (New England style), cream of potato, cream of shrimp, fish chowder, green pea with ham, old-fashioned vegetable with beef, snapper, lobster langostino, oyster stew.

In mid-1966 the largest U.K. food freezer launched the first three Q/F soups on the British market. This had apparently been preceded by a test launch of a U.S.-made counterpart some time previously. One of the new soups was 'Home Make Vegetable and Chicken' and, in effect, it was a 'super-concentrated' soup since the carton contents of 5 oz. were added to $\frac{3}{4}$ pint (15 oz.) of water to make, after simmering for ten minutes, one pint of ready-to-eat soup. After this first introduction of U.K.-produced Q/F soups they were quietly withdrawn from the market.

By the use of modern quick-freezing methods it is possible to produce soups of very high quality and with the delicate flavours of sea foods and certain vegetables fully preserved. These soups are usually of better quality than the equivalent canned or dried variety. The lack of development of the sales of Q/F soups in the United Kingdom is probably partially due to the past low incidence of consumer refrigerators and to the relatively low price of canned and packet soups on the market. A contributing factor may also be the high capital cost of quick-freezing equipment for the traditional canned and dried soup manufacturers in the U.K., who have not diversified as much as their U.S. counterparts.

Canned soups suffer from the disadvantage that they have to be heated to a high temperature for quite a time in the can in order to render them commercially sterile. This means that they may be easily overcooked. Dried soups cannot easily be made to contain certain types of solid garnish, e.g., a piece of oxtail. On the other hand, frozen soups can be made to contain anything required and, as they are preserved by freezing, they need not be overcooked or overspiced, but can be preserved just in the condition in which they leave the kitchen of the soup manufacturer.

There is no doubt that the cost of preserving soup by freezing and then keeping it cold through all stages of distribution, is slightly greater than that involved in canning or drying, but with the growth of distributive facilities for frozen foods the gap is narrowing rapidly. Indeed, it is safe to say, that when the frozen food industry has grown a little more and turnover is greater and distributive profit margins smaller, there will be nothing in it as regards price between canned or frozen soups. Probably the greatest disadvantage of frozen soup is that it cannot be put on the larder shelf and kept like canned soup, and soup is essentially something which the housewife likes to keep in stock. Nevertheless there is and will be a growing demand for this kind of product, especially in the higher class type of soup, as if the housewife is buying other frozen foods for a meal, she will not mind buying her soup in the same way at the same time.

Perhaps at this stage it should be pointed out that foods which are preserved by quick-freezing, pass through the following stages. Firstly the foods are cooked or otherwise prepared, and they are then cooled and packaged. The degree of cooling will depend upon the product, the method of packaging and the method of freezing. The packaged foods are then frozen in a special machine and placed into cold store at 0° F. or less. During transport from cold store to shop the foods must be kept frozen at 0° F. by refrigeration or dry ice, and again the foods must be held at 0°F. in the retail shop conservator until they are sold. When once purchased by the housewife, these foods must in general be used before they are completely thawed and warmed to room temperature. The various steps in production and distribution will be dealt with in detail later, but the necessity for refrigeration at all stages must be clearly understood from the start.

Undoubtedly comparatively low priced, savoury types of soup, such as are used for canning, could be produced and preserved by freezing and may be in the future. For the moment, however, because quick-freezing is different and to some extent a luxury trade, the tendency is to produce higher class soups or other foods, of a type which cannot readily be canned or dried. Thus for example, real cream soups, which cannot be canned, lend themselves to quick-freezing.

If frozen soups were to be produced on a very large scale as in a modern cannery, then the same equipment and to some extent the same production technique would be applied. However, as has been stated, this new preservation method is being applied mainly to higher class soups and in most cases therefore something more on the lines of a very large hotel kitchen is called for.*

In general, the soup to be frozen is made exactly the same as it would be for immediate consumption in an hotel, although certain allowances have to be made for changes which are likely to take place during storage in the frozen state and during heating up. Some of the changes which are likely to take place, and the methods which must be applied to counteract them, are as follows:

1. Soups tend to become slightly 'flat' during storage and the sharpness should therefore be increased at the time of manufacture to allow for this.

2. Most soups tend to taste less salt when stored for some time than they do when tasted fresh. This is because the salt becomes more evenly spread throughout the mixture during storage and extra salt should therefore be added.

3. Pepper increases in flavour and should be added sparingly.

4. Celery gets very much stronger and only delicately flavoured celery should be used. Coarse old stalks tend to give the product a strong odour and bitter flavour.

5. Curry tends to develop a musty flavour in long-term storage, but if the time is reasonably short and a good fresh mix is used this will not happen, in fact curried foods do

---

* Ref.: *Production of Pre-Cooked Frozen Foods for Mass Catering* by John L. Rogers, 1969, Food Trade Press Ltd., London.

improve owing to the gradual permeation of the flavour through the mass of the dish.

Most soups and especially those containing a lot of fat tend to separate during defrosting. This does not matter as the soup will mix again during heating, but the following steps may be taken to overcome the trouble, which may affect sales:

1. It has been observed that it is better to use a smaller percentage of real cream in a mix, plus water, rather than all milk.

2. Whole egg or egg yolk added to a soup acts as a valuable stabilizer, but egg yolk is better than whole egg. Never use egg white alone as this will tend to toughen the product during storage. When egg yolk alone is used, never heat to more than 160° F., or if whites are included, to not more than 145° F.

3. Such stabilizers and emulsifying agents as glyceryl monostearate are most useful, and the common ice-cream stabilizers can be used with benefit.

4. Wherever possible, it is most desirable to emulsify soups before freezing.

Where starchy vegetables such as potatoes are added to soup, which is perhaps unlikely, or more particularly if extruded dough products like macaroni are used for garnish, then great care must be taken not to heat these too much before adding to the soup and freezing. Never cook dough products or starchy vegetables at a temperature higher than 145° F. or they will soften and disintegrate during storage.

Where root vegetables such as carrot are used for garnish, these are best if they are parted from the liquid element of the soup before the liquid is cooled and then added back to the cooled liquid for freezing whilst they are still hot. The hotter the vegetables are when frozen, and the lower the freezing temperature used, the more 'crisp' will be the vegetables when finally heated and served.

Where sugar is a part of the recipe, it is as well to add 10 per cent of this sugar content in the form of a reducing sugar, as oxidation is one of the worst enemies of frozen foods. For this reason also, it is most desirable to remove as much air from the soup as is possible. To a certain extent the actual cooking of the soup will drive off the air, but where reasonably large-scale operations are undertaken, it does undoubtedly pay to use a deaerator. Care must also be taken to drive as much air as possible out of the package used.

The actual steps involved in making frozen soups and the plant required are as foollws:

1. The usual stock-making and other kitchen equipment with which high-class soup is made in the ordinary way. The soups should be cooked to a degree just right for serving and no allowance is made for the cooking which will take place during reheating and there is of course no cooking in the container, as in canning so that vegetables, etc., must be properly cooked.

2. Where large-scale operations are in progress and the cost is justified, the hot liquid soup should definitely be deaerated at this stage. Deaeration is carried out in a special piece of equipment which consists of a vertical cylinder in which a very high vacuum is maintained by a steam jet vacuum pump. The hot soup is fed into the top of this cylinder and flows down through it over a series of baffle plates which spread the liquid very thinly. The thin layer of soup is thus subjected to high vacuum flashes and gives up much of its occluded oxygen. The initial and final temperatures of the liquid have to be very carefully adjusted to prevent too much loss of moisture, and the whole piece of equipment is both elaborate and costly.

3. The liquid element of the soup should then be cooled, although where a type of package is being used which permits hot filling this step may be omitted and the cooling done in the freezer, although this is rather costly. The best method of cooling is to use an ice-cream type cooler, which must, however, be totally enclosed and preferably of the plate type. The cooling plates or grids must not be too cold, as the soup is usually thicker than ice cream and may therefore clog up. For this reason a brine type cooler is better than direct expansion types. For very thick soups, water cooling is adequate, unless a drum-type cooler with a scraper is available.

4. After cooling, the liquid and the solids, if any, are filled into packages, either by hand or on a machine.

Packages vary a great deal, but the best type is that which

lends itself best to ultimate reheating. The cheapest form of package is of course a simple film or waxed paper bag and this is perfectly satisfactory so long as the housewife removes the block of soup while it is still frozen. If, however, she allows the soup to become partially or wholly defrosted, then the soup does tend to stick to the bag. Waxed or plastic-coated boxes are quite good for this purpose, but only the plastic-coated type can be filled hot and neither type lends itself to the application of heat for thawing and warming up. Undoubtedly the best container for frozen soup is an aluminium foil bag or rigid box, and not only can the soup be filled in hot, but at the same time the soup may be thawed and heated in the bag or box, thus simplifying the whole procedure in the kitchen and making the emptying of the container easier.

Whatever type of container is used, it should be filled carefully and sealed so that it is both airtight and moisture-vapour-proof. In most cases a heat seal is best. Whilst some headspace must be left to allow for expansion during freezing, this space should not be too great, as this means more air entrapped in the bag. Vacuum sealing would of course be ideal.

As an alternative to freezing in the container, the soup may be frozen in blocks in suitable moulds, and then put into the package afterwards. Where film bags are used, this system has the merit that it standardizes the size and shape of the pack.

5. The actual freezing process may be carried out in any one of a variety of machines made for the purpose, but in general there are three possible methods of quick-freezing: by immersion of the goods in a low temperature freezing medium; by contact with a very cold surface; or by subjection of the food to a very cold air blast.

Immersion freezing is not really suitable for soup freezing, so that there is a choice of contact or blast freezing.

The contact freezer, giving both top and bottom contact, is a machine in which there is a series of large flat shelves placed one above the other in a suitably insulated cabinet. These shelves are cooled by direct expansion of a refrigerating gas and are mounted on guides so that they may be moved up or down to close or open the gaps between the shelves. In operation the packages of food to be frozen are placed on the shelves, either singly or on trays, the shelves are then closed together so that

I

contact is achieved with both the top and bottom of each package. In these machines a slight pressure is applied to the packages. Heat is then extracted from the packages and the foods frozen by means of the top and bottom contact of the packages with the cold shelves or plates, as they are usually called.

One of the great advantages of these machines is that by reason of the slight pressure which is applied to the packages, these are kept in good shape and do not curve or bulge during freezing. This in turn simplifies packing the frozen units into shipping cases. However, as will readily be realized, the necessity for both top and bottom contact over the entire area of the package means that only rectangular packages may be used and these may not have lid or bottom end recesses. These machines may of course be used for soups in film bags, if these bags are held in shape in formers of the right dimensions to allow the bag to expand outwards under pressure to the right degree, but they do not allow of the use of round pots with lid and bottom recesses nor of the freezing of sundry lines of odd shape, outside the soup range.

In view of the fact that any manufacturer who makes quick-frozen soups is also likely to use the plant for freezing other pre-cooked food lines, some of which may not be of very regular shape, it seems possible that in most cases a blast freezer, or one which combines blast and contact will be the most suitable.

Blast freezers are made in many different forms by various manufacturers, but essentially a blast freezer consists of two large insulated boxes, or rather one box divided into two sections. In one section is the space for the foods to be frozen, either on shelves or on trolleys as the case may be. In the second section are cooling coils of a suitable size to deal with one load of food. Air is circulated over the cooling coils, over the food and back to the coils again, by means of a fan and thus the heat from the food is carried by the air to the coils and eventually by way of the compressor down the drain or into the atmosphere by way of the condenser water.

In some cases, contact as well as blast is used, by means of using cooled shelves on which to place the goods. In this case, however, there is no top contact, but only a cold blast passing over the top of the goods.

Whilst this description may make the blast freezer sound a very simple piece of apparatus, it is in fact most complicated in design, as the size of the cooling coils, the rate of air flow, the expansion temperatures and so on, have to be most carefully balanced to give the best effect and to avoid drying out the foods being frozen or excessive frost formation on the coils. There are a number of small blast units made in this country which are highly suitable for new, small-scale operations and a number of these machines are already being used for various types of pre-cooked foods.

6. Proper storage and transportation of frozen foods and especially pre-cooked frozen foods is essential. The foods must be stored at all times at zero or preferably below and, above all else, the temperature must not be allowed to vary. Variations in temperature, by even a degree or two, will lead to the drying out of the foods and serious loss of flavour.

In general, it must be said that the processing and handling of any type of pre-cooked frozen food is a most delicate operation, certainly much more delicate than the handling of ordinary frozen fruits or vegetables. Once food is cooked, it develops all its volatile flavours to the full, and unless the food is handled carefully and quickly at all stages prior to freezing, and is then stored properly, at low and even temperatures, these precious and all-important flavours will be lost.*

* Ref.: *The Freezing Preservation of Foods* by Dr. Donald K. Tressler, W. B. Van Arsdel and Dr. J. Copley, 1968. Published in 4 volumes. U.S.A.: Avi Publishing Co. Inc. London: Food Trade Press Ltd.

CHAPTER VIII

LEGAL ASPECTS

THE composition of canned soups in the United Kingdom is not controlled by legislation at the time of writing (1969), but only by adherence to the Code of Practice for Canned Soups adopted by the Canned Soup Section of the Food Manufacturers' Federation Inc. (FMF), having been in operation, as a manufacturers' code, since February, 1965. The Non-Liquid Soups Section of the FMF has produced a code but it has not been brought into operation.

To keep matters in perspective the various codes and reports are listed in chronological order, starting with the Code of Practice for Canned Soups, published February, 1965, and negotiated between the then Ministry of Food and the food manufacturers.

FOOD MANUFACTURERS' FEDERATION INC. CODE OF PRACTICE FOR CANNED SOUPS

(Operative on and from 1st February, 1965)

To secure that canned soups are not falsely described or sold under names which might mislead as to their nature, substance and quality, the Food Manufacturers' Federation has agreed the following Code of Manufacturing and Labelling Practice for canned soups packed for retail sale. The Code shall not apply to catering packs in cans of A.2½ size or larger, provided that these are labelled 'Specially packed for catering purposes only', nor to dry soup mixes.

In the absence of any reference to dilution on the label, the soup in the container shall conform to any minimum quantity prescribed in the following specifications. If the label bears a reference to dilution, that reference shall be specific and the relative minimum quantities shall be increased proportionately in accordance with the dilution recommended.

When the description states or implies that the soup is condensed or concentrated, directions for dilution shall be given and these shall be specific.

For the purpose of this Code, other than in Clause 2, 'meat' means raw, lean, boneless edible flesh, containing not more than 10% of ether-extractable fat. Meat extracts, hydrolized protein or yeast extract are not equivalent to meat and shall not be reckoned as such.

Where an extract of meat is present and is described as 'meat extract', this shall be beef extract. Where any other extract of meat is used the animal origin of the meat shall be specified in the list of ingredients, e.g. mutton, whalemeat, etc.

1. Meat Soups (excluding Clear Soups, Poultry and Game Soups)

(a) 'Meat Soup' (excluding Real Turtle Soups)

A product sold under this description unqualified, shall contain not less than 6% by weight of meat.

A meat soup sold under a specific name, e.g. 'Beef Soup', shall contain not less than 6% by weight of the named meat except in the case of oxtail soup or kidney soup mentioned below.

(b) 'Oxtail Soup'

Products sold under this description shall contain not less than 2% of oxtail (including bone). The total meat content shall be equivalent to not less than 6% by weight of meat.

(c) 'Mock Turtle Soup'

A product sold under this description shall contain not less than 6% by weight of meat.

(d) 'Kidney Soup'

A product sold under this description shall contain not less than 6% by weight of meat or permitted offal of which not less than two thirds shall be kidney (excluding capsule).

(e) 'Mulligatawny Soup'

A product sold under this description shall have a meat content of a meat soup, i.e. not less than 6% by weight of meat. It shall be flavoured with curry and may be garnished with an appropriate cereal.

In this variety of soup, the meat content may be replaced in whole or in part by poultry meat.

2. Poultry and Feathered Game Soups

In the preparation of a product sold under a specific name, e.g.

'Chicken Soup' not less than 6% of the raw, eviscerated, dressed carcases should be used.

3. Cream Soups

A product described as 'Cream Soup' shall contain not less than $2\frac{1}{2}\%$ by weight of butter fat; but no exception will be taken to a product sold under this description:

 (a) which contains less than $2\frac{1}{2}\%$ but not less than $1\frac{1}{2}\%$ by weight of butter fat if the total fat content is not less than 3%; or

 (b) which contains no butter fat or less than $1\frac{1}{2}\%$ by weight of butter fat if the total fat content is not less than $3\frac{1}{2}\%$.

4. Vegetable Soups

The word 'weight' shall be taken to mean the weight of the vegetable prepared for use, i.e. peeled, trimmed or shelled, or the equivalent weight of dehydrated vegetables or (for tomatoes) of tomato paste. In the case of dehydrated vegetables being used, the weight refers to the equivalent in fresh vegetables. For tomato purée added as purée, the amount can be calculated back to fresh tomatoes for the purpose of a reference to weights in the following paragraphs (except in (d)).

(a) *Vegetable Soup*

A product sold under this, or similar description, e.g. 'Mixed Vegetable Soup', 'Windsor Vegetable Soup', shall contain at least four different varieties of vegetable and no one variety should unduly predominate. Should the weight of one vegetable be more than 40% of the total weight of the vegetables, the descriptions of the soup shall include the name of the predominant variety (e.g. 'Potato and Vegetable Soup').

(b) *Single-Named Vegetable Soups (e.g. 'Celery Soup', 'Lentil Soup')*

In a product sold under such a description the weight of the named vegetable shall exceed the sum of the weights of the remaining vegetables (if any).

(c) *'Pea Soup' and 'Green Pea Soup'*

The description 'Green Pea Soup' implies a soup made from fresh, canned, frozen or dehydrated green peas, but not from processed or harvest dried peas. Dehydrated green peas are peas which have been dehydrated from the same fresh state required for canning or freezing as green peas. A soup made from processed or harvest-dried marrowfats or blues, or pea flour, shall be described as 'Pea Soup' without any suggestion that fresh green peas have been used.

(d) *'Tomato Soup'*
A product sold under this description shall contain not less than 3% tomato solids.

5. Clear Soups (*excluding Real Turtle*)

For the purpose of the following definition, a clear soup is considered to be the thin clear liquid obtained by the suitable extraction of meat, poultry or feathered game, or by the dilution of their extractives, or, in the case of clear vegetable soups, by the suitable extraction of selected vegetables.

(a) *Single-Named Meat Consommés (e.g. 'Beef Consommé')*
A product sold under one of these descriptions shall be a clear soup in the preparation of which the named meat, e.g. Beef, has been the predominant ingredient.

(b) *'Consommé'*
A product sold under this description shall be a clear soup in the preparation of which meat (or an equivalent amount of meat extractives) has been the predominant ingredient.

(c) *'Julienne'*
A product of this description shall be a suitably flavoured clear soup containing not less than 3% of strip or diced vegetables.

(d) *'Noodle'*
A product sold under this description shall be a clear soup as described above, garnished with noodles.

6. Broths

A broth as canned shall contain meat or bone extractives, derived from meat, bones, meat extractives or bone extract, used either singly or in any combination of two or more, in such proportion that the 'nitrogen' content shall be equivalent to not less than 1% by weight of 'meat protein' ($N \times 6.25$). The broth may contain optionally meat fibre, vegetables, farinaceous material, spices, herbs and suitable colourings and flavourings.

Single-Named Meat Broths (e.g. 'Beef Broth')
A product sold as 'Beef Broth' shall be a broth as defined above in the preparation of which only beef, beef extractives, or beef bones have been used as the meat ingredient.

(*Explanation:* The figure for the nitrogen content, which is given in the definition of broth relates not merely to the liquid part but to the complete product including solids. Thus the protein content of a 16 oz. can of broth, of which 12 oz. is liquid and 4 oz. solids, shall be 1% of 16 oz.).

7. Miscellaneous Soups

(a) '*Minestrone*'
A product sold under this description shall contain appreciable amounts of strip or diced assorted vegetables and may or may not contain meat. A pasta product (Macaroni, Spaghetti, Vermicelli) shall be present.

(b) '*Scotch Broth*'
A product sold under this description shall contain not less than 6% by weight of meat, including bone and fat, or 3% boned meat. It shall contain barley and an assortment of vegetables.

(c) '*Meat/Poultry/Feathered Game and Vegetable Soups*'
A specifically named meat and vegetable soup (e.g. 'Beef and Vegetables'), shall contain not less than 3% of the named meat. In the case of poultry or feathered game and vegetable soups (e.g. 'Chicken and Mushroom Soup') there shall be the use of not less than 3% of raw, eviscerated, dressed carcases of the named bird.

The FMF Revised Draft Code of Practice for Soup Mixes was as follows:

FOOD MANUFACTURERS' FEDERATION INC.

REVISED DRAFT

CODE OF PRACTICE FOR SOUP MIXES

To ensure that soup mixes and soup powders packed for retail sale are not falsely described or sold under names that might mislead as to their nature, substance or quality, the following Code of Manufacturing and Labelling Practice has been prepared. The Code shall not apply to:
    (a) Catering packs, provided that these are so labelled.
    (b) Bouillons not described as Soup Mixes.
    (c) Soup Powders, whether compressed or not, sold under a

description in which the word 'flavour' appears immediately following, and as conspicuously as, the name of the variety. The description of such an article may denote an ingredient present primarily for flavouring purposes and in relatively small proportion (e.g. 'Celery Flavour') or absent altogether but whose flavour is simulated (e.g. 'Kidney Flavour').

All other dry mixes intended to produce soup after mixing with water shall be described by the generic term 'Soup Mix'. The description 'Soup' is not permissible.

All packs of soup mixes shall bear a statement of the dilution or dilutions recommended for use when water alone is the diluting fluid. References in this Code to the soup made from a soup mix are to be interpreted as referring to the product obtained when the mix is made up with water according to the maximum dilution pre-scribed on the label.

If a product is described as 'cream' soup mix or 'cream of —' soup mix, the soup made from it shall contain not less than $2\frac{1}{2}\%$ by weight of butter fat; but no exception will be taken to a product sold under this description:

(a) which contains less than $2\frac{1}{2}\%$ but not less than $1\frac{1}{2}\%$ by weight of butter fat if the total fat content is not less than 3%; or

(b) which contains no butter fat or less than $1\frac{1}{2}\%$ by weight of butter fat if the total fat content is not less than $3\frac{1}{2}\%$.

Where an extract of meat is present the origin of the extract shall be specified, e.g. beef, mutton, whalemeat, etc.

The soup resulting from soup mix, when made up with water according to the maximum dilution prescribed on the label, shall conform to the following requirements.

1. Meat Soup Mixes (excluding Poultry and Feathered Game)

(a) General

For the purpose of the definition of meat soup mixes 'Meat' means raw, lean, boneless edible flesh (containing not more than 10% ether-extractable fat), or its equivalent of dehydrated meat when reconstituted.

Meat soup mixes which are specifically described shall produce a soup containing at least 2% of the named meat and of which the minimum total creatinine content shall be 45 mg. per pint derived from meat and/or meat extract.

(b) *'Clear Meat Soup Mix' (excluding 'Julienne Soup Mix')*

A clear meat soup mix shall produce a clear liquid obtained by the dilution of an amount of meat extract as appropriate, with or without garnish. The minimum total creatinine content in the case of a clear meat soup mix shall be 90 mg. per pint, derived from meat and/or meat extract.

(c) *'Meat Broth Mix' (excluding 'Scotch Broth')*

A meat broth mix shall produce an unclarified meat soup with or without garnish, the consistency of which is mainly liquid.

(d) *'Oxtail Soup Mix'*

A product of this description shall produce a meat soup with a total minimum meat content of 2% of which at least one-third shall be boneless lean oxtail meat.

2. Vegetable Soup Mixes

For the purpose of the definitions of vegetable soup mixes, 'vegetables' may include tomatoes and mushrooms but not herbs, and references to 'vegetable content' are to be interpreted as 'raw trimmed vegetables'.

(a) *'Vegetable Soup Mix'*

A product of this or similar description, e.g. 'Assorted Vegetable Soup Mix', 'Windsor Vegetable Soup Mix', shall contain at least four different varieties of vegetable and no one variety shall unduly predominate. If the weight of one vegetable be more than 40% of the total weight of vegetables, excluding cereal flours and edible starches for thickening purposes, the description of the soup mix shall include the name of the predominant variety (e.g. 'Potato and Vegetable Soup Mix').

(b) *Single-Named Vegetable Soup Mixes (excluding 'Tomato Soup Mix')*
    (e.g. 'Celery Soup Mix', 'Lentil Soup Mix')

In a product of such a description the weight of the named vegetable shall exceed the sum of the individual weights of the remaining vegetables, if any, excluding cereal flours and edible starches for thickening purposes.

If the description 'Green Pea Soup' is used, it shall contain dehydrated peas derived directly from green peas.

(c) *'Vegetable Broth Mix'*

A vegetable broth mix shall produce an unclarified vegetable soup, the consistency of which is mainly liquid.

(d) *'Clear Vegetable Soup Mix'*
   A clear vegetable soup mix shall produce a clear liquid obtained by the dilution of an amount of vegetable extract, with or without garnish.

3. Poultry and Feathered Game Soup Mixes

(a) A product of specific description (e.g. 'Chicken Soup Mix') shall produce a soup containing not less than 2% of the appropriate meat and fat and of this not less than 60% shall be lean meat.

(b) *'Clear Poultry Soup Mix'* *(excluding Noodle Soup Mixes)*
   A clear poultry soup mix shall produce a soup containing fat and extractives of meat derived from such an amount of whole dressed poultry that is not less than 2% of the finished soup.

4. Miscellaneous Soup Mixes *(Not covered in preceding paragraphs)*

(a) *'Minestrone Soup Mix'*
   A product of this description shall contain strip or diced assorted vegetables and may or may not contain meat. A pasta product (Macaroni, Spaghetti, Vermicelli, etc.) shall be present.

(b) *'Chicken Noodle Soup Mix'*
   A product of this description shall produce a clear soup in which the flavouring is primarily derived from chicken meat and chicken fat; it shall also contain noodles.

(c) *'Julienne Soup Mix'*
   A product of this description shall produce a suitably flavoured clear soup containing not less than 3% of strip or diced vegetables.

(d) *'Scotch Broth Mix'*
   A product of this description shall produce a soup with a boned meat content of not less than 2%. It shall contain barley and an assortment of vegetables.

In 1968 the Food Standards Committee Report on Soups was published. The enforcement authorities expressed their preference for statutory standards and stressed the need for compositional requirements to apply to all products. They also thought that analytical control should be reinforced by inspection of factories and methods of manufacture. The trade, naturally enough, considered a Code of Practice as the best method of ensuring control and that they were near agreement on draft codes with the Local Authorities' Joint Advisory Committee on Food Standards (LAJAC). The manufacturers further stated that soup was not now a major part of the modern diet and that composition did not therefore require to be controlled for health reasons or to prevent consumer deception.

The Committee reported that, as it is not at present possible to determine accurately by analysis the meat content of canned soups, disclosure of recipes would be essential. They therefore recommended that the 'manufacture' as well as the 'sale' of non-standard soups of all kinds be made an offence. They also recommended that basic compositional requirements for the most important soups should be embodied in regulations. Regarding other requirements in existing or proposed Codes of Practice, the Committee recommended that as soon as any regulations are made a revised Code of Practice for canned soups and a new code for soup mixes should be drawn up by negotiation between the LAJAC and the manufacturers.

The Report also contained the following recommendations:

1. The appropriate designation for Powdered Soup should be 'Soup Mix'.
2. Meat Soups should have the following minimum percentages of meat:

> Canned Soups—6%
> Soup Mixes   —3%

3. Minimum meat contents of named meat soups should be 6% of the named meat; Oxtail or Kidney Soups should contain at least 6% total meat and not less than $1\frac{1}{2}$% oxtail (excluding bone) or not less than two-thirds kidney (excluding capsule) respectively.
4. The minimum meat content of named soup mixes should be 3%; Oxtail Soup Mix and Kidney Soup Mix should contain at least 3% total meat and not less than 1% of oxtail (excluding bone) or not less than two-thirds kidney (excluding capsule) respectively.

5. The definition of 'meat' should be as recommended below.* For soup mixes this should be the meat used in the preparation of the mix or its equivalent in dehydrated meat.

6. The minimum meat content of Poultry and Game Soups should be 3%, with a proviso that it shall be sufficient compliance if the meat from an amount of raw, eviscerated, dressed carcase was incorporated as an ingredient so that the amount of carcase used shall be not less than 8% by weight of the soup when prepared for consumption.

7. The minimum meat content of Poultry and Game Soup Mixes should be 3%.

8. Regulations are not necessary for Clear Meat Soups or Broths, except for Scotch Broth.

9. Meat and Vegetable Soups and Soup Mixes (including Scotch Broth) should have the following minimum meat contents:

(i)   Meat and Vegetable Soup   — 3%
(ii) Poultry and Vegetable Soup   — $1\frac{1}{2}$%
(iii) Meat and Vegetable Soup Mix   — $1\frac{1}{2}$%
(iv) Poultry and Vegetable Soup Mix — $1\frac{1}{2}$%

provided that for Poultry and Vegetable Soup the proviso in paragraph 47 (i) shall apply with 4% substituted for 8%.

10. Soups or soup mixes described as 'Cream of . . .' or 'Cream' should be required to contain either:

(i) not less than $2\frac{1}{2}$% by weight of butter fat; or
(ii) 1% butter fat if the total fat content is not less than 3%.

Soups described as 'Creamed' may either comply with (i) or (ii) above, or may contain no butter fat, but in this instance they must have at least $3\frac{1}{2}$% total fat content.

11. Tomato Soup should contain not less than 3% tomato solids; Tomato Soup Mix should contain not less than 2% tomato solids.

12. The term 'Condensed' should be restricted to products which require dilution to at least double the volume. Only the word 'Condensed' unqualified should be permitted.

13. Unambiguous dilution instructions should appear on the labels of all soups and soup mixes.

14. Ingredients of canned soups and soup mixes should be declared.

---

* 'Meat' means raw, lean, boneless, edible flesh, of any animal or any bird, which is normally used for human consumption, containing not more than 10% of ether-extractable fat. Meat extracts, hydrolised protein or yeast extract, are not equivalent to meat and shall not be reckoned as such.

Where an extract of meat is present and is described as 'meat extract', this shall be beef extract. Where any other extract of meat is used the animal origin of the meat shall be specified in the list of ingredients, e.g. mutton, whalemeat, etc.

An interesting case involving soup mixes was reported in Britain some years ago (Brit. Food J., 1959, *61*, 69). A company was summoned on the ground that their mushroom soup mix did not contain dried mushrooms and that the prime ingredient, the fungus *Boletus edulis,* was falsely described on the label. Their defence was that they used *B. edulis* because the dried English mushrooms are dark in colour and do not have the real mushroom flavour, and hence are unsuitable for mushroom soup mixes! The magistrates decided that *B. edulis* is properly described as a mushroom and that any company using this product was putting mushrooms in their soup mixes. The case was dismissed with costs for the defendant and it was stated that three other soup mix manufacturers in Britain were also using *B. edulis* in their soup mixes.

However, in view of the possibility of the U.K. joining the Common Market (EEC) in due course readers must bear in mind the standards promulgated by the EEC which relate solely to minimum composition of various types of soup products based on chemical constituents of various ingredients rather than specific minimum quantities of the ingredients themselves.

The Draft Council Directive concerning the Harmonization of Member States Laws for meat, yeast and protein extracts, spices in soups and foods, broths, soups and meat sauces (presented to the council of the EEC, October 30th, 1968) contains the following appendix:

APPENDIX I

DEFINITIONS OF PRODUCTS

1 *Meat Extract*

Product derived by concentration of aqueous extracts of fresh beef
(1), obtained by extraction of the coagulable protein and the fat;
also after the addition of sodium chloride.

If the meat extract is intended for direct consumption, it must
conform with the following criteria:

Water	not more than 20%	
Total creatinine	not less than 7%	determined on dry matter
Total nitrogen	not less than 10%	
Sodium chloride	not more than 5%	
Water insoluble matter after defatting with ethyl ether	not more than 1%	
Fat	not more than 2%	

(1) 'Fresh Beef', according to the meaning of these rules are all parts
from skeletal muscles, of domesticated cattle, which were given no
other treatment for preservation except refrigeration.

2 *Yeast extract*

Product derived solely from yeast by physical or biochemical
procedures, also after addition of sodium chloride.

If the yeast extract is intended for direct consumption it must
conform with the following criteria:

Water	not more than 22%	
Total nitrogen	not less than for brewer's yeast extract 7% not less than for other yeast extracts 8%	determined on dry matter
Sodium chloride	not more than 20%	
Water insoluble matter after defatting with ethyl ether	not more than 1%	

3 *Protein extract*

Product derived by concentration of protein hydrolyzates. If the
protein extract is intended for direct consumption it must conform
with the following criteria:

Water	not more than 20%	
Total nitrogen	not less than 5·8%	
Amino acid nitrogen	not less than 3·4%	determined
Ammonia nitrogen	not more than 1·25%	on dry
Sodium chloride	not more than 35%	matter
Water insoluble matter after defatting with ethyl ether	not more than 1%	

4   Seasonings in Soups and Foods

Liquid products derived by hydrolysis of proteins or protein rich materials; also after addition of meat extract, yeast extract, other extracts obtained from suitable protein-rich substances, sodium chloride, spices or their natural extracts and—for improvement of the flavour—of other foods, of glutamic acid and its salts, as well as sodium and potassium salts of inosinic and guanylic acids.

It conforms to the following criteria:

Specific gravity at 20°C	not less than 1·24%	
Total nitrogen	not less than 5%	
Amino acid nitrogen	not less than 3%	determined
Ammonia nitrogen (1)	not more than 2%	on dry
Sodium chloride	not more than 45%	matter
Matter insoluble in water and ethyl ether	not more than 1%	

(1) Obligatory requirements as soon as an analytical method is worked out by the Community.

5   Broth

Product derived from protein-rich substances or their derivatives; also after addition of seasonings, suitable fat substances, sodium chloride, spices or their natural extracts or distillates, aromas (1) and—for improvement of flavour—of other foods, of glutamic acid and its salts, as well as sodium and potassium salts or inosinic and guanylic acids.

It conforms to the following criteria:

Total nitrogen	not less than 350 mg.	per litre of broth
Amino acid nitrogen	not less than 210 mg.	prepared according
Sodium chloride	not more than 12·5 mg.	to directions

(1) As long as the national regulations are not harmonized, it is only permitted to use natural aromas and such synthetic aromas that are chemically identical to the naturals.

6 *Meat Broth*

Broth derived by use of fresh beef and/or meat extract (in the sense of paragraph 5) also by use of other meat and/or extracts of meat other than beef.

It conforms to the following criteria:

Total creatinine from beef   not less than 70 mg;
                             of which this creatinine
                             must not make up less than   per litre
                             $\frac{2}{3}$ of the sum of the   of broth
                             total creatinine content   prepared
                             of the product   according
                                                              to
Total nitrogen   not less than 100 mg.   directions
Sodium chloride   not more than 12·5 mg.

7 *Consommé*

Broth which conforms to the following criteria:

Total creatinine from beef   not less than 110 mg;
                             whereby this creatinine   per litre
                             may not make up less   of meat
                             than $\frac{2}{3}$ of the sum of   consommé
                             the total creatinine   prepared
                             content of the product   according
                                                              to
Total nitrogen   not less than 160 mg.   directions
Sodium chloride   not more than 12·5 mg.

8 *Poultry Broth*

Broth derived by the use of poultry meat in the sense of paragraph 5.

It conforms to the following criteria:

                                                              per litre
                                                              of poultry
                                                              broth
Total nitrogen   not less than 100 mg.   prepared
Sodium chloride   not more than 12·5 mg.   according
                                                              to
                                                              directions

9 *Fatty broth, fatty meat broth, fatty consommé, fatty poultry broth*

Broth, meat broth, consommé or poultry broth, which contain at least 2·5 g. of fat substance per litre of product prepared according to directions.

K

10   *Soups*

More or less liquid products or products presented in this form when prepared according to the directions for use, also with a more or less high content of solid pieces, which yield preparations of similar flavour and appearance as soups derived from the customary kitchen procedure.

If the information or pictures on the container, the wrapper, or the label indicate the presence or use of beef or meat (without more specific designation) or of meat extract, the soups must contain per litre of the product prepared according to direction at least 70 mg. of total creatinine from beef, whereby this creatinine must represent not less than $\frac{2}{3}$ of the sum of the total creatinine in the product.

11   *Meat sauces*

Products more or less liquid, based on preparation according to the directions for use, derived from fresh beef and/or meat extract, as well as possibly also from the substances listed under paragraphs 5 and 6 for consumption in a warm state together with other foods. Their content of total creatinine from beef must not be below 140 mg. per litre of the product prepared on the basis of the directions for use; whereby this creatinine must not represent less than $\frac{2}{3}$ of the sum of the total creatinine contained in the product.

Antioxidants

Antioxidants have been permitted in certain fats and oils since the promulgation of the Antioxidants in Food Regulations 1958. In 1963 the Foods Standards Committee (FSC) made certain recommendations for revised legislation and these were modified by the Food Additives and Contaminants Committee (FACC). The FSC had recommended that butylated hydroxytoluene (BHT) be no longer permitted because of doubts about safety of this compound. The FACC proposed that the legal levels of BHT be halved until further investigations could be made. It was also suggested that antioxidants be permitted in partial glycerol esters. In 1965 the British Ministry of Agriculture, Fisheries and Food (MAFF) issued proposals for revised regulations, and the following is a summary of the contents which are of interest to soup manufacturers:

(see table opposite)

Specified Food	Description of Antioxidant	Parts per Million
(a) Anhydrous edible oils and fats, whether hardened or not and vitamin oils and concentrates other than preparations containing more than 100,000 IU's vitamin A per g.	n-propyl gallate or n-octyl gallate or n-dodecyl gallate or any mixture thereof or	100
	Butylated hydroxyanisole (BHA) or	200
	Butylated hydroxytoluene (BHT) or	100
	any mixture of BHA and BHT	200
		(except that BHT must not exceed 100)
(b) Partial Glycerol Esters	n-propyl gallate or n-octyl gallate or n-dodecyl gallate or any mixture thereof or	100
	Butylated hydroxyanisole (BHA) or	200
	Butylated hydroxytoluene (BHT) or	100
	any mixture of BHA and BHT	200
		(except that BHT must not exceed 100)
(c) Butter for manufacturing purposes	n-propyl gallate or n-octyl gallate or n-dodecyl gallate or any mixture thereof or	80
	Butylated hydroxyanisole (BHA) or	160
	Butylated hydroxytoluene (BHT) or	80
	any mixture of BHA and BHT	160
		(except that BHT must not exceed 80)
(d) Essential oils and isolates from and concentrates of essential oils	n-propyl gallate or n-octyl gallate or n-dodecyl gallate or any mixture thereof or	1,000
	Butylated hydroxyanisole (BHA) or	1,000
	Butylated hydroxytoluene (BHT) or	500
	any mixture of BHA and BHT	1,000
		(except that BHT must not exceed 500)

The Antioxidants in Food Regulations 1966 (SI No. 1500) came into operation on 9th December, 1966 and superseded the 1958 regulations. They contained similar provisions to those recommended by the FSC in 1963, with the exceptions that the permitted BHT levels for foods were *double* the earlier recommended levels and that no restriction on BHT level in the BHA/BHT mixtures was laid down. The *total* amounts of antioxidants permitted were laid down as 300 p.p.m. for foods in items (a) and (b) above, 240 p.p.m. for item (c), and 1,000 p.p.m. for item (d).

Food intended mainly for babies or young children is prohibited from containing any added antioxidant.

Artificial Sweeteners

In 1966 the FACC recommended that sodium cyclamate and calcium cyclamate be permitted as artificial sweeteners in foodstuffs. This is of interest to manufacturers of soups for dietetic purposes.

The Artificial Sweeteners in Food Regulations 1967 (SI No. 1119) included provision for the use of cyclamate compounds in foods in addition to the continued use of saccharin preparations.

Author's Note:

In October 1969 the US Government banned the manufacture of foods and soft drinks containing cyclamates and set a deadline for the withdrawal of all food items containing cyclamates of February, 1970. Similar action also followed in Sweden, Denmark, Germany, and Finland while the British Ministry of Agriculture, Fisheries and Food banned the use of cyclamates and set a final sale date of January 1st, 1970.

Colouring Matter

In 1964 the FSC issued a report which recommended the withdrawal of six colours from the permitted list. In 1965 the MAFF issued proposals for revised regulations which would control the use of colouring matter in foods. It is thus becoming somewhat difficult for manufacturers of certain foodstuffs to achieve precisely the range of colours they want, since the list of permitted colours is being reduced all the time. It is obviously time for an international colour standard to be agreed on and enforced.

The Colouring Matter in Food Regulations 1966 (SI No. 1203) laid down a list of statutory permitted food colours. This included twenty-five coal tar colours and a number of colours of vegetable origin. Caramel, carmine and some metallic lakes were also permitted.

Flavouring Agents

The FSC was asked to study the use of flavouring agents in food, and in 1965 this body issued a report in which it recommended prohibition of the use of sixteen substances used as flavouring agents. This was done on grounds of probable toxicity and because of pharmacological properties. At the time of going to press no regulations had been promulgated in the U.K., but these may be expected in the near future, possibly along the lines of the permitted lists in force in the U.S.A.

Mineral Oils

The Mineral Oil in Food Order 1949 (as amended) was revoked in early 1965 by the Mineral Hydrocarbons in Food Regulations 1964. Later, in 1965, the MAFF issued proposals for amending these regulations and it issued a revised test for polycyclic hydrocarbons. These legal steps were considered necessary because of the carcinogenic nature of certain hydrocarbons.

The Mineral Hydrocarbons in Food Regulations 1966 (SI No. 1073) prohibited the use of any mineral hydrocarbon in the preparation or composition of food, with certain exceptions. Specifications for mineral hydrocarbons were included plus a test method for polycyclic hydrocarbon.

Solvents

The FACC published a report on the use of solvents in food in 1965. This body recommended that solvents in food be subjected to control and that eight substances would be permitted. These were: ethyl alcohol, ethyl acetate, glycerol,

glycerol mono-acetate, glycerol di-acetate, glycerol tri-acetate, isopropyl alcohol, and propylene glycol. These materials are used as solvents or carriers for flavouring and other substances in canned and packet soups.

Following a FAAC Report on Solvents in 1966 the Solvents in Food Regulations 1967 (SI No. 1582) were promulgated. The regulations prohibited the use of all but nine solvents in food. The list included diethyl ether plus the eight chemicals listed above.

Labelling

In 1964 the FSC issued a report on food labelling. This was very comprehensive, some 72 recommendations being made. The items of special interest to soup manufacturers are as follows:

1. The use of a registered trade mark should not be allowed as an alternative to the name and address of the labeller or packer.

2. The ingredients of a foodstuff should be listed in the order present when the food was first compounded. This is to give the consumer an idea of the order of ingredients used at the 'mixing bowl' stage of manufacture. It was also recommended that for dehydrated food-stuffs such as soup mixes the manufacturer should have the option of declaring the ingredients in order as in the packet or as they will be when reconstituted with water. In the latter case a heading should indicate that they are in order by weight when reconstituted. These recommendations give the consumer information which should theoretically simplify the confusion which exists between items which have to be dehydrated substantially before inclusion in a dry mix and those which are used in a dry state in any case.

3. Ingredients on a label should be in certain point sizes of type.

4. Deodorized fatty oils should be declared as of animal or vegetable origin. A generic term for herbs and spices should be allowed, as at present, where they do not form more than 1 per cent of the food concerned. Generic terms for dried fruits and nuts should be discontinued.

5. The generic terms 'edible gums' and 'fruit acids' should be permitted. The latter would cover citric, tartaric and malic acids. The terms 'seasoning', 'meat extract' and 'fruit juices' should be replaced by more precise descriptions.

6. Additives used as processing or manufacturing aids should be declared. If there is a statutory permitted list a generic term may be used, e.g., 'permitted emulsifier'. A special declaration should be made of preservatives, antioxidants, colours, artificial sweeteners and flavourings. Until flavourings become the subject for a permitted list they should be designated as 'natural' or 'synthetic'.

7. Where a permitted preservative, antioxidant or mineral oil is present in a compounded food by reason of a carry over from an ingredient, it is not necessary to declare its presence, provided it is not present in excess of 5 per cent of the maximum amount permitted in the ingredient by the relevant regulations.

8. The word 'instant' should not be used in the designations of foods.

9. Where liquid glucose is used, it should be declared as 'glucose syrup'.

10. Food vending machines should carry a clear statement of their contents. This is of interest in view of the growing use of these dispensing aids in the United Kingdom and on the Continent.

11. Canned and powdered soups should be specially labelled and compositional standards should be drawn up as soon as possible.

12. Hydrolysed protein should be declared as of vegetable or animal origin and that salt in it should be declared. A wide variety of animal and vegetable proteins are used in the manufacture of hydrolysed protein and in some cases proteins from both classes are used. This would create some difficulties. Since hydrochloric acid is the normal hydrolysing agent, neutralization with sodium hydroxide or sodium salts means that a substantial amount of common salt is present in the final product. In fact, salt is often added to the usual hydrolysed protein paste in order to assist in drying to produce a powder. The salt declaration would apparently only apply to the sale of the raw material. This information has always been available to soup manufacturers in the technical information supplied by manufacturers and importers.

In 1965 the MAFF issued proposals for a revision of the Order based on the FSC report, and these implemented most of the above recommendations. Foods intended for export and for Armed Forces contracts will be exempt from the proposed regulations.

The International Association of the Broth and Soup Industry met in Vienna in 1965 and proposed a standard for soups and bouillons within the European Economic Community and their relationship with work to be carried out under the FAO/WHO Codex Alimentarius Commission. In 1961 the Association of Swiss Soup Manufacturers had published *Analytical Methods for the Soup Industry*. This volume was issued by the Technical Commission of the International Association and it contained tests for meat extract, bouillon products, soup seasonings, soups and antioxidants. More detailed reference is made to this work in Chapter IX.

In 1967 the Labelling of Food Regulations (SI No. 1864) were promulgated. Apart from applying to any food containing cyclamate (operating from 1st January, 1968) they come into operation on 4th January, 1971. Included in the regulations:

1. Ingredients of foods should be listed on the label in descending order of magnitude.

2. Where a name has been used for not less than 30 years (before 4th January, 1971) to describe any food, then that name shall be deemed to be an appropriate designation of that food.

3. Hydrolysed starch in liquid form shall be designated 'glucose syrup'.

4. Water as an ingredient need not be declared.

5. The name of the packer or labeller with a business address shall be declared.

6. For dried foods, the ingredients may be listed as if they had first been reconstituted by the addition of an appropriate quantity of water. For soup mixes, and other foods for reconstitution before consumption, ingredients may be listed in order of weight as reconstituted by the addition of water.

7. Declaration of permitted preservatives, antioxidants, stabilizers, artificial sweeteners, solvents and flavourings as constituents of an ingredient allow the word 'permitted' to be used if desired, or the substances themselves may be declared. Preservatives and antioxidants in ingredients, in a proportion of less than five per cent, need not be declared.

8. Oils, as part of a food, may be described as 'edible oils', 'oil', 'shortening', 'edible fat', 'fat' or 'shortening'.

9. Sodium citrate, sodium phosphates and sodium tartrate, when used as ingredients, may be declared as 'emulsifying salts'.

10. Purified starch, as an ingredient, may be designated 'edible starch', 'food starch' or 'starch'.

11. Citric, tartaric and malic acids may be designated 'fruit acids' when used as ingredients.

12. Spices, when not more than one per cent of a food, may be declared as 'spices' or 'mixed spices'.

13. Acacia, carob, ghatti, guar, karaya and tragacanth gums may be declared as 'edible gums' when their level of use in a food is not more than one per cent.

14. The actual manner of marking or labelling pre-packed foods is listed.

In August 1966 the FSC reported on claims and misleading descriptions. This was followed, on 6th November, 1967, by the MAFF proposals for new regulations to control claims and misleading descriptions on labels and advertisements of food.

It was proposed that detailed control of general claims would be legislated for, as well as claims for: benefit due to energy or protein content; presence of vitamins and minerals; benefits for slimming; suitability for diabetics; benefit for invalids; and tonic, restorative and medicinal properties. Control of the use of certain special descriptions would be obtained as well.

The effect of the proposed regulations would be substantial on the practice of marketing, advertising and labelling of food and, in some cases, would exceed the effect intended by the earlier FSC report.

Certain prohibitions were proposed:

1. Any claim that vitamins hasten recovery from colds and influenza or confer protection against these illnesses.

2. Suggestions that a food does not contain sugar if it contains carbohydrate (other than sorbitol).

3. Suggestions that a food has slimming properties.

4. The use of the word 'slim', or any similar word, in the name of a food product.

In the definitions proposed it was stated that if the name of a food was used to indicate a specific flavour, or a picture of the same was used, then the flavour designated must be derived wholly or mainly from the food. If the word 'flavour' is used with the food name then this restriction would not apply.

The words 'home-made' and 'home-baked' were proposed for use solely for foods made in a domestic kitchen.

Emulsifiers and Stabilizers

The Emulsifiers and Stabilizers in Food Regulations, 1962 (SI 720), became effective in England and Wales in July of that year. A list of permitted emulsifiers and permitted stabilizers was established as follows:

Stearyl tartrate
Complete glycerol esters
Partial glycerol esters
Partial polyglycerol esters
Propylene glycol esters
Monostearin sodium sulphoacetate
Sorbitan esters of fatty acids and their polyoxyethylene
    derivatives
Cellulose ethers
Sodium carboxymethyl cellulose
Brominated edible vegetable oils

Many other materials were already permitted for use in foods and raw materials, including: many hydrophilic colloids such as agar, alginates, and edible gums; lecithin; pectin and pectates; caseinates; starches; proteins; malt extract; sorbital; sodium and potassium salts of certain organic acids. Substances on the new permitted list are not allowed in flour and cream but they are permitted in any foodstuff which contains them naturally. The substances used in bread are limited to stearyl tartrate and partial glycerol esters.

At the time of going to press the MAFF was reviewing the regulations.

In 1965 the European Food Law Research Centre, with headquarters in Brussels, was set up by the Institute of European Studies for the comparative study of food laws in Western European countries. It is hoped that a uniform code of food regulations will eventually be evolved for Western Europe with the ultimate goal of international law to replace the present chaotic situation.

Tomato Paste or Purée

The Medical Officer of Health for the Port and City of London in 1962 limited the amount of mould (determined by the Howard Mould Count) which imported tomato purée and paste may contain. Some shipments were refused entry. When the British food trade proposed a standard for tomato purée it was rejected on the ground that it was really a trade specification. The food trade organized a conference on the subject called The London Tomato Purée Conference, of which the senior author of this book, Mr Raymond Binsted, was chairman. The conference was attended by manufacturers of tomato purée from the principal producing countries, London importers, and food manufacturers in the U.K. using large tonnages of tomato purée. The technical papers presented at the conference were published in *Food Trade Review 33* Nos. 7 and 8 and subsequently reprinted. This proposed standard has, however, been submitted to the Codex Alimentarius Committee, which is producing an international standard for these tomato concentrates. The United States Government has been invited to prepare a draft for a world-wide standard and it is co-operating with the United Kingdom and French Governments. This is of paramount importance to canned soup manufacturers in view of the very large amounts of tomato paste used in this country, for tomato soup still appears to be the most popular processed soup in the Western world. It will be a happy day when the whole vexed question of mould count techniques can be rationalized in relation to processsing quality.

Weights and Measures

The Weights & Measures Act, 1963, and the Weights & Measures (Marking) Regulations, 1964, became fully effective at the end of July 1965. These lay down the types of foods which must bear a quantity declaration and also how the declaration must be made. For canned soups and soup mixes the net weight of contents should be declared in the Imperial system although many manufacturers are now giving the equivalent weight in the metric system as well. This is to assist in smoothing the path to conversion of the United Kingdom to the metric system by Government action by about 1975.

Fruit and Vegetables

A new Code of Practice on canned fruit and vegetables was made effective on 8th October, 1965. This is only of interest to soup canners who are using canned vegetables for use in manufacture, where it will be of assistance in maintaining standards for purchasing specifications.

Trace Elements

Apart from the basic food law of the United Kingdom, the Food and Drugs Act, 1955, there exist certain Statutory Instruments (SI) which deal legally with trace elements in some foods and raw materials. The various reports of the Food Standards Committee have no legal sanction but they are often used in court proceedings as a guide. Manufacturers therefore use these reports, even where no regulations are issued, as giving reasonable upper limits so that their compliance with them will obviate the need for statutory ones.

General Limits

The Lead in Food Regulations, 1961 (SI No. 1931), prescribed 2 parts per million (p.p.m.) for foods.

The Arsenic in Food Regulations, 1959 (SI No. 831), as amended by SI 1960: No. 2261 prescribed 1 p.p.m. as a general limit.

FSC-recommended limits of 20 p.p.m. of copper, 50 p.p.m. of zinc and 250 p.p.m. of tin (for canned foods only) have been made for foods in general.

Specific Limits

Those materials of interest to the manufacturer of canned soups and soup mixes are listed in the table opposite with the specific statutory and recommended trace element limits:

	(PARTS PER MILLION)			
	Statutory		*Recommended*	
	Lead	*Arsenic*	*Copper*	*Zinc*
Agar	10			
Alginates	10			
Apples	3			
Caramel	5			
Carrageen	10			
Chemicals	10	2		
Colours	20	5	30	
Curry Powder	20			
Dextrose	0·5			
Fats	0·5			
Flavourings	10		30	
Gelatine	5	2	30	100
Glucose	5			
Herbs, dried	10	5		
Lecithin	5			
Lemon and Lime Juice	2			
Meat Extract	5			
Molasses	5			
Mustard		5		
Mustard, ground	20			
Oils, edible	0·5			
Onions, dehydrated	10	2		
Protein, hydrolyzed	5			
Spices	10	5		
Spices, ground	10			
Sugar (ash content less than 0·03 per cent)	0·5			
Sugar (ash content more than 1 per cent)	5			
Tomato juice	1		100 (on dry solids)	
Tomato paste, purée			100 (on dry solids)	
Tomato purée & paste (solids 15–25 per cent)	3			
Tomato purée & paste (solids more than 25 per cent)	5		6	
Vegetables, dried (except onions)	5			

Where there are gaps in the above table the general limit may apply. Readers are referred to the specific regulations and to the excellent summary which has been published by M. S. Davis (*Food Trade Review*, 1966, *36,* No. 3, 53) and from which the above information has been abstracted.

Preservatives

In 1959 the FSC published their Report on Preservatives in Food. This led, in 1962, to legislation as SI No. 1532, The Preservatives in Food Regulations 1962.

Apart from the regulations governing the use of SO_2 in dehydrated vegetables, referred to in Chapter IX, the following are of interest to soup manufacturers:

Specified Food	*Permitted Preservative*	*Maxima* (*p.p.m.*)
Cheese	Sorbic acid	1,000
Cheese (other than Cheddar, Cheshire or soft cheese)	Sodium nitrate or Sodium nitrite	100 10
Colouring matter (in solution)	Benzoic acid or Sorbic acid	2,000 1,000
Fish, raw	Tetracyclines	5
Flavouring emulsions & flavouring syrups	Sulphur dioxide or Benzoic acid	350 800
Fruit, dried	Sulphur dioxide	2,000
Gelatin	Sulphur dioxide	1,000
Ginger, dry root	Sulphur dioxide	150
Meat, pickled, cooked	Sodium nitrite	200
Meat, pickled, uncooked	Sodium nitrite	500
Potatoes, raw, peeled	Sulphur dioxide	50
Sausages or sausage meat	Sulphur dioxide	450
Starches, prepared	Sulphur dioxide	100
Sugar or sugar syrups	Sulphur dioxide	70
Tomato pulp, paste or purée	Sulphur dioxide or methyl p-hydroxybenzoate or propyl p-hydroxybenzoate	350 800 800
Vinegar	Sulphur dioxide	70

Additionally, nisin was permitted in cheese, clotted cream and any canned food; nitrates and nitrites of sodium and potassium were allowed in bacon and ham; nitrates of sodium and potassium were permitted in cooked and uncooked pickled meat; a maximum of 5 p.p.m. of formaldehyde was allowed in any food where formaldehyde is used in the manufacture of the packaging material.

At the end of 1964 the FACC started a review of the preservative regulations, and the views of the FMF were sought. The latter organization requested the extended use of certain preservatives. No new regulations were issued at the time this book closed for press.

Manufacturers of soups, and indeed of all foodstuffs intended for sale in the United Kingdom, should also make themselves familiar with the following:

The Butter Regulations 1966 (SI No. 1074)

The Dried Milk Regulations 1965 (SI No. 363)

The Margarine Regulations 1967 (SI No. 1867)

The Trade Descriptions Act 1968

The Weights and Measures Act 1963

The Weights and Measures (Marking) Regulations 1964 (SI No. 1140)

The Weights and Measures (Abbreviations of Units of Measurement) Regulations 1964 (SI No. 1139)

Memorandum on Procedure for submissions on Food Additives and on Methods of Toxicity testing 1965

The Imported Food Regulations 1968 (SI No. 97)

CHAPTER IX

THE SEASONING OF SOUPS

H. B. Heath, M.B.E., B. Pharm., F.P.S., F.I.F.S.T.
(Bush Boake Allen Ltd.)

THE IMPORTANCE OF SEASONING

THOSE concerned with the marketing of food products, whatever the nature of these may be, are well aware that flavour is of particular importance for continuing sales. Initial sales are more readily affected by advertising and by eye-catching packages, but the housewife will only buy a food product a second time if she sees pleasure in the faces of her family when the dish is served to them on the table.

Now flavour is a complex subject and although it is primarily composed of the sensations of taste and smell it is also very closely connected with such secondary considerations as texture, colour and heat. Not only must the food product taste right, it must also look right and when eaten be really appetizing. The past decade, in particular, has seen tremendous strides in the practice of food technology and today a large proportion of the nation's food is supplied in ready prepared forms involving the minimum of time and effort in preparation and presentation. There is always some degree of nostalgia about the past and perhaps in no other field is this expressed so forcibly as with food. Somehow mother's cooking tasted better—or at least this is what we think. Certainly at the turn of the century every family meal was prepared with meticulous care and attention to the details of the recipe, however tedious and time-consuming this may have been. At that time every kitchen had its collection of herbs and spices, not just as a set of pretty jars to decorate a corner shelf but to be used. Every cook knew the secret of adding these in just the right amounts at just the right stage of the cooking so as to give a distinctive character to each dish. Today few can afford the long hours spent over the kitchen stove. At our present rate of life we demand speed in all things, but even so we are not prepared to sacrifice the undoubted quality of those well-established recipes and mouth-watering dishes. Unfortunately the most flavourful dishes are often those which take the longest to prepare. It has fallen to the lot of the food technologist to give the housewife a meal similar to one which, under normal circumstances, would have taken her hours to prepare in the kitchen, that she can be proud to put before her family. All this to be done with the minimum of cost in money, time and effort. That is the problem.

In spite of these acknowledged difficulties, the consumer is not prepared to accept any lowering of standards, particularly when it comes to quality. The food technologist is expected to produce the answer and the excellence of many of our nationally and internationally distributed food products is in itself evidence of the considerable success of those concerned with product development, and not least those involved in the development of flavours. We are all learning to appreciate good, well-flavoured foods and this tends to be a progressive process, for as our palates become trained and conditioned so do they become more discriminating.

The flavour of any food product will depend upon all the ingredients used in its preparation. So far as the soup manufacturer is concerned, virtually anything that can be eaten can be used in the making of a soup. It is one of the basic forms of presenting food and may be used as an appetizer or as a main meal. Indeed this is well reflected in the dictionary definition which describes 'soup' as 'a well-seasoned broth of meat or vegetables or both; a food in the form of a liquid broth . . .'. The flavour of such a product will be determined not only by the seasonings added intentionally but by the quantity, quality and variety of the main food ingredients used and the method by which these are processed.

The question of the actual flavours to be achieved in any given soup is largely a matter of opinion, between one manufacturer and another. The range of blends is so varied that it is impossible to discuss this aspect of formulation other than in terms of the general principles involved. Apart from the main food items, what then is available to the manufacturer to enhance or modify the flavour of his finished product? These may be classified as follows:

L

(a) the basic taste modifiers—salt, sugar, vinegar and wine.
(b) the herbs and spices—either as whole spices, ground spices, spice oils, spice oleoresins, emulsions and essences or as standardized spice products on a salt or other base.
(c) the flavour enhancers—MSG, disodium guanylate or inosinate.
(d) the meat flavours—meat extracts, hydrolysed vegetable protein and yeast extracts.

THE BASIC TASTE MODIFIERS

Salt

Common salt (sodium chloride) is an ingredient of all soup mixes, the amount used being determined by the type of soup and also to some extent upon customer preference, particularly in certain countries and areas and among certain ethnic groups. Unless a fair proportion of salt is present, nearly all starchy and protein foods are uninteresting and even unpalatable. Salt is just noticeable at 0·5 per cent and in most foods is used at about 1 to 1·25 per cent, rarely above this, except in the U.S.A. where there appears to be a decided preference for high salt contents in soup mixes. In the formulation of soup concentrates, due allowance should be made for the salt level in the soup ready for consumption. If dehydrated vegetables are used in the recipe it may be necessary to increase the initial salt level slightly to counter their somewhat insipid taste.

Sugar

Sugar (sucrose) should be used with care; a little used correctly can considerably enhance the natural flavour of many ingredients, particularly that of tomatoes and vegetables which are naturally sweet. If sugar is used in excess it can seriously detract from the rounded flavour of the soup, making it unnatural and slightly sickly. The usage level in any particular formulation is best determined experimentally as this will depend so much upon the raw materials present.

Vinegar

In almost all soups a little vinegar, or diluted acetic acid, is required to add a sharp piquancy to the flavour and the skilful manufacturer uses this ingredient to 'carry' the spices and other flavour notes to the nose. Ordinary malt vinegar is, in most cases, just a little too coarse and obvious, but there are many other types available such as cider vinegar and the several wine vinegars.

The spiced vinegars, such as tarragon vinegar, are also very useful in soup formulations. These may be purchased from one of the many supply houses or the soup manufacturer can quite readily make up his own brews of blended spices and herbs for later addition to soup by simple maceration of the crushed spices, etc., in vinegar over a long period. However, this is not a simple process when it comes to the blending of the herbs and spices and this aspect requires a good knowledge of the relative strengths of the aromatic materials. It is not difficult to use single spices, even if these are very strong such as garlic, but when these are blended together with much milder herbs the flavour of the resulting vinegar will be far from what is expected. As a general rule always use about one quarter the amount of the strong spice to one of the milder spices or herbs, and check the flavour of the product at intervals until the right flavour balance is obtained. During the maceration period the flavours gradually mature and change and conditions must be standardized if continuity of flavouring character and strength is to be obtained.

The simple process is one of direct maceration of the ground or broken material in a closed vessel with the vinegar for a period of several months. The vessel is stirred or otherwise agitated at regular intervals to ensure good mixing. This process is allowed to continue until the vinegar attains maximum flavouring strength. Care should be taken when using such vinegars as their strength can be very variable, due not so much to the conditions of manufacture but to variations in both the vinegar and the spices. A far better way to prepare spiced vinegars is to add one of the specially developed essences which are completely soluble in this medium. By this means one not only saves considerable time but gets a product which is of a consistent flavouring effect.

Along with the simple malt and distilled vinegars go the more complicated vinegar products or sauces such as Worcester Sauce, etc. These are highly seasoned but if used with care they form an invaluable additive as the product of any one manufacturer should have a constant flavour effect in the soup mix. One cannot, of course, use such liquids in the dry soup mixes and in these cases the additional flavour can be obtained by the use of blended seasonings based on standardized products such as the SAROMEX* range of herbs and spices.

Wine

Although not one of the primary taste modifiers, it is convenient to consider wine in this section. There is no doubt that the addition of wine to a soup formulation can work wonders to the flavour and aromatic appeal, producing a smooth rounded effect. The best type of wine to use as well as the quantity is best determined by trial and error, not forgetting that wines do change in character during cooking and what may seem to be a good flavour when added during initial trials may turn out to be quite unpleasant when the soup is autoclaved or processed under bulk factory conditions.

THE HERBS AND SPICES

Nature has provided a very considerable range of flavours in the herbs and spices and by skilful blending there are few flavour effects that cannot be achieved with them. Unfortunately the use of spices is often based on a vague notion of the quantity actually required. Far too often the expression 'seasoning to taste' is meaningless and less than helpful. The 'pinch of this or a teaspoonful of that herb or spice' is frequently translated with equal uncertainty into a manufacturing formulation. It is for this reason that so often food products are either grossly under-seasoned and hence not as good as they could be or else are over-seasoned and the true flavour almost destroyed. It is not uncommonly assumed, of course quite incorrectly, that if a little of a particular seasoning is good then a bit more will be a lot better. This may be the case if the original dosage was too low, but generally the addition of more seasoning can result in the total loss of the main flavour of the delicate primary notes of the meats and vegetables present. A good seasoning should be subtle, not obvious, as its main effect is to enhance those pleasurable flavour characteristics of the principal food items present and only in a very few cases to impose an entirely new

* Registered trade name of Bush Boake Allen Ltd.

flavour effect. When the housewife buys tomato soup she wishes to taste tomatoes, not a strong seasoning of clove or cinnamon, etc.

Herbs and spices are used by food manufacturers either whole, ground, or in the case of herbs, rubbed. In addition there are available the various processed forms such as the essential oils, oleoresins, seasoning emulsions, spice essences, dry soluble spices and spray-dried spice concentrates. There are pros and cons about the use of each of these and the decision which one to use in any particular formulation is somewhat difficult to make. A review of each of these forms will emphasize certain points which must be taken into consideration.

Whole Spices

In soup manufacture there are few occasions in which the whole spices can be incorporated into the product as such. However, it is a very old and long established practice to hang a muslin bag of spices into the stock-pot during its cooking period. In general the flavouring effect achieved by this method is unreliable and whereas this simple procedure may be quite acceptable to the housewife or restaurant chef it is far too uncertain for manufacturing use in which flavour continuity is essential. In addition, this is a most wasteful way to extract the flavour from spices as most of the volatiles are lost in the steam and many of the other flavouring components are not water soluble. In this respect it should be remembered that the household recipe for soups generally has a higher meat and vegetable content than the commercial product and that, in consequence, such soups do not require so much or so careful seasoning as the cheaper product manufactured in bulk. If sufficient spices are added to a commercial soup to give to it the exciting flavour of the kitchen-produced article there is a grave danger of the product tasting like a Christmas pudding. One cannot just scale up a spice formulation, for processing conditions vastly alter the final flavour effects.

Ground Spices

In order to liberate more of their available flavour, spices are ground to varying degrees of fineness as required by the food manufacturer and in this form they blend well into the product mix and impart more flavour than the same weight of whole spice. The natural ground spices have been used in the seasoning of foods for so long that they are now taken for granted. There are, unfortunately, many inherent disadvantages in the use of these flavour adjuncts, not the least important of which is their variability. Many of the difficulties of usage are well appreciated by food technologists but for convenience these may be summarized as follows:

    (a) variability of odour and flavour strength.

    (b) variability of odour and flavour character.

    (c) the presence of undesirable bacteria, and in particular thermophilic bacteria and mould spores.

    (d) the presence of 'filth' in one form or another.

    (e) sophistication with less valuable or useless materials.

    (f) the presence, in many spices, of lipase enzymes or other enzyme systems affecting product stability.

    (g) instability on storage, particularly when ground.

    (h) certain production difficulties, particularly in respect of the appearance of the finished product, waste of flavour due to inefficient extraction of the spice during processing, etc.

Most of these are self-explanatory and require no elaboration, but all should be taken into account when deciding to use ground spices or to adopt one of the processed forms of spices in a seasoning formulation.

Rubbed Herbs

Usually the rubbed herbs are combined into 'bouquets garnis' to season particular dishes. For this purpose it is usual to use the rubbed herb from which the hard woody material has been removed and the leaves broken down to a coarse mass. In certain dishes it is customary to allow the herb particles to remain in the soup, the herbs being eaten with it. It is a more common culinary practice to suspend the broken herbs in a muslin bag as with the spices and this has already been commented upon.

Spice Essential Oils

With certain very important exceptions (i.e., pepper, ginger and capsicum) the herbs and spices depend largely for their flavouring effects upon the essential oil present and its recovery by distillation is long established. The use of such essential oils as flavouring agents certainly overcomes some of the difficulties listed above. They are comparatively constant in flavour strength, though of course their flavour quality will depend upon the source of the spice from which they are obtained. They are free from bacteria, contamination and enzymes. If correctly stored they are, in most cases, reasonably stable. For these reasons there is much to commend the use of the essential oils in spice formulations. However, the essential oils are mere shadows of the full flavour of the spice itself for they lack the many non-volatile flavour components which contribute so much to a roundness of flavour which is obtained when one uses the ground spices.

As was mentioned above, in certain cases such as pepper and ginger, the volatile oil only gives the aroma of the spice, the pungent principles being non-volatile and therefore not present in the oil which is almost bland to the taste. In the case of capsicum there is no essential oil component and the pungency, like pepper and ginger, is non-volatile. In these three cases it is necessary to use the extractives which will contain both the volatile aromatics and the non-volatile pungent constituents.

When using the essential oils it should always be remembered that they are very concentrated and almost invariably must be diluted in some way before being incorporated into a product mix.

Spice Oleoresins

Since the essential oils fall short on several counts, the next alternative to the use of ground spices is the use of oleoresins, which represent, in concentrated form, the flavouring components soluble in the particular solvent used in their preparation. This point is stressed as no one solvent dissolves all the flavouring ingredients present in the ground spice, so that different solvents can produce so-called 'oleoresins' of quite different character. However, such oleoresins do generally approach more nearly the flavour balance of the natural spice and by the nature of their manufacture they are free from many of the disadvantages of ground spices. Like the essential oils, there are certain reservations to their use, particularly in such liquid food products as soups and flavouring materials such as the spiced vinegars. Oleoresins are prepared from the ground herbs and spices by solvent extraction and unless great care is taken with the purity of such solvents it is quite likely that any high boiling fractions may remain in the product and give rise to off-notes in the aroma and flavour when these are used in foodstuffs. Excessive treatment to remove the last traces of solvent, as is required by the very stringent regulations in force in the U.S.A., almost invariably ruins the fine balance of heat-labile flavour components, leaving the final oleoresin lacking in characteristic top-notes. Examples of such products are commonplace, and the addition of essential oil fractions does not remedy this type of damage.

Spice oleoresins are extremely powerful in their flavouring effects, and being in most cases either solid or very viscous liquids which are insoluble in an aqueous medium, they are difficult to incorporate into soup mixes. Incomplete dispersion can lead to insoluble specks which are very unsightly and may, particularly in the case of the pungent spices, be dangerous to the consumer.

Spice Essences and Emulsions

Because of the high concentration of the essential oils and the oleoresins and their limited solubility, most food manufacturers make use of dilutions in one form or another. This overcomes the grave danger of weighing out numerous small quantities of powerful flavours, a small error in which can have a profound effect upon the final product. Such dilutions are achieved by the use of acceptable solvents such as glycerol, propylene glycol and isopropyl alcohol, all of which are harmless in foodstuffs. The liquid essences have enjoyed long popularity and are most suitable for use in soups for canning. Their main disadvantage is the presence of a solvent to which many manufacturers have an objection. They cannot readily be used in dry soup mixes owing to the difficulties of dispersion.

An alternative to the use of solvents such as those mentioned is to present the blended oils and oleoresins as water-dispersible emulsions. These would appear to have a real practical application in liquid soup manufacture but it should be remembered that most of the essential oils are composed of highly reactive chemicals and that hydrolysis, with a consequent change in flavour character, readily occurs in such emulsions during storage. Unfortunately many of the seasoning emulsions available at present make use of low-grade essential oils only, mostly because the oleoresins are more difficult to emulsify and hence more costly to process. Such emulsions are nothing like the best seasonings obtainable.

Another alternative liquid product is prepared from the essential oils and certain of the oleoresins by admixture with such acceptable solubilizing agents as TWEEN-80. These products are water-soluble depending upon the concentration used, but in addition to their lack of stability they impart a very definite flavour to the product depending upon the grade of solubilizer used. Under certain conditions there is also the tendency to produce slightly frothy products.

Dry Soluble Spices

The really satisfactory alternative to the use of ground spices is the range of what are now called 'dry soluble' or 'dispersed' spices. These products, of which SAROMEX spices are typical, are standardized and have been developed to give food technologists an essential control over the raw materials used in their seasoning formulations. One of the greatest advantages of using this type of product is continuity of both flavour strength and quality. Consumers are very conscious of changes in the flavour of a food product, particularly that of soups in which the aromatic character is so prominent, and rapidly lose confidence in a brand that is not consistent. With the standardized spices there is complete control over flavour but in addition to this the dry soluble spices are free from all the other objections listed under ground spices and, in the case of SAROMEX for example, being of equal flavour strength to a good quality ground spice, they can be replaced directly in formulations, and are easily incorporated into both wet and dry soup mixes.

It should be remembered that the flavour of the dry soluble spices is instantly available and being sterile there is no need for further heat treatment or cooking. In fact it is an advantage to add such seasonings after the completion of any such cooking stage. In the case of canned goods, of course, they are incorporated with the main mix. The final processing is carried out after canning and involves no volatile loss.

There are many grades of dry soluble spices available, some making use of the essential oils only instead of complete flavour extractives. Generally the colour of such products indicates whether or not total extractives are present, although in itself the colour of the dry solubles is of less importance than the aroma and flavour.

Spray-dried Spices

Spray-dried products under various trade names have been available for the flavouring of food products for many years and in view of the very aromatic nature of most flavouring raw materials such encapsulated products show many advantages, particularly from the point of view of their stability on storage. The base used in the drying operation is usually one of the natural edible gums (i.e. gum acacia or arabic) or a blend of these, or it may be one of the many starch products designed for this purpose and now readily available.

Spray-dried products are usually fine dried powders having a particle size of approximately 30 microns. As the flavouring materials are encapsulated such products do not usually possess as strong an aroma as the dry soluble spices of freshly ground spices. As the base is expensive when compared with, say, salt which is the most widely used carrier for the dry soluble spices, the spray-dried products are usually offered as concentrates, being up to ten times the flavour strength of the equivalent freshly ground spice. The flavour strength of these products can, however, be misleading as it is not easy to obtain a direct correlation between them and the natural spices which they are designed to replace. The reason for this is that many of them are made from essential oils only and not from the total flavour extractives and hence lack the full flavour character of the spice. In addition, during the spray-drying process microdistillation, usually of the more volatile terpinoid compounds, is unavoidable so that the flavour profile of the resulting pro-

duct lacks some of the lighter aromatic character usually associated with the freshly ground spice. However, this partial removal of the terpenes does contribute to the improved shelf-life of
these products but it means also that the determination of the
volatile oil content does not directly correlate with that of the
ground spice or dry soluble spice. The quoted flavour strength
of such products should, therefore, be checked by sensory means
against a freshly ground sample of the genuine spice so as to
establish the true comparative usage rate in the particular
product being seasoned. On occasions the concentrations
quoted on the label do not work out correctly after processing
and, in certain instances, the product may be of even greater
strength than the equivalent ground spice or dry soluble spice
product. Once the equivalent usage rate has been established,
then there are no further problems and these encapsulated
materials can be used with great advantage, particularly in
dry soup mixes.

These then are the considerations that must decide what type
of spice to use in seasonings. For most commercial purposes
there is little doubt that the standardized forms, and in particular the dry soluble spices dispersed on a salt, dextrose or
cereal base, offer the greatest advantages. If the factory is large
and can afford the space and labour to handle whole spices
directly and an expert to evaluate them, grind them as required
and blend them into formulations, then obviously this gives the
processor the control he wants, always assuming that he can get
the spices he wants at the time he wants them. Even in the case
of the smaller manufacturer there are certain techniques which
may be employed by which he can make standardized products
from the whole spices rather than using the ground ones, but,
again, time, facilities and available knowledge must be taken
into account in comparative costings. For the majority of soup
manufacturers the choice is fairly obvious—stick to the stan-
dardised spices which will give you continuity of product,
involve the minimum of control in the factory and are not
subject to the vagaries of the spice market.

If one is using any of the dry soluble spices it should be
remembered that these are on a soluble base such as salt or
dextrose or an insoluble base such as rusk or starch. Such bases

must be taken into consideration when formulations are being evolved, otherwise it will be found that the salt content of the finished soup, if salt-based spices are being used, may be too high, or, again, if starch-based products are included, the final soup may be too thick.

Spice Blends

In modern manufacturing techniques, the addition of accurately weighed small quantities of numerous herbs and spices to a soup mix is just out of the question. Such an operation is too time consuming, uneconomic and open to serious errors. To overcome this, most manufacturers resort to the use of stock blends which are made in bulk from time to time either by the manufacturer himself or by one of the spice houses who specialise in this work. Such blended seasonings can be incorporated into the rest of the soup mix at an appropriate stage and involve one simple weighing and checking process. One word of warning. As each soup produced is likely to have its own seasoning, designed especially for that particular product, there is always the danger of adding the wrong seasoning, so that a fool-proof system of labelling and checking must be used to obviate this.

One of the disadvantages of using the ground spices is that they lose aroma and hence flavouring power on storage. Since spices do not all degrade at the same rate there is a good chance in a blended seasoning that the balance of flavour will alter significantly on storage. Storage conditions are of considerable importance and stocks of all seasonings should be kept to reasonable levels and turned over regularly.

In the above, emphasis has been laid upon the dry soluble spices such as SAROMEX, but similar considerations apply to the many essences and emulsion seasonings offered by the leading houses in these products. Although working within a very broad framework, no two essence compounders will produce exactly the same seasoning for any particular soup and details of the range available should be obtained directly from the literature of the supplier concerned. In most cases careful instructions about usage rates are quoted and these should be followed if the correct flavour effect is to be obtained.

The proof of the pudding is in the eating and the manufacturer should establish for himself the correct usage level, taking the supplier's information as a starting guide only. This is a very necessary precaution as the final flavour will be largely determined by the other raw materials used in the formulation. Again, overstocking is not recommended, it being far better to order in regular amounts which will give a reasonable usage and turn-over period.

HERBS AND SPICES—THEIR SOURCES AND CHARACTERISTICS

Herbs

Although there are a large number of herbs listed and described in the many popular books on the subject, only about eight of these are widely used in the seasoning of soups. Some are related botanically or by the nature of their principal aromatic constituents and care should be taken when formulating these into a seasoning that the effects do not add together or cancel out so as to give an unbalanced flavour effect.

The herbs fall into four main flavour groups:

(a) sweet and anise-like   BASIL and TARRAGON
(b) thymol   MARJORAM, SAVORY, THYME and ORIGANUM
(c) thujone   DALMATIAN SAGE
(d) cineole (eucalyptol)   ROSEMARY, SWEET BAY and SPANISH SAGE

For convenience, the herbs will now be described in alphabetical order.

Sweet Basil

The dried leaves and flowering tops of a strongly aromatic annual of the mint family (*Ocimum basilicum* L.). This herb grows in most temperate climates and has a peppery undertone to a most pleasing sweet and warm flavour with a suggestion of clove overlaid with aniseed. It is difficult to describe this very characteristic flavour. Basil is particularly good in soups based on beef or tomatoes. As it is a powerful flavour its usage level should not exceed 0·03 per cent in the soup ready for tasting, but half this amount will probably be quite sufficient to give a herby background flavour.

Bay Leaves—Sweet Bay Laurel

The true bay or bay-laurel (*Laurus nobilis* L.) is a large evergreen shrub which grows throughout the Mediterranean countries. The dark green shiny leaves are very pleasantly aromatic and give a delicious flavour to tomato, onion, and vegetable soups and also to meat stocks. The flavour is strong and if over-used is somewhat bitter. In the finished soup the usage suggested is between 0·01 and 0·05 per cent, although much less than these quantities will give the necessary 'lift' to the flavour without being too obvious.

West Indian bay is often sold as 'bay oil'; this is derived from a quite different tree (*Pimenta acris* L.) and has a bitter flavour very reminiscent of clove, as one of its principal constituents is eugenol.

Marjoram

Sweet marjoram is the dried leaves and flowering tops of the cultivated variety of *Majorana hortensis* M., but there are many sources of so called marjoram, the bulk of which is derived from wild marjoram (*Origanum majorana* L.) which grows extensively throughout southern Europe and northern Africa. In some countries the name 'marjoram' also includes the wild plants of *Origanum vulgare* L., or indeed yet another species called *Thymus mastichina*. There is much confusion over the correct designation of this herb and in consequence great care should be exercised in its assessment. The odour and flavour of cultivated marjoram is quite distinctly aromatic, spicy, warm and somewhat bitter. It in no way compares with the other forms of so-called 'marjoram', all of which are predominantly cineolic with an overtone of thymol.

Sweet marjoram is a very useful herb in seasonings as it blends so well with the other herbs and spices without overpowering them. It is particularly good in the seasoning of chicken, oxtail, turtle and onion soups. The usage rate is usually between 0·01 per cent and 0·03 per cent in the finished soup.

Origanum and Oregano

Considerable confusion exists over the nomenclature of these two herbs and as they are so different in aroma and flavour character it is necessary to define the correct terms so that when purchasing one can be sure of getting what is wanted.

Origanum is the Italian or Spanish name for wild marjoram (*Origanum vulgare* L.) although the origanum oil of commerce is more often derived from a species of wild thyme (*Thymus capitatus*). Origanum oils are characterized by containing approximately 70 per cent of phenols, most of which is carvacrol. It is this which gives to the herb its harsh tar-like woody flavour.

Oregano is derived from Mexican Sage herb (*Origanum majorana*) and is much more like marjoram in aroma and flavour, although much stronger than sweet marjoram.

Both of these herbs are pleasantly aromatic on dilution but those containing carvacrol can be overpoweringly strong in blended seasonings and should be used with care. They go well in formulations based on tomatoes and in vegetable soups.

Parsley

Although not primarily considered as a flavouring herb, parsley herb (*Petroselinum sativum* H.) is probably one of the most widely used of the culinary herbs. Both the bright green fresh leaves and the duller dried leaves, finely chopped, are an essential garnish to many dishes and are a traditional ingredient in chicken noodle soups. Parsley can contribute a definite fresh herb note to soups and is of particular value in those having an inherent delicate flavour such as chicken or fish.

Parsley essences and dry soluble parsley are available for use as flavouring agents and in purchasing these one must ensure that the product has been made with parsley herb oil and not parsley seed oil. This latter completely lacks the fine fresh notes of the herb and even on dilution is no replacement for the herb.

Rosemary

This is the dried leaves of an evergreen shrub (*Rosmarinus officinalis* L.) which grows profusely in the sunny climate of southern Europe and in particular in Spain. Rosemary is most widely used in 'bouquets garnis', combined with basil and marjoram, in the seasoning of soup stocks. In flavour character it is akin to sweet bay laurel and, like it, is a good seasoning for use in chicken and turtle soups. The usage rate should be restricted to about 0·01 per cent to 0·05 per cent in the finished soup otherwise the very light top-notes can readily be distinguished and this detracts from the overall flavour effect.

Sage

Sage herb is the dried leaves of *Salvia officinalis* L., a member of the mint family. Like most of the other herbs that are native to the Mediterranean region, it is now cultivated throughout the temperate countries and in consequence there are some 500 varieties. It is not surprising, therefore, to find very wide variation in flavouring power and character between sage grown in the different countries. There are three prime sources, each having a quite distinct flavour quality. These are:

(a) Dalmatian Sage—derived from Jugoslavia, the leaves of which are strongly aromatic and have a quite distinctive note due to the presence of a ketone called thujone. Dalmatian sage is the most important variety from a commercial point of view and is widely used in seasonings of products based on meat. Care is necessary in its usage otherwise it has a tendency to swamp other flavours present and if used excessively it leaves an unpleasant bitter after-note.

(b) English Sage—derived from cultivated plants, the leaves of which have a more delicate aromatic character than those of Dalmatian sage. English sage is preferred in spice blends as it is more subtle and does not give to the finished soup an unpleasant herby note suggesting that the manufacturer has something to hide.

(c) Spanish Sage—derived from the leaves of the wild growing *Salvia lavandulaefolia*. This herb is usually distilled in Spain and it is the essential oil that is offered to food manufacturers. This oil has a very pronounced eucalyptol-camphoraceous note which is very reminiscent of rosemary. It is not really like sage at all and cannot truly replace sage herb in a formulation.

Most cream soups are improved by the judicious use of sage in the seasoning—not sufficient to be noticeable as such but rather to give a fuller and more rounded background to the overall flavour and aroma.

Summer Savory

This is another herb (*Satureia hortensis* L.) of the mint family, cultivated in southern France. The aroma and flavour is closely reminiscent of both sage and thyme and is a very pleasing herb for use in the seasoning of vegetable soups and stocks. The flavour has a certain fresh sharpness but if overdone is rather bitter so that care is necessary in its usage which should be limited to about 0·01 per cent in the finished soup. In bean soups and fish chowder, the addition of a little savory in place of the more usual parsley herb gives a most interesting and acceptable flavour to the product.

Tarragon

The dried tops of the perennial herb *Artemisia dracunculus* L. grown mainly in the south of France. This herb has a strong and quite characteristic odour and has been used for a very long time in the making of traditional tarragon vinegar. Tarragon is used in the seasoning of chicken consommé, fish chowder, mushroom, tomato and turtle soups, to which it adds a fresh piquancy.

Thyme

The last of the herbs to be considered is derived from *Thymus vulgaris* L. and is amongst the most widely used of the culinary herbs and spices. Herb lovers grow many varieties of thyme, but the principal source of the commercial crop is Spain where it grows wild over the lower mountain slopes. True thyme is characterized by its essential oil which contains up to 60 per cent of phenols, most of which is thymol. The strong, pungent flavour of thyme can be most useful in a blended seasoning when used with restraint. Its warm, slightly phenolic character, coupled with a sharp and lasting mouthfeel, makes it an excellent seasoning in meat stocks and vegetable soups. A suggested usage level would be about 0·05 per cent in the finished soup, but this will be determined by the strength and flavour of the other raw materials present.

M

Spices

Like the herbs, the spices are best considered according to their primary flavour effects which may be classified as follows:

(a) the pungent spices   CAPSICUM (CAYENNE), GINGER, PEPPER and MUSTARD.

(b) the aromatic fruits   ALLSPICE or PIMENTO, NUTMEG and MACE, CARDAMOM and FENUGREEK.

(c) the umbelliferous fruits   ANISEED, CARAWAY, CELERY, CORIANDER, CUMMIN, DILL, FENNEL and PARSLEY.

(d) other aromatic spices   CINNAMON, CASSIA and CLOVE.

(e) the coloured spices   PAPRIKA, TURMERIC and SAFFRON.

Each of these classes shows a broad flavour relationship although the individual spices within each group will have quite distinct and characteristic aroma and flavour qualities. Again, for convenience, these spices will now be described in alphabetical order.

Aniseed

The dried ripe fruits of *Pimpinella anisum* L., a small annual plant that grows in all temperate countries, although the main commercial crops are produced in Spain, southern France and Jamaica. On the Continent the fresh herb is used for the flavouring of vegetable soups, the seeds having only a limited use owing to their rather 'pharmaceutical' flavour. Aniseed oil is also obtained from a quite unrelated plant *Illicium verum* Hook, which is cultivated in China and is known commercially as China Star Aniseed.

Capsicum

Capsicum, Cayenne Pepper and Chillies are all names given to the fruits of various capsicum species and varieties. Considerable confusion arises over what is meant by 'cayenne pepper', which is an item in many soup formulations. The capsicum family is widely distributed and exists in innumerable sizes, shapes, colours and pungencies. The most pungent species are the small fruited varieties of *Capsicum minimum* and *C.*

frutescens, the fruits of which are the small dirty-looking chillies
from Mombasa. The least pungent are the large fleshy pimien-
toes or red and green peppers which are extensively used as a
vegetable. In between these there is a whole spectrum of
varieties many of which are offered in the spice trade as
'cayenne pepper'. The larger and less pungent types of capsicum are derived from *C. annuum* and are often known as Chilli
pepper; this should not be confused with a product called
Chilli powder which is a blend of spices consisting of a mild
variety of capsicum ground together with cummin seeds,
oregano and garlic. This form of pungent seasoning is used
throughout the U.S.A. and Central America in the formulation
of specialist meat products.

The pungency of capsicum is determined by its capsaicin
content and whereas Mombasa chillies may contain upwards of
0·5 per cent most commercial samples of cayenne pepper
contain less than a half of this amount. Great care should be
exercised when including cayenne in formulations as the
pungent effect is cumulative and if overdone the product will
become progressively unpleasant to take, leaving a painful
burning-sensation in the throat long after the soup is finished.

Caraway

The dried fruits of *Carum carvi* L., commercial crops of which
are grown in northern Eruope. The aroma and flavour of
caraway is pleasantly warm and characteristic. It is not widely
used as a soup seasoning but is favoured in Continental recipes
and in particular in cabbage soup.

Cardamom

Dried cardamom fruits obtained from the perennial herb
Elletaria cardamomum M., and imported from India, are the
usual article in the spice trade, but it is the mass of dark brown
seeds enclosed in the tough husk which contain all the aromatic
character of the spice. The aroma and flavour of these is
warmly spicy with a cineolic-camphoraceous note and, if used
in excess, a very slight pungency. Cardamom can readily give
to a seasoning an unbalanced aroma which is often described
as 'perfumed', but if used carefully it contributes a suggestion of
curry and is of particular use in the seasoning of meat-based

soups. This flavour also enhances the fresh notes of pea soup, but in this its usage should be limited to not more than 0·02 per cent, otherwise it becomes too obvious.

Celery

The dried ripe fruits of *Apium graveolens* L., cultivated throughout northern Europe and the northern states of India. The aroma and flavour of celery seed is very much more powerful than that associated with the culinary celery sticks but if used with care it adds considerable character to soups containing meat. The usage rate should be limited to about 0·05 to 0·1 per cent in the finished soup otherwise the aroma may override that of the main food constituents present. The flavour of celery goes well with that of onion and leek to which it adds an attractive 'green' note. It also adds a certain fullness of flavour to a vegetable soup, particularly if this has been formulated with dried vegetable pieces.

Cinnamon and Cassia

These two spices are dealt with together as they are closely related and in the spice trade cassia is frequently sold under the general name of cinnamon, qualified by its source (e.g., Saigon Cinnamon). True cassia is the bark of *Cinnamomum cassia* L., a large tree which grows wild in south-east China. This is a coarser and much cheaper spice than genuine cinnamon with which it is often confused. True cinnamon is the thin inner bark of *C. zeylanicum* L., obtained from cultivated coppiced trees growing in Ceylon.

The aroma and flavour of cassia is similar in general character to that of cinnamon but is much coarser and more evident in blended seasonings. With this limitation, the flavour of both is sweet and tenacious and if used with discretion enhances the flavour of soups based on tomatoes and adds zest to any soup containing bacon or ham.

Cinnamon products, because of their cost and certain restrictions on availability, especially in the U.S.A., are open to considerable sophistication. Unfortunately, cinnamon leaf oil is often offered under the simple description of 'cinnamon oil', from which it is entirely different in aromatic character and flavour. The prime constituent of genuine cinnamon bark oil is

cinnamic aldehyde whereas cinnamon leaf oil has a high
phenol content and is more reminiscent of clove than of
cinnamon.

Clove

Cloves are the dried unopened flower buds of a large evergreen tree *Eugenia caryophyllata* L. (also called *Caryophyllus
aromaticus* by some authorities). The flavour is very strong,
pungent and aromatic and because it is so powerful it readily
swamps other aromas and flavours in a seasoning. The usage
level is usually in the order of 0·01 per cent but even this may
be a little prominent if the other ingredients are mildly flavoured.

Again, the flavour and character of clove bud oil is far
superior to that of clove leaf or clove stem oils, both of which are
much cheaper and are offered commercially in seasoning
blends. These latter oils have a marked 'inky' taste which
detracts from the overall flavour effect.

Coriander

The dried ripe fruits of *Coriandrum sativum* L., the main
commercial source of which is Russia and the eastern European
countries, although considerable crops are raised in Morocco.
The Russian variety has the finest flavour. The aroma and
flavour is mild but distinctive and blends well with clove, sage,
nutmeg and mace for the seasoning of meat-based soups. A
little ground coriander sprinkled on the surface of green pea
soup adds a most attractive flavour note. Coriander is usually
used at 0·02 to 0·05 per cent in soups, depending upon the base
materials used in the formulation.

Cummin

The dried ripe fruits of *Cuminum cyminum* L., a small herb
which grows in Cyprus, Morocco and Spain. The aroma and
flavour is very strong, faintly pungent and quite characteristic.
It is usually associated with the flavour of curry, in which it is
one of the more important ingredients; it thus finds its use in
the flavouring of mulligatawny soup. In other seasonings it
should be used warily and limited to about 0·005 per cent in the
initial development trials.

Dill

The dried fruits of *Anethum graveolens* L. are of limited use in the seasoning of soups as the flavour is too characteristically 'pharmaceutical'. A very little may be used in the seasoning of tomato and bean soups and on the Continent the fresh herb is used in the flavouring of cabbage and turnip soups.

Fennel

The dried fruits of a perennial herb *Foeniculum vulgare,* Miller, which may be obtained either from wild or cultivated plants. There are two main types of fennel—bitter fennel and sweet fennel. Care should be taken in purchasing this spice to ensure that one gets the correct variety. Fennel has an agreeable, aromatic flavour reminiscent of both liquorice and aniseed which blends well with fish, cheese and vegetable-based soups.

Fenugreek

The dried seeds of the leguminous plant *Trigonella foenaum-graecum* L., which grows in Egypt, Greece, India and Morocco. The odour of fenugreek is characteristic and is both strong and persistent. Only minute quantities are usually required in a seasoning to which it imparts a fullness not achieved with any other spice. Its usage should be limited to about 0·01 per cent in the finished soup otherwise it becomes unpleasantly obvious and sickly.

Ginger

Ginger is a widely used spice obtained from the dried rhizomes of *Zingiber officinale,* Roscoe. Like pepper, the total flavour is a combination of the aromatic constituents of the essential oil and the non-volatile pungent principles which are generally known as gingerine. The oil is found principally in the outer layers of the rhizome and as this is peeled off in the case of Jamaican ginger this variety lacks the harsh notes imparted by the essential oil but still retains the lighter terpenoid fractions which characterize the oil from the deeper tissues. As a result, Jamaican ginger has a subtle and more delicate flavour than is found in any of the other varieties.

African ginger, most of which is cultivated in Sierra Leone, and Nigerian ginger are both unpeeled or at the most only lightly peeled on the flat surfaces of the 'hands'. These gingers have a relatively high essential oil content and their aroma is coarse and very strong. Because of this, care must be exercised in their use in seasonings otherwise the ginger note will predominate. Ginger should not be recognizable as such. Ginger from Cochin in India is also used in seasonings, but the flavour is quite different and is characterized by a marked lemony note.

In seasonings, too much ginger tends to flatten the overall features of the blended flavour making it dull and lifeless. Being a pungent spice an excess of ginger leaves an unpleasant after-flavour and a very lingering feeling of warmth in the throat. It is usually included with the other hot spices such as pepper and cayenne. It should be remembered that all these tend to build up as the product is being eaten, and one should not judge the pungency on one mouthful alone. In most seasonings its use should be restricted to the order of 0·05 per cent in the finished soup mix, although 0·01 per cent will probably be quite adequate for the effect required. The final usage level will depend upon the other spices present.

Mace

This spice is directly related to nutmeg and is the dried arilus which surrounds the nutmeg shell. When fresh this is scarlet but on sun-drying the colour changes to a yellowish brown and the texture becomes horn-like and brittle. The better the quality of the mace the paler its colour. The aroma and flavour of mace are very similar to that of nutmeg, as one would expect, but it imparts a certain amount of bitter after-flavour when used in excess. Again, the cheaper grades are more bitter than the pale coloured selected grades. The usage rate suggested in seasonings for soups would be in the order of 0·01 to 0·05 per cent in the finished product.

Mustard

The yellow powdered mustard of commerce is obtained from the seeds of either *Sinapis alba* L. or *Brassica juncea* L., the annual plants known as white and black mustard respectively. Most commercial mustard powders are a blend of both so as to make best use of the strong coarse notes of black mustard and the more delicate flavour of the white. The flavour is sharp, hot and very pungent and is formed by enzyme activity in the presence of water. Mustard is of more use as a table condiment than as an ingredient in seasonings.

Nutmeg

Nutmegs are the seeds of a large tropical evergreen tree (*Myristica fragrans* Houtt.) which grows throughout the East and West Indies. Nutmeg is a very powerful flavouring agent so that too much in a seasoning can quite easily upset the flavour balance. If used correctly nutmeg imparts a full creaminess to the overall flavour effect, giving an impression of warm spiciness. Nutmeg may be used up to about 0·05 per cent in the finished soup but this must be reduced if mace is also used so that the combined amount present is only of this order.

Paprika

One of the most colourful of the spices is paprika, the dried ground stemless pods of specially mild varieties of capsicum (*C. annuum* L.). It is produced mainly in Hungary and Spain. The flavour, though mild, is distinctive and in certain varieties (e.g., Rosen Paprika) there may be a little pungency, although this is usually very small. The flavour of paprika, in moderation, is good, particularly in cream soups, but if overdone the effect is to 'lay a dead hand' over the total flavour of the product resulting in a slightly musty and distinctly unpleasing taste. Paprika is most often used for its colouring effects and a small quantity incorporated into the mix gives a richness to the colour of cream soups. Continuity of colour effect is best achieved by the use of one of the standardized oleoresins of paprika that are available. These are incorporated into any of the fats present in the soup mix. Again, if too much is used the product will have an unnatural colour and the flavour of the paprika will mask any other delicate flavours present.

Pepper

Black pepper and white pepper are derived from the fruits of

the vine *Piper nigrum* L. As there is some confusion about the
origin of these two extremely important spices the following
definitions may not be amiss:

Black pepper—the berries are picked while they are still green
and before they are fully ripe. The whole berries are sun-dried
and cleaned.

White pepper—the berries are left on the vines until they are
almost ripe and changing their colour through yellow to red.
The berries are then water-soaked and the loose outer skin is
removed by rubbing. The white inner kernel is sun-dried.

Decorticated pepper—a white pepper produced from whole
black pepper by mechanically removing the brown outer hulls.

Pepper has a twofold use in seasonings, imparting a mild
aromatic and characteristic flavour and also a distinctive 'bite',
different from that given by capsicum. It is the essential oil
content of the peppercorns that contributes the aroma, and the
non-volatile constituents, mostly piperine, which are the source
of the pungency. The unique value of pepper lies in the combined effects of these two qualities and it is the balance between
them that is of prime importance. It is this differing balance
between aroma and pungency that distinguishes peppers from
different sources—Indian peppers (Malabar, Tellicherry and
Alleppy) are very aromatic, whereas those from Malaysia and
the East Indies (Indonesia, Lampong, Sarawak and Singapore)
are less aromatic but much more pungent. Brazilian pepper,
most of which is imported into the U.S.A., is not unlike that
from Singapore and finds wide favour in seasonings in the
U.S.A.

It is the pungency of pepper which has made this spice world
famous and its use in seasonings takes more account of this than
of the aromatic character, most of which is overlaid by the
other spices present in the blend. Black pepper has rather more
flavour and aroma than white but both are very pungent. Care
should be taken in using pepper as this pungency tends to be
cumulative and many people object to the residual warmth in
the mouth after taking a 'hot' soup.

The main objections to the use of ground black pepper in
soups is that the black specks detract from its appearance,
particularly in a cream soup where they show up so much more
clearly. In addition to this, ground pepper is notoriously bad

from a bacteriological point of view and is one of the 'dirtiest' of the spices. Both of these objections can be overcome by the use of a standardized pepper product dispersed on a salt or rusk base.

Pimento (Allspice)

Pimento, or as it is more generally called in the U.S.A., allspice, is the dried unripe berry of the tree *Pimenta dioica,* and is an excellent blending spice as it contributes an aroma which is at once reminiscent of clove, nutmeg and cinnamon (hence its name). The flavour of pimento is freshly warm and slightly peppery and in view of its phenolic content is reminiscent of clove. It is not over-powerful so that its usage rate can be adjusted within fairly wide limits.

A word of warning may not come amiss here. Other parts of the pimento tree also yield an essential oil when distilled and pimento leaf oil is readily available. This oil lacks the fullness and fresh character of the berry oil and has a much weaker flavouring effect. It also tends to impart a certain sourness to seasonings in which it is used.

Saffron

This expensive spice is the dried stigmas of the purple-flowered crocus (*Crocus sativus* L.). Each blossom yields three thread-like orange yellow stigmas which must be collected by hand. It takes some 250,000 of these to make just one pound of saffron spice. The flavour of saffron is rich but somewhat bitter so that a very little goes a long way. Saffron is more used for the water-soluble colouring matter it contains and is not often included in soup seasonings. Mexican Saffron is often used in place of true saffron. This is prepared from the stigmas of Safflower (*Carthamus tinctorius*) which is quite unrelated to saffron.

Turmeric

Like saffron, turmeric is primarily used for its yellow colour but it does also have a well defined aroma and flavour. Turmeric is the dried rhizomes of *Curcuma longa* L., a member of the ginger family which is cultivated throughout India and the East Indies. The aroma of turmeric is powerful and persistent and is that associated with curry powder. The flavour effect is warmly aromatic with a rather bitter back-note.

Turmeric is mostly used for the colouring of such soups as chicken noodle and mulligatawny; again a little goes a long way.

SPICE QUALITY CONTROL

The ground spices and rubbed herbs are notoriously bad from a hygienic point of view and the examination of samples for purchase as raw materials for seasonings should really include a microscopic examination for filth as described in the A.O.A.C. In addition spices should be assayed for moisture content, total ash, water-soluble ash, acid-insoluble ash and ether-soluble extractives (both total and non-volatile). Most important of all the tests required is that for the essential oil content. This is normally carried out by the method described in the British Pharmacopoeia 1968, the separated oil also being available for examination by G.L.C. and T.L.C. techniques.

Obviously all this testing takes time and at present is a very costly item, so much so that very little testing is actually carried out and much is left to the experience and judgement of the purchaser—not a truly satisfactory state of affairs for large-scale food production in which almost everything else is controlled to within clearly defined limits. What really matters in quality control of spices? There are three prime considerations:

1. Does the spice look right? In the case of powdered spices this is almost impossible to judge.

2. Does the spice smell right? This depends upon having a genuine sample freshly ground with which to compare it.

3. Does the spice taste right? This can only be evaluated properly under normal usage conditions and this is, in most cases, impracticable for routine control.

All other tests, as listed above, are really secondary to these considerations. To ensure satisfactory continuity, and this is essential in modern food manufacturing methods, it is far better to rely upon the integrity of the well-established supply houses whose reputation has been built on quality and who are fully equipped and experienced to carry out detailed quality control on these very variable commodities. Better still, the use of one of the standardized forms of spicing should be seriously considered, even if this involves some changes in present manufacturing procedures.

Curry Powder

Curry powder is a well recognized commercial term and one which often appears in the list of ingredients in a soup formulation. Yet there are as many curry powders as there are compounders of these useful spice blends. Curry was originally an essentially Indian flavour based on the grinding together of such locally produced spices as cardamoms, cummin seeds, pepper, turmeric, etc., all of which were readily available. Curries have now become universally popular and in India it is recognized that different food products require quite different blends of curry powder to achieve the best effect—hence the wide variety available. The term 'curry powder' in a formulation is, therefore, rather meaningless.

Curry is used as an ingredient of mulligatawny soup and it must be emphasized that the final flavour of this will depend almost entirely upon the type of curry powder used. On the other hand, curry may be added to such soups as oxtail and meat, in which case it is used in very small amounts to give only a hint of the full curry flavour relying upon the spices to enhance the character of the meat constituents. In such soups the flavour effect of the curry type is nothing like so marked but even so the blend, once established, should not be changed. Curry powders differ widely in pungency, making full use of pepper, ginger and capsicum. As everyone does not necessarily like this type of product a compromise must be reached in establishing the level of pungency so as to obtain a maximum sales appeal.

The pungency of any curry powder is likely to be as variable as that of the spices used in its manufacture. This can, however, be overcome by standardization using such products as SAROMEX Cayenne or SAROMEX Pepper, both of which are of constant pungency effect. Unfortunately curry powder is essentially a cheap flavour, but even so one should insist on purchasing one which is made with the highest grade of powdered spices so as to get the minimum of flavour variation.

Curry flavour can, of course, be produced in dry soluble

form on, say, a farinaceous base, in nut oil or hardened nut oil or again as a soluble essence. Such blends are primarily intended for special application in the making of sauces and are not really the right source of curry flavour for soups.

Curry tends to develop a musty flavour on long-term storage but if the time is reasonably short and a good fresh curry powder mix is used then the soup will tend to improve in flavour as the numerous aromatic constituents blend more intimately with each other.

Stock Seasonings

Mention has already been made of the advantages of using seasonings prepared to a stock formulation. Throughout this book you will find recommendations for the spicing of all types of soups and it is a simple matter to abstract this information and blend together the appropriate spices into a seasoning for use in several batches. This, however, should be restricted as most ground spices rapidly lose strength on keeping and the process of blending tends to accelerate this. Any such blended seasonings should, of course, be kept in airtight containers and stored in a cool dry place until required on the factory floor.

Similar stock formulations in the dry soluble spices and any of the liquid seasonings offered can be used in a similar way. In all cases it is better to hold minimum stocks and ensure a fairly rapid turn-over so as to minimize the effects of deterioration.

Spice formulations can be, and usually are, developed from the individual spice and herb components by trial and error to suit a particular product or market. This is a tedius process and it is often far better to seek the advice of spice experts in the early stages of product development. The larger supply houses offer a technical service and discussions with their technical staff cannot fail to be of considerable assistance and a saving of valuable time in arriving at a satisfactory formulation. The spice blends in the various formulations should, therefore, be taken more as a guide than as a final answer.

THE FLAVOUR ENHANCERS

Apart from the herbs and spices there are several other

acceptable and widely used food additives which have a considerable effect upon flavour and must be considered when formulating a soup base. Some of these impart a definite flavour of their own—such as the hydrolysed proteins, etc., but others have little intrinsic flavour but are capable of bringing out any latent flavours already present in the other ingredients in the soup mix. Of these the most important, and the most extensively used, is monosodium glutamate (M.S.G.). More recently the Japanese have produced the 5′-nucleotides as flavour modifiers and as synergists for M.S.G. Each of these materials is worthy of careful consideration.

Monosodium Glutamate (M.S.G.)

Chemically M.S.G. is the sodium salt of the naturally occurring L-form of glutamic acid which was formerly produced by the acid or enzymic hydrolysis of vegetable proteins such as wheat gluten, sugar beet wastes or soya bean protein, but is now manufactured in large tonnages by a process of fermentation. It is a white powder or fine needle-like crystals which are very soluble in water. Over the past few years M.S.G. has become very popular not only in manufacturing practice but in kitchen usage. It is a comparatively cheap food additive which needs to be used in only small concentrations and the optimum for most products is between 0·1 and 0·5 per cent, although as little as 0·05 per cent will enhance existing flavours particularly in the presence of salt. Because of this effect, M.S.G. is a most useful ingredient and in many purified grades now available it adds neither flavour nor aroma of its own when used in foods. Some of the less pure grades may have a slight meaty note and some people are particularly sensitive to the slight metallic after-taste that it leaves when used in excess.

The main effects of using M.S.G. are:

(a) it intensifies and enhances the natural flavour of foods, particularly in the presence of a little salt.

(b) it prevents the loss of flavour, particularly in canned goods.

(c) it produces a sense of satisfaction in the mouth that persists for quite a long time after the meal is finished.

(d) it increases the acceptability of foods which would otherwise be monotonous or uninteresting.

(e) it can, in certain circumstances, subdue undesirable flavour effects. It is particularly effective in reducing the sharp unpleasant notes of onions, the earthiness of potatoes, the bitterness which can so easily develop in cooked vegetables and the slightly metallic taste which is sometimes formed in canned goods containing spinach and tomatoes.

(f) it tends to produce a more uniform blend of flavour giving the product a richer fullness than is achieved without it.

It is small wonder that M.S.G. can be included with great advantage in almost all formulations—but do not overdo it as the effect is not proportionately increased.

The Flavour Nucleotides—Disodium Inosinate and Disodium Guanylate

Recent research in Japan has led to the introduction of the 5′-nucleotides as food flavour enhancers. Of these disodium inosinate has experienced the greatest commercial development initially as a by-product of the Japanese fishery industry but is now processed from yeast nucleic acid. A second compound, disodium guanylate, either by itself or in admixture with the inosinate, is also gaining in popularity.

Like M.S.G., these compounds have little taste *per se*, being only very slightly salty with a faint sour back-note. Their prime effect is upon the mouthfeel of the product. They give to it a mouthfilling sensation resulting in a feeling of complete satisfaction of having eaten the product. Like M.S.G., this feeling is persistent long after the food is eaten. The effect of using the nucleotides will depend upon the type of food in which they are to be used and the comments just made must not be taken to mean that the addition of inosinate or guanylate will convert a poor tasting product into a superb one. What they do achieve is to make a good product into a better one. In liquid products, such as soups, it results in a fuller flavour and an impression of increased viscosity in the mouth. The suggested maximum and optimum usage range is 0·015 to 0·02 per cent, but even as little as 0·01 per cent is sufficient to bring about significant flavour improvements. In some products the nucleotides tend to increase the saltiness but it is reported that this is not predictable and can only be ascertained in flavour trials during product development.

THE MEAT FLAVOURS

The flavour of meat is of great importance in many soup formulations. Normally this is obtained directly from the meat used during the processing and the preparation of meat and bone stock is essential in the making of quality soups. In some cases, however, particularly where the product will not stand the high costs of meat or natural meat extracts, it is necessary to supplement this by the addition of flavouring materials such as the hydrolysed proteins or yeast extracts. These may be used in two ways, either to add their specific flavour to the product or in much smaller amounts as flavour modifiers or enhancers. In certain soups nothing effectively replaces meat and any attempt to cheapen the product at the expense of this ingredient cannot fail to produce an inferior flavoured article.

The Protein Hydrolysates

Numerous commercial grades of vegetable protein hydrolysates are now available, the standards for which are best obtained from the manufacturers concerned. In selecting the grade of hydrolysate most suitable to any particular product it is necessary to decide whether one wants a dark, meaty product with a high degree of inherent flavour or whether a light and somewhat bland material which will act more as a flavour enhancer is more suited. Again one has to decide whether it is more convenient to use the hydrolysate in paste, powder or liquid form. Each has its advantages for certain products and as these are described in the manufacturer's literature reference should be made to this for more detailed information about usage and applications.

If any of the powdered hydrolysates are incorporated into soup seasonings it should be remembered that they are very hygroscopic and that about 1 per cent of tricalcium phosphate might well be added to prevent lumping during storage. All such blends should, of course, be kept in tightly closed containers which should only be open for the time taken in weighing out the required quantity.

Most hydrolysates are offered for particular food products and, as with the herbs and spices, it is usually better to seek technical advice during product development. In all cases

M.S.G. and salt occur in the final product; the levels of these should be ascertained for the grade selected and this must be taken into account when determining the total amounts present in the formulation.

Yeast Products

In the production of soups, yeast extracts are invaluable as flavour emphasizers either by themselves or in conjunction with M.S.G. Numerous grades of these are available for this purpose and the manufacturers' literature should be consulted for details of usage. Clear soups, consommés and light broths can be much improved by the addition of 2 to 3 per cent of yeast extract to the basic stock. In the case of cream soups a more satisfactory flavour effect is given by the addition of about 5 per cent of the dried powdered yeast extract to the other dry ingredients.

As with the other speciality flavouring materials, the manu-facturers are in the best position to give technical advice on formulation and this often saves considerable time during product development.

Beef Extract Substitute

Another product recently introduced by a Japanese company is claimed as a complete replacement for natural beef extract, although in conjunction with beef extract it is said to have a well defined flavour enhancing effect. Because of this it is recommended that this product be used with beef extract in the proportion of 23 parts of the product with 30 parts of beef extract so that the mixture will be equivalent in meat flavour to 100 parts of the beef extract if used alone.

The constitution of this product is not disclosed in the literature but it is claimed that it fully complies with food regulations as a safe food additive. It is recommended for use in chicken soups in which it contributes an increasing 'mouth-fulness' as well as accentuating the true chicken flavour. It is also claimed that its use cuts the feeling of fattiness from the mouth coating and thereby improves the palatability of many soups.

N

In view of the great importance of proper control over the amount of each type of flavouring ingredient which is added to a batch of soup, as it is made, it is a good practice to have a small room set aside from the remainder of the main factory floor, in which spices, flavours and colours, etc., can be handled correctly from the time of receipt to the time of issue to the process operative. If such a room is conveniently arranged all the necessary seasoning ingredients for one batch can be weighed out and placed in a standard container, clearly marked so that no mistake in identity can occur. These containers can then be issued to the process chemist or operative so that the entire contents are added to one particular batch of soup mix, the empty container being checked back into the issuing room. Such a system obviates the risk of double lots being added to the soup or one or other ingredient being omitted or indeed of the wrong seasoning altogether being added.

In the realm of manufactured foodstuffs, and in particular in such products as soups, flavour is probably the most important item to be considered and carefully controlled. It does not matter how attractive the packaging, however attractive the price, the product will only sell a second time if the family likes what it tastes. Most people prefer to eat food in which the seasoning does not override the accepted flavour of the main ingredients—tomato soup should taste like tomatoes, not of clove or cinnamon as is so often the case. In formulating soups always remember that the seasoning should enhance, improve or elaborate the natural flavours present and not swamp them. If it does, then all products tend to taste the same and will rapidly lead to customer rejection. If in doubt, seek the advice of the expert.

BIBLIOGRAPHY

Spices by John W. Parry. 1969. Vol. I, *The Story of Spices—Spices Described*. Vol. II, *Their Morphology, Histology and Chemistry*. Food Trade Press Ltd., London.

CHAPTER X

TECHNICAL ASPECTS OF RAW MATERIALS

IN this chapter it is proposed to discuss, in the light of modern food technology, the various raw materials used in the manufacture of canned soups and dry soup mixes. The materials are classified for convenience in the following sections:

1. Dehydrated Meat, Poultry and Sea Foods
2. Dehydrated Vegetables
3. Flours, Starches and Thickeners
4. Flavourings
5. Fats and Oils
6. Sugars
7. Dairy and Egg Products

In certain sections, information on laboratory testing is provided and, in general, the manufacturing aspects of ingredient production are dealt with.

1. Dehydrated Meat, Poultry and Sea Foods

Virtually every type of meat, poultry and sea food is dehydrated by soup mix manufacturers or supplied to them in ready-to-use form by dehydrators. In recent years the trend has been away from dehydration by the soup manufacturers who are developing into blenders and packers of soup mixes. There are certain advantages in this system. Firstly, the supply of dehydrated products means that capital, labour and factory space are not tied up in the blending factory. Secondly, with quality control allied to a good buying policy it is possible for the customer firms to buy first-class materials at an economical price, the responsibility being on the many dehydrators, world-wide, to provide an extensive variety of dehydrated items. As the range of soup mixes widens, and as the number of raw materials and new processes increases, the soup mix firms can always be assured of a good supply of dehydrates; apart from supplying technical and research assistance for new products, they need only exercise stringent quality control coupled with sound purchasing policies.

Dehydrated chicken meat is one of the largest commodities in this section. This product, for economic reasons, is often prepared by the soup mix companies although a lot of the preliminary work can be avoided by purchasing the chicken meat in partly processed form. Eviscerated chickens are supplied in fresh or frozen form and these are then retorted to provide the cooked meat for dehydration with chicken stock which can also be utilized by drying. The chicken meat is stripped by hand from the carcase before being diced mechanically. The chicken dice are dried on trays by conventional hot air dryers, after which they are ready for use in soup mixes. The stock can be used serially until the solids content is high enough to warrant subsequent evaporation to a syrupy liquid or paste. This can then be incorporated in the soup mix directly or by further drying with salt, flour, etc. Chicken fat is normally supplied additionally, with or without antioxidant. Chicken skins, livers and other edible offals are also utilized by grinding or milling them to a fine textured paste and then drying this as above.

Certain companies are supplying manufacturers with cooked chicken meat in pieces, dice and other forms, already prepared and quick-frozen so that the constituents are free-flowing. This is often carried out on a contract basis according to a specification laid down by the customer. The entire carcase, minus bones, can be supplied in this way, and the products can be quite economical even though the delivered prices may appear at first sight to be high. One must take into account the fact that there is a high bone/meat ratio in young chickens and broilers and that there is a shrinkage of the meat which occurs in retorting. Further, there is a small percentage of white meat available, although the dark meat has more flavour, apparently. Skin has a flavour, being normally eaten as such in many countries as a matter of course. Chicken fat appears to contribute more to aroma than to flavour in a soup.

Other kinds of dried meat products available include minced beef, mutton, oxtail, kidney, liver powder, minced pork and turkey. Bone fragments should be absent from all material and the final moisture content of the meat ingredients should be of the order of 3–4 per cent by weight. Meat ingredients prepared by accelerated freeze-drying (AFD) are much in evidence, but their relatively high price often tends to mitigate against their use, particularly since a quality premium is not always evident in such products. Dehydrated meat for use in soup mixes is normally in the form of a pre-cooked mince containing little fat. This fat content should be low since this hinders dehydration and because fat is naturally a low-priced commodity. Meat in the form of pieces is occasionally used and meat powders have their place in some formulations. Dried meat materials should have a good bacteriological status on receipt at the factory and they must be manufactured under strict hygienic conditions. Bacteriological testing techniques are outside the scope of this book; the reader is referred to modern manuals of practical bacteriological testing for guidance in this important area of food technology.

The moisture content of dried meats can be determined by grinding the material to a fine powder and measuring the loss in weight of a small weighed sample after drying for 4 hours at a temperature of 105° C. in an oven. Other suitable methods are discussed in the section dealing with dehydrated vegetables.

A few dehydrated sea foods are available. These include clams, shrimps, prawns, crab, lobster, which, on account of their properties and delicate flavour, are best preserved by the AFD process.

2. Dehydrated Vegetables

These are nearly always purchased by the soup mix manufacturer and soup canner because of the great variety required, the capital cost of adequate drying equipment and the non-availability of many fresh items for dehydration in the soup manufacturing countries. Soup canners are also tending to use dried vegetables quite often at this time to 'fill the gap' when the fresh varieties are unavailable.

Some idea of the range of dehydrated vegetables available is given by the following admittedly incomplete list:

Dehydrated Vegetable	*Form in which used*
Asparagus	Green powder
	White powder
	Tips
Beans (Green)	Slices
Beetroot	Powder
Cabbage (Savoy)	Flakes
(*Brassica oleracae Sabanda L.*)	
Carrots	Dice
	Powder
	Flakes
Cauliflower	Florets
	Part florets and part stalks
Celeriac	Flakes
(Roots of *Apium graveolens L.*)	Powder
Leek	Flakes
	Powder
Mushrooms	Powder
	Slices
	Kibbled
Onions	Powder
	Kibbled
	Slices
Parsnips	Dice
	Flakes
Peas	Powder
	Whole
Peppers (Bell)	Flakes
Potatoes	Granules
	Flakes
	Dice
Shallots	Slices
Spinach	Powder
	Slices
Tomatoes	Powder
	Flakes
Turnips (White and Swede)	Dice
	Flakes

The Drying of Vegetables

At present there are a number of drying methods used for the preparation of vegetables for inclusion in soup mixes. Air drying is the most usual method, there being two main types of air dryers in operation:

(i) *Tunnel Dryers*

These consist of long tunnels inside on which slatted trays of vegetables are stacked on trucks. Loaded trucks are introduced at one end and the dried material taken out at the other. Hot dry air is usually blown through the tunnel in a counter current direction, i.e., the air flow is in the opposite direction to the movement of the trucks. A variation of this method is the conveyor tunnel, in which a metallic mesh belt is used to convey the vegetables. In this case the air also flows through the vegetables.

(ii) *Cabinet Dryers*

The drying chamber in this model holds stacks of perforated trays of vegetables and hot air is blown across and through the trays. Discharged air is dried and reheated or blown out of the system.

Vacuum drying is used for some vegetables where rapid drying at low temperatures is required. One type consists of a cabinet fitted with hollow shelves heated by steam and supplied with a powerful vacuum pump, ejector and compressor. This form of drying is more expensive than air drying, but improved quality, lower final moisture content and, in some cases, improved reconstitution, results.

Where powdered vegetables are required these may be obtained by a simple comminution or milling process until the particles of dried vegetable are reduced to the required fine particle size. Size grading is effected by the use of vibratory screens. Alternatively a purée may be made by milling the fresh product and drying on a drum dryer or in a spray dryer.

(i) *Drum Dryers*

These consist of two contra-rotating steam-heated metal drums on to which the purée or slurry is fed. As the drums revolve the purée is dried in the form of a sheet and this is removed by the action of a scraper or doctor blade. Starches may be added to the purée to assist in sheet formation and this has to be allowed for in the formulation of the soup mix. This sheet is then broken down mechanically to produce a fine flake or powder. Where heat-sensitive products are concerned, the apparatus may be enclosed in a high vacuum chamber.

(ii) *Spray Dryers*

The raw material is prepared in the form of a slurry which is atomized in a large heated drying chamber. The hot dry air evaporates the moisture in the material and the resulting powder is left behind to be collected. Agglomerating devices may be incorporated to change the powder structure and give 'instant' products. These materials wet out easily on addition of water, do not 'ball-up', are relatively dust-free and dissolve very quickly. There are many kinds of spray dryers in operation, these being differentiated by the directional flow of the hot air and by the direction of the spray dispersal.

A method of fairly recent introduction to the food field is that of accelerated freeze-drying (AFD). This was developed right up to production stage for all kinds of foods by the British Ministry of Agriculture, Fisheries and Food at Aberdeen, and subsequently it has been commercially exploited by a number of companies throughout the world. The principle of AFD is that the frozen foodstuff is heated in a high vacuum. The moisture is removed by sublimation from the solid to the gaseous phase giving a product which retains the shape of the original material, but which is porous in structure. This latter feature allows speedy reconstitution in water, giving the foods so prepared an 'instant' character. In many cases flavour, colour and nutritional properties are virtually unchanged, but the relatively high cost of the process makes it more suitable for items such as sea foods, poultry, meats and certain fruits. Mushrooms and onions are currently being processed by AFD techniques, the quality being considered excellent.

Quality Factors

Dehydrated vegetables are normally purchased according to company specifications laid down by the purchaser. Such a specification takes into account the following factors:

1. *Freedom from foreign matter*
   Foreign matter is defined as literally everything but the edible

parts of a dehydrated vegetable. Scorched, burnt and discoloured pieces are considered unwanted; metallic fragments, insect parts, rodent excreta and other materials due to insanitary preparation or storage are usually sufficient to ensure rejection of the sample or parcel. For harmless discoloured pieces of vegetables it is usual to set a maximum limit in practice of, say, 0·2 per cent.

2. *Physical state*

The size of the pieces is specified; if a powder is used, the particle size by sieve classification is defined. It is also usual to state the exclusion of certain unwanted parts of a vegetable, e.g., the stalks of cauliflower, the butts of asparagus, the roots of onions, and so on, where applicable.

3. *Organoleptic factors*

The subjective factors of flavour, texture, appearance, colour and odour are normally evaluated by trained laboratory personnel acting as expert individual tasters or in tasting panels.

Cooking tests, to determine the suitability or otherwise of samples, are necessary and in this case the reconstitution ratio (R.R.) should also be determined. The R.R. will increase with time until complete reconstitution is achieved and the time when the R.R. is at a maximum will not necessarily coincide with the cooking time, i.e., the time when the vegetable is judged to be fully 'cooked' as in soup. Ideally the maximum R.R. should approximate to the yield factor from the prepared fresh vegetables but in practice this is rarely so, since irreversible physical and chemical changes play a part in determining the magnitude and rate of reconstitution.

The R.R. is determined experimentally by simmering weighed samples of dried vegetables in water and draining them on a sieve at timed intervals. The sample and sieve are re-weighed each time and eventually the time is reached when no further increase in weight of the sample is noted. The R.R. is then expressed as the maximum weight of reconstituted vegetable divided by the weight of the dry sample. This ratio varies considerably with different vegetables and, in general, is between 4 and 12. Variety, maturity, blanching and drying conditions all affect the ratio and, in general, the more the vegetable has been pre-cooked before dehydration the shorter the period of time before the maximum R.R. is achieved.

As one of the advantages of soup mixes is the saving of preparation time it is obvious that vegetables requiring a relatively short period of cooking should be selected. Furthermore, all the vegetable ingredients in a soup mix should cook in approximately the same time, so that a pleasant 'mouthfeel' is experienced by the customer. It should further be borne in mind that the cooking time may be increased by the presence of other ingredients in the soup mix, notably by common salt.

4. *Moisture content*

Moisture is extremely important, both in the dehydrated vegetable and in the complete soup mix, since the moisture content of the entire mix will, to a large extent, determine the shelf life of the product. This value is very difficult to determine in absolute terms because volatile substances other than water are usually additionally obtained by the normal heating techniques of the laboratory.

From a research angle, optimum stability of a dehydrated product can be related to equilibrium moisture content by means of moisture sorption data. It can be calculated by using the Brunauer, Emmett and Teller (BET) theory of multi-molecular adsorption. This monomolecular layer of adsorbed water can be regarded as a film protecting the product from oxidative degradation. In practice, the dried vegetables are exposed to atmospheres of differing relative humidity until the equilibrium moisture content is achieved. Saturated solutions of inorganic salts placed in the bottom of desiccators at constant temperature provide the range required; the exposed ground vegetables are periodically weighed. When the moisture contents, calculated for each stage, are plotted against the relative humidities, a curve is obtained. This is the equilibrium moisture content curve. BET values are calculated from this and the optimum moisture content follows. Strolle and Cording (1965. *Food Technol. 19,* 171) studied the moisture equilibria of dehydrated mashed potato flakes in this way and found optimum moisture contents of 5·0–6·6 per cent for six months storage of the air-dried product at 75° F. When the flakes were dried to 4 per cent moisture, or to 9·6 per cent moisture, the storage life was only one month under the same conditions.

For routine control it is sufficient to determine the approximate moisture content under standard conditions each time. The dried vegetable is ground to a powder and a weighed sample is heated for a number of hours in a hot-air oven or in a vacuum oven. The cooled sample is re-weighed, the loss in weight being expressed as a percentage loss of the original sample. Temperatures of 98°–105° C. and above, are used for hot-air ovens, and 70° C. for *in vacuo* determinations. Other volatiles besides water are included in values so determined, but these figures are used on a comparative basis for routine work. Absolute values can be obtained by long exposure (days) *in vacuo* of the sample to powerful desiccants such as phosphorus pentoxide or concentrated sulphuric acid. Rapid methods of moisture determination include: (a) entrainment distillation, (b) chemical titration and (c) electronic techniques.

(a) Organic liquids immiscible with water (toluene) are distilled with the ground sample in a flask. The vapours are condensed in a special graduated receiver, where the volume of the water is measured, the solvent being recycled continously. There is a BSS available for the apparatus.

(b) The Karl Fischer technique (McComb, E. A., & McCready, R. M., 1952, *J.A.O.A.C. 35*, 437) utilizes a special reagent which reacts with the water in the sample to give an end-point which is determined potentiometrically.

(c) Various 'moisture meters' are available which instantly measure moisture content by means of specific inductive capacity. They usually require a calibration curve constructed from regular moisture determinations of the specific material under test.

5. *Storage requirements*

These include packaging specifications for the product and recommendations for the best factory storage of it.

Testing for the presence or absence of enzymes should be carried out on all vegetables except onions, since the latter are not blanched before dehydration. Enzymes, therefore, are always present in dried onions but the finished product has a good storage life. Enzymes may be considered as biochemical catalysts, essential to all life, and they are present in all living plant tissue. If blanching prior to dehydration is inadequate these enzymes are not inactivated and hence they may catalyse chemical reactions in the dried vegetables on storage, and in the soup mix, and thereby give rise to off-flavours and off-odours. Testing for the presence of peroxidase and catalase is carried out as follows:

Peroxidase Test

Soak a small sample (5 g.) of dried vegetable in 25 ml. of distilled water in a test-tube for one hour. 1 ml. of freshly mixed equal volumes of an aqueous 1 per cent solution of guaiacol and 5-volume strength hydrogen peroxide is added to the vegetable mixture. If a red-brown colour develops in under one minute then peroxidase is present.

Catalase Test

A test-tube is fitted with a rubber stopper through which a capillary tube projects down about one inch into the body of the tube. A sample of the vegetable is ground to a fine powder in a hammer mill or in a mortar and 3 g. are placed in the test-tube. The tube is completely filled with hydrogen peroxide solution so that, on inserting the stopper, the surplus liquid overflows through the capillary. No air-pockets should be present at the top of the test-tube. After one hour the presence of catalase is confirmed by the presence of oxygen bubbles ascending through the mixture and often a layer of oxygen is present at the top of the tube if the activity is considerable.

In both enzyme tests controls should be carried out simultaneously with samples of dried vegetables which have been boiled, in order that non-enzymic reactions may not give false positive reactions. Typical positive reactions can always be observed with fresh vegetables.

Preservatives

Samples of dehydrated vegetables should be examined for sulphur dioxide (SO_2) content. Since the last edition of this book there has been a slight change in the regulations relating to the limits permitted by law in the United Kingdom. Following on the FSC Report on Preservatives in Food (1959), the Preservatives in Food Regulations 1962 were promulgated, the following maxima being permitted for dehydrated vegetables:

	Parts per million of SO_2
Potatoes	550
Vegetables other than potatoes and cabbage	2,000
Cabbage	2,500

It appears that, as a general principle, a soup mix is permitted to contain a preservative to the extent that it is within the prescribed limits in the constituents of the mix, i.e., in the dehydrated vegetables, according to the above table.

The method adopted as an official test is that of Monier-Williams (1927. *Analyst, 52,* 343, 415). A useful rapid accurate method is described below.

Determination of SO_2 in Dehydrated Vegetables

An all-glass distillation assembly, consisting of a 1-litre flask with side-tube, a stillhead with side-arm, a double-surface condenser and absorber unit, is used. 10 g. of powdered dehydrated vegetable are soaked in 300 ml. of distilled water in the flask and 25 ml. of concentrated hydrochloric acid are run into the contents after steam has been admitted via the side-tube. The absorber tube is immersed in 300 ml. of distilled water in a beaker to which 10 ml. of 2 N. hydrochloric acid, a few crystals of potassium iodide and 2 ml. of starch solution have been added. Once the steam distillation has commenced N/32 potassium iodate solution is run into the beaker by burette so that the sulphur dioxide is titrated on stirring. Completion of the distillation (five minutes or so) is indicated by a permanent blue colour. The titre of potassium iodate solution multiplied by 100 gives the sulphur dioxide content in parts per million.

Sulphur dioxide plays a large part in retarding the browning reaction of dried vegetables during storage. If vegetables are processed without the use of sulphur dioxide storage of soup mixes containing them will often produce brown discoloration and off-flavours of the 'scorched' type. The main reactants in the browning reaction are the amino acids and reducing sugars in the vegetables and SO_2 blocks intermediates in the reactions and thus prevents or retards the complex storage deterioration.

The method described above determines the total SO_2 content, i.e. free SO_2 available for retarding the browning reaction plus bound SO_2 which has chemically reacted already with various constituents in the dried vegetable. It is thus important to determine the relative amounts of free and bound SO_2 in vegetables.

Determination of Free SO_2

10 g. of powdered dehydrated vegetable are reconstituted in cold water and then a few crystals of potassium iodide, 2 ml. of starch solution and 10 ml. of 2 N. hydrochloric acid are added. The mixture is rapidly titrated with $N/32$ potassium iodate solution until a blue colour is produced. The titre multiplied by 100 gives free SO_2 plus other reducing substances, such as ascorbic acid, etc. The procedure is repeated except that 10 ml. of formaldehyde are added to the mixture before titration. This result gives the equivalent SO_2 of the other reducing substances. When the latter figure is subtracted from the former the free SO_2 in p.p.m. is obtained.

When the free SO_2 is subtracted from the total SO_2 figure the bound SO_2 is obtained and the ratio of free to bound SO_2 in a dehydrated product will give a sound idea of its storage life under various conditions.

Microbiology of Dehydrated Vegetables

All too often the possibility of introducing micro-organisms into food products via the use of dehydrated vegetables is overlooked. Poor plant sanitation and the improper selection of suitable vegetables can result in material with an appreciable 'bacterial load'. Incorrect processing is another predisposing factor and dehydrated vegetables with a high bacterial count can confer inherent quality defects on soup mixes.

It is interesting to note that Vaughn (1951. *Food Res. 16,* 429) isolated starch-fermenting species of the genera *Aerobacter* and *Bacillus* from samples of spoiled dehydrated potatoes. The predominant organisms were *A. aerogenes, B. subtilis* and *B. cereus.*

Incidentally it is noteworthy that the free SO_2 is also available in treated dehydrated vegetables for bactericidal purposes and the incorporation of SO_2 during processing will tend to prevent bacterial build-up and spoilage.

Eschmann *et al.* published details of laboratory tests for the bacteriological examination of soup mixes of many kinds (1967, *Alimenta*, 6, 77). Standards agreed by Swiss health organizations were presented in the paper.

In an American study by Nakamura and Kelly (1968 *J. Food Sci.*, 8, 33, 424) they examined fifty-five samples of retail soup mixes, sauce and gravy mixes for the presence of *Cl. perfringens*. Although this organism was found in over 18 per cent of the total samples, only one of the twenty-eight soup mixes tested was contaminated with it. No common ingredient was detected as the source of contamination; it was suggested that these findings may have epidemiological significance in some food poisoning outbreaks in the United States.

3. Flours, Starches and Thickeners

Starches, like edible fats and oils, can be 'tailored' for specific uses in the soup industry. Starches, as the polysaccharide isolates of flours, are the primary thickeners of canned, frozen and packet soups.

Starches contain two polysaccharide fractions, the amylose (linear) unit and the amylopectin (branched) one. The proportion of each type in a starch determines its behaviour in a soup. Gelatinization in liquids occurs over different temperature ranges for the various starches and swelling patterns vary too. Chemical treatments giving cross-bonding of the starch granules confer swelling resistance to starches normally containing only the amylopectin fraction. Starch granules consisting mainly of the amylose fraction hardly swell at all during prolonged cooking and therefore do not produce viscous pastes.

Potato and tapioca starches have fragile over-swollen granules on heating; these break down on prolonged cooking to produce a highly viscous unstable paste. Corn starch does not swell on cooking so readily; hence it gives a more stable but less viscous paste. When a chemically cross-bonded 'tailored' starch is used in soup canning the limited swelling and solubility makes it ideal for viscosity retention during retorting. Crossbonding also confers stability to low pH (high acid) conditions. This is of particular importance in tomato soups where the

acidity would normally hydrolyse part of the starch on processing.

Of associated interest is the use of enzyme-inactivated flour
in canned soups, where this material gives better pasting
quality than ordinary wheat flour or low amylase flour. The
α-amylase content of the flour is responsible for amylose
breakdown and the British Food Manufacturing Industries
Research Assocaition (BFMIRA) has investigated this problem
in canned soups (Technical Circular No. 236, 1963). This work
confirmed the increased viscosity, reduced curdling and settling
out produced by enzyme-inactivated flour.

The following thickeners and flours are given in descending
order of thickening power: farina, arrowroot, cornflour,
tapioca, oat flour, wheat starch, barley flour, sago, wheat flour.
Other products used include pea flour, potato flour, rice flour,
barley, and many other speciality products.

Producers of soups of all kinds are referred to the manufacturers of starches for expert advice on the best product to use
for a particular type of soup.

PHYSICAL PROPERTIES OF COMMERCIAL RAW STARCHES

| | Temperature (°F.) at which gelatinization begins | | Starch paste | |
	5 Per Cent solution	33⅓ Per Cent solution	Texture	Clarity
Corn	176	156	Gel	Opaque
Amioca	165	162	Cohesive	Sl. clear
Tapioca	145	136	Cohesive	Clear
Sago	165	160	Soft cohesive	Sl. clear
Potato	147	142	Soft cohesive	V. clear
Wheat	170	140	Soft	Cloudy
Rice	178	167	V. Soft	Cloudy
Arrowroot	167	164	Soft cohesive	Sl. clear

Corn starch is the most abundant of all United States
commercial starches and is the base for more speciality starches
than any other starch.

Amioca is produced from a special 'waxy' corn or maize. It is quite dissimilar to corn starch since it gives a clear, fluid and cohesive paste and is non-gelling. It also has less cereal flavour than corn starch.

Tapioca is obtained from the root of a tropical plant called cassava. It is a typical root starch giving cooked pastes which are clear, fluid and cohesive. Tapioca pastes are very stable and it has a bland non-cereal flavour.

Sago starch is refined from sago flour, a native food product from the West Indies. This is, in turn, made from the sago palm. Cooked sago starch pastes are semi-clear, fluid and fairly stable.

Potato starch granules are unusually large and are oval in shape. Potato starch, and converted or processed starches made from it, are used extensively in soup mixes.

Wheat starch gives cloudy, slightly cohesive, soft cooked pastes. It is used a great deal in soup mixes for its lack of flavour and viscosity.

Rice starch has the smallest granules of any commercial starch and cooked pastes made from it are soft and opaque.

Arrowroot comes mainly from the West Indian island of St. Vincent. It is a root-type starch and is similar to tapioca, but has a less cohesive, cloudier and softer paste. Its high price prevents it from being used more widely.

Sorghum starch is now being produced in the United States and it is similar in properties to corn starch.

Sweet potato starch is quite different from white potato starch, resembling a mixture of corn and tapioca starches in properties. Cooked pastes of sweet potato starch are soft, cloudy and relatively stable.

In evaluating these items for use in soup mixes the following factors should be investigated: moisture content, thickening power, and stability. The moisture content is usually determined by oven drying, as in the case of dehydrated vegetables. The thickening power or viscosity characteristic is determined by determination of the viscosity in a Redwood viscometer under controlled conditions. This property is of great value in formulation problems as well as in raw material evaluation.

The stability of a farinaceous material is of interest where the storage life of a mix requires evaluation. Certain flours contain enzymes known as lipases (fat-splitters) which catalyse the

o

splitting of fats on storage to give free fatty acids. Oat flour is particularly prone to a high lipase content and, on storage, the lipolytic action of the enzyme can give rise to typical 'soapy' off-flavours. In a soup mix not only the natural flour fat but also the added fat can be affected in this way. The lipase value of a flour can be determined by incubating the sample of flour with fat, intimately mixed, at a temperature of 80°–100° F. for a period of time, and then determining the free fatty acid content by titration with standard alkali. The results can be expressed as a percentage of oleic acid, for example, and correlated with taste tests to determine the onset of off-flavour development.

The fat fraction of flours and soup mixes containing fat is also liable to undergo oxidative rancidity in which the fatty fraction is autocatalytically split into substances giving rise to typical 'stale' and 'cardboard' odours and flavours. A similar reaction also occurs with the small fat or lipid fraction of dehydrated vegetables. The course of oxidative rancidity can be followed by determining the peroxide value which again should be correlated by taste tests with the onset of perceptible rancid flavours. During storage there is an induction or lag period at the beginning during which little peroxide formation occurs. At the end of this period a very sharp rise in peroxide value usually occurs, often accompanied by rancidity perceptible by odour and flavour.

The peroxide value can be conveniently determined by extraction of the material with a chloroform-acetic acid solvent and subsequent titration with $N/500$ sodium thiosulphate solution. A starch-iodide indicator is used and the titration is carried out in the absence of air.

Noodles, as a speciality flour product, require to be tested for cooking quality as well as for structural strength. In all cases the farinaceous products should be tested for behaviour on cooking in the actual soup mix after various storage periods, as sometimes physical changes take place in the starch fraction. These changes are sometimes apparent as separation of the flour or starch on cooking, giving rise to 'watery' soups. Retrogradation of the starch is responsible for this type of fault.

Ref. *Macaroni Products*, Dr Ch. Hunmell 1961. Food Trade Press Ltd., London.

Final check tests on batches of flour products should include examination for presence of extraneous matter, which would be evidence of insanitary practices during processing.

Soya flour is a very useful product for use in soup mixes and canned soups since it possesses a high fat and protein content and a relatively high phosphatide content. This latter property is responsible for its good emulsifying properties and for its long storage life. Certain extracted soya protein 'flours' and isolates are now available for adding to the protein contents of soups and this they do at low cost. These products are usually bland buff-coloured powders and they are finding an increasing place in the food industry in general.

COMPOSITION OF SOYA AND WHEAT FLOURS

	Wheat Flour per cent	Soya Flour per cent
Moisture	12·00	6·14
Ash	0·42	5·24
Fat	1·00	20·71
Fibre	0·25	1·72
Protein	12·50	39·56
Carbohydrate	73·83	26·63

Hydrocolloid vegetable gums are used in the formulation of soup mixes for special dietetic purposes, e.g., the so-called 'low calorie' foods. They also have a limited use in ordinary soup mixes, where they are used to give special texture effects in addition to the use of flours and starches. These materials vary greatly in their properties of solubility, viscosity in solution, effect of heating, gel formation and resistance to acid. The most commonly available are: gum arabic, gum tragacanth, gum karaya, guar gum, locust bean gum, carrageenan (Irish moss extract) and agar. Another very useful thickener is carboxymethyl cellulose (CMC).

4. Flavourings

The properties and uses of herbs, spices and condiments are dealt with very fully in Chapter IX. It is considered necessary, however, to give additional data on the flavour enhancers and meat flavours in this section.

Monosodium Glutamate

Monosodium glutamate (M.S.G.), the sodium salt of L-glutamic acid, is produced in very large quantities in Japan, the United States and Formosa. Smaller tonnages are produced in Europe, the world annual production being of the order of 90,000 tons. Since the manufacture of this flavour enhancer changed in recent years to one based on fermentation and synthesis techniques, the price has dropped dramatically to about 2s. 6d. per pound (CIF London basis) at the time of writing (1969).

M.S.G. is available to the soup manufacturer in a range of crystal sizes and as a fine powder. For canned soups any crystal size is suitable, whereas for dry soup mixes the fine crystal or powder grades are best for blending. M.S.G. is stable at all processing temperatures, very soluble in water (73·9 g. per 100 ml. of water at 25° C., 114 g. per 100 ml. of water at 60° C.), but virtually insoluble in organic liquids. It can be easily stored at normal temperatures and it is non-hygroscopic. Available at normal 99·5 per cent purity, M.S.G. contains no other amino acids, not more than 0·2 per cent of moisture and less than 0·1 per cent of salt. The normal test in the laboratory is a simple total nitrogen determination, which should give 7·48 per cent. Specific enzymic methods are rarely used because of the reliability of suppliers' warranties.

The potassium salt of L-glutamic acid is manufactured on a small scale as monopotassium glutamate for use in foods which are part of a low sodium dietary.

5'-Ribonucleotides

While there is a good deal of research and development interest in these products at the present time, their relatively high price and minute level of use have precluded widespread use in the food industry. These flavour potentiators and enhancers consist of disodium 5'-inosinate and disodium 5'-guanylate; they are being produced in commercial quantities from yeast nucleic acid in Japan, the United States and in Europe. They are available as separate compounds, as 50/50 mixtures, and as 50/50 mixtures at the 5 per cent level with M.S.G. Apart from their flavour enhancing effect at very low levels (thus making blending more difficult), the phosphate linkage in each compound is easily broken by phosphatases present in meat and other foods. This imposes a restriction on their use, since they must be added after a meat product has been cooked. The latest forms of the 5'-ribonucleotides available are coated with a hardened fat to protect the compounds from enzyme attack. The 5'-ribonucleotides are synergistic with M.S.G. and their effect is similar. The mixture of the two compounds is effective at levels purported to be as low as 0·001–0·005 per cent, but actual levels for canned soups are probably about 0·02–0·05 per cent.

It would appear that exaggerated claims have been made for these very interesting products and, as usual, it will be some time before a true evaluation can be made for them. The very high price will undoubtedly fall as production increases and competition occurs and a factor may well be the large drop in M.S.G. prices, which has mitigated against the sparing and synergistic effects claimed for these materials.

It should be noted that M.S.G. and 5'-ribonucleotides both occur in very many foodstuffs and that these compounds should never be considered as artificial in any way. In fact it has been shown that the natural levels of these compounds usually fall on processing or storage of foods and that the addition of small quantities to a processed food will restore part of the pre-processing flavour.

Protein Hydrolysates

Synonymous terms for this low cost savoury flavouring are: hydrolysed protein, vegetable extract, H.V.P. (hydrolysed vegetable protein) and hydrolysed plant protein. Whereas throughout the book the term 'H.V.P.' is used it should be noted that protein hydrolysates may also be obtained from animal proteins, mixed animal and vegetable protein sources being quite common.

The normal food grades of H.V.P. are made by hydrolysis of a blend of selected proteins. Occasionally, a single protein may be used to give a grade with a special flavour effect. The most commonly used vegetable proteins are: wheat gluten, soya meal, maize gluten, groundnut meal, cottonseed meal, yeast.

Typical protein sources of animal origin include: meat meal, casein, and whalemeat meal. Hydrolysis is effected in autoclaves at elevated temperature and pressure by strong mineral acids such as hydrochloric acid. After hydrolysis, the excess acid is neutralized with an alkali hydroxide or salt (to produce common salt with sodium compounds) and this is followed by various filtrations and carbon treatments to produce a 'clean' clear liquor. Certain amino acids, such as leucine, phenylalanine and tyrosine, may be removed during processing, since they give rise to unwanted flavours in the finished product. The remaining amino acids (and their sodium salts) are mainly responsible for the flavour-producing and flavour-enhancing properties of H.V.P. One of these is glutamic acid, the monosodium salt of which is M.S.G.

The liquor may be used directly in canned soups since it is cheaper than the paste and powder grades, always provided that cartage costs of the liquor are not excessive. To produce the normal paste grades of H.V.P., the liquor is concentrated in evaporators *in vacuo*. A further stage consists of either tray-drying in vacuum ovens to give a granulated powder or spray-drying to produce a fine powder. In both cases the H.V.P. powders are very hygroscopic.

H.V.P. is used extensively in the production of canned and packet soups, the liquor and paste for the former, and powder grades for the latter. Sometimes H.V.P. paste is dried with farinaceous materials, beef extract, yeast extract, salt, etc., by soup mix manufacturers to produce a dry granulated savoury base. H.V.P. can be produced virtually salt-free by use of special chemical techniques and by enzymatic hydrolysis. These expensive grades are used especially for dietetic purposes.

H.V.P. powders usually contain appreciable amounts of salt by virtue of the neutralization procedure, and salt is sometimes added as a drying aid. As H.V.P. is used in foods where salt is a common ingredient, and since the level of use is low, this factor is quite unimportant. Purchasers of H.V.P. however should always test the salt content and the moisture content to arrive at the organic or flavour solids content—a criterion of value, apart from flavour!

It is not considered pertinent to discuss the deeper implications of the use of H.V.P. products within the scope of this book, but the following table gives an idea of the analytical characteristics of just a few of the many grades available in the United Kingdom and in the United States at the present time.

HYDROLYSED VEGETABLE PROTEINS

	Pastes							Powders		
Moisture (per cent)	12·3	15·0	17·0	15·0	14·0	17·0	—	5·0	3·0	2·0
Salt (per cent)	32·5	29·0	37·0	33·5	39·8	24·5	37·2	43·0	39·0	34·5
pH Value	5·0	5·4	5·2	5·4	5·3	—	6·6	4·7	4·9	5·0
Total Nitrogen (per cent)	6·1	6·8	6·9	6·8	6·1	7·0	5·8	5·3	5·3	7·0
Amino Nitrogen (per cent)	4·1	5·6	5·5	5·4	—	—	3·6	4·0	—	5·1
M.S.G Content (per cent)	16·1	8·3	7·0	7·5	1·07	—	—	7·0	14·7	19·8

Some of the very variable M.S.G. contents can be explained by the fact that M.S.G. is sometimes added to H.V.P. grades before the final process. The amino nitrogen value is a measure of the amino-acid content of the material; this will be low if undue degradation has occurred during processing. The total nitrogen figure is a measure of the nitrogen-containing compounds contained in the H.V.P. and a high figure is not necessarily indicative of a good grade of H.V.P. This value will of course be depressed by very high salt and moisture contents.

Bishov, Masuoka and Henick (1967, *Food Technol.*, *21*, 446) suggested that H.V.P. has a stabilizing effect on chicken fat in a chicken flavoured soup and gravy base. The composition of the base (U.S. Army specification, 1962) was given as:

	%
Salt	31·0
H.V.P·	18·0
M.S.G.	12·0
Sugar	10·0
Starch	10·0
Dried Chicken Meat	6·0
Chicken Fat	5·0
Hydrogenated Shortening	4·4
Onion Powder	3·0
Garlic Powder	0·3
Turmeric	0·2
Ground White Pepper	0·1
	100·0

Yeast Extract

Yeast extract (YE) is a savoury flavour used extensively in the soup industry. The product is actually the concentrated extract (in paste or powder form) of autolysed brewers' yeast. Its use has been greatly extended in recent years as the price of beef extract has increased. Apart from contributing a rich meaty flavour to canned and packet soups, YE possesses flavour-enhancing effects by virtue of its *natural* content of M.S.G. and 5'-ribonucleotides. Since it is of purely vegetable origin, it is also acceptable to consumers of varied ethnic groups and it is used as an ingredient of soups made for dietetic purposes. In most consumer packs the levels of use are such that the high content of the vitamin B group of vitamins is of limited value. However, this nutritional aspect of YE is of value where relatively high usage in a formulation can be maintained.

The starting point of manufacture of YE in the United Kingdom is normally brewers' yeast, the different sources of which play a large part in the flavour of the final product. Other kinds of yeast can be used, such as bakers' yeast and food yeast, giving rise to a wide range of end products.

The yeast is first treated to remove any impurities and hop

bitters, then the yeast cell liquor is allowed to autolyse at a controlled elevated temperature of about 50° C. After subjection to an inactivating temperature of 80° C., the solids are filtered off and the liquor is concentrated, the pH value adjusted, the liquor clarified and the pH adjusted again before it is finally evaporated *in vacuo* to the familiar paste. Vegetable juices, herbs and spices (and extra vitamins) are sometimes added to provide extra flavour for the consumer product. Vacuum drying and spray-drying provide YE powders, which are used in soup mixes directly. Salt-free YE is available for special dietetic soup preparations.

Laboratory tests for YE include:

(i) *Moisture*

A 1 g. sample is heated for 30 minutes at 146° C. in a Carter-Simon oven, the result expressed as a percentage weight loss.

(ii) *Salt Content*

The Volhard method is used—see below.

(iii) *Trace Metals*

These include tests for arsenic, copper and lead, the maxima for which should be 2, 10 and 5 p.p.m., respectively.

(iv) *Bacteriological Status*

A total plate count of 1,000 or less is usual. Coliforms, E. Coli and H_2S-producing organisms should be absent.

Typical analyses of YE pastes and powders are given as a guide in the accompanying table.

YEAST EXTRACTS

	Pastes						Powders		
Moisture (per cent)	26·5	25·0	20·0	37·0	27·4	29·5	20·0	4·0	3·5
Salt (per cent)	11·2	10·8	17·0	10·5	0·3	13·0	16·0	11·0	45·4
pH Value	5·6	5·6	—	5·2	—	5·6	—	—	—
Total Nitrogen (per cent)	6·6	6·7	6·9	4·5	7·8	6·5	7·5	8·0	5·9
Thiamin (p.p.m.)	25	13	—	90	48	18	20	40	—
Riboflavin (p.p.m.)	60	58	—	75	68	18	75	28	—
Nicotinic Acid (p.p.m.)	600	500	—	500	553	400	300	430	—

As in the case of H.V.P., the salt and moisture contents when subtracted from 100 per cent will give the flavour or organic solids content. YE should give a clean meaty flavour in solution when tasted at the 2–5 per cent level. The solution should be yellow-to-brown in colour and it should be clear. No unpleasant 'yeasty' flavours should be present in the extract and the high nitrogen figure, particularly the amino-nitrogen one, should indicate no undue breakdown of essential amino-acid components during the processing of the material.

———

Soup Stock

An inexpensive but useful ingredient for canned soup manufacture is soup stock. Beef bones, with residual meat adhering to them, are autoclaved to provide a stock which is then evaporated to provide a viscous, rather intractable, material with the following typical analysis:

Moisture	22–25 per cent
Salt	5–7 per cent
Fat	Trace
TCC	0·5–0·1 per cent

The soup stock has a neutral flavour and is very useful indeed in providing the 'body' for many types of canned soup. The normal pack is the 56 lb. can, as for meat extract.

Meat Extract

The generic term 'meat extract' covers extracts of beef, mutton and whalemeat, but beef extract is the most important item in this connection in present-day soup manufacture, and it is the ingredient usually referred to when extracts of meat are discussed.

Beef extract, as normally produced, is a by-product of the manufacture of corned beef although it can be made specifically as an end-product. At present it is produced in South America, Australia, New Zealand and in Africa. Although beef extract is considered a by-product, the price obtained for it usually dictates the economic viability of the corned beef processing operation itself. This is self-evident when one considers the present high cost of beef.

The basic method of manufacture of beef extract consists of leaching out the extractives from fresh beef by means of water. The manner in which this is accomplished determines the quality of the finished product as does the method of concentration of the liquor. Extraction of the beef by counter-current techniques is practised and control of the temperature of the extracting water is most important. The primary stage of concentration is carried out by the use of vacuum evaporators, which may be of the triple effect type. This condensed liquor is then concentrated to a paste by the careful use of open steam-heated jacketed pans or kettles. Again, control of temperature is extremely important if the product is not to be scorched. Throughout the processes above, various filtration, skimming and clarification operations are carried out to remove any fat, precipitates and insolubles which may be present. The ideal is to produce a beef extract which is easily soluble in hot water, which has a good rich beefy flavour and aroma and which is free from any traces of off-flavour. This unique and invaluable extract is obtained normally at less than 2 per cent yield from beef, this factor emphasizing again the present high price.

Creatine from the lean beef muscle changes to creatinine during extraction whilst creatinine slowly reverts to creatine on storage of the beef extract. Creatine and creatinine are usually determined together in the laboratory as equivalent creatine to give the total creatine content (TCC). The following method is the one laid down by the International Association of the Broth and Soup Industry ('Analytical Methods for the Soup Industry', Berne, 1961):

Determination of Total Creatinine
Hadorn Method

Reagents:
HCl about 2 normal
Aluminium oxide for adsorption analysis by the Brockmann method.
Aqueous saturated picric acid solution (saturation at 20° C).
10% sodium hydroxide.
Control solution: 1.5 ml picric acid solution + 1 ml NaOH solution made up to 50 ml with water.
Peroxide-free ether.

Procedure:

5 ml of a solution of 1 gr of meat extract in 100 ml of water, to which is added 10 ml of HCl, is evaporated to dryness in a small porcelain dish. The residue is taken up in 25 ml of water and treated as follows:—

The solution is passed slowly through a layer of aluminium oxide contained in an Allihn tube closed with a cotton plug. Weak suction by means of a water-jet vacuum pump can be applied.

Five ml of the colourless, or possibly pale yellow eluate acidified with 1–2 drops of hydrochloric acid is evaporated in a small porcelain dish almost to dryness. The residue is rinsed twice with ½ ml of water into a ground glass stoppered test tube. Levulinic acid is removed by extracting four times with 5 ml peroxide-free ether. The ether layer is best sucked off with a capillary tube into a receptacle connected to a vacuum. The extracted solution is returned to the porcelain dish, carefully evaporated to dryness and determined colorimetrically. For this purpose the residue is dissolved in 2 ml water, to which is added 1.5 ml picric acid solution and 1 ml NaOH solution. The mixture is stirred and allowed to stand exactly five minutes. The solution is then transferred into a 50 ml volumetric flask and made up to the mark. The colorimetric determination is performed immediately in a 0.5 or 1.0 cm cell using a green-blue filter (500 mμ) against a picrate solution as the blank. The creatinine values obtained are proportional to the extinction, provided this remains below 1.

For each type of colorimeter a corresponding calibration curve has to be plotted: 1.603 gr of creatinine zinc chloride c.p., or 1.322 gr creatinine hydrochloride c.p., is dissolved in about 500 ml distilled water, 100 ml N hydrochloric acid is added and the solution made up to one litre with distilled water. 1 ml of this solution contains 1 mg of creatinine. In order to obtain the readings for the calibration curve 20 ml of the solution is again diluted to 100 ml. Of this solution 0.0, 0.5, 1.0, 1.5 and 2.0 ml—corresponding to 0.0, 0.1, 0.2, 0.3 and 0.4 mg of creatinine—are pipetted into 50 ml volumetric flasks. Sufficient distilled water is added to make all these volumes up to 2 ml, and, after addition of 1.5 ml of picric acid and 1 ml of sodium hydroxide solution, the flasks are left to stand exactly 5 minutes. Water is then added to bring the volumes up to the mark, the solutions are vigorously swirled, and the absorption is immediately measured in a 1 cm cell at 500 mμ, using the reagent mixture without creatinine as a blank. The readings obtained (absorbance values) are plotted to give the calibration curve, which should be a straight line.

The results are given in per cent by weight to one decimal place.

Limits of error: ± 0.1%.

Although the TCC is a useful guide to the genuineness of a beef extract, the latter is best expertly assessed on flavour and aroma, there being no substitutes for these characteristics. The reader is referred to the international standards for the determination of dry weight and ash content, and for sampling procedures.

The following method for chloride content (salt) is also taken from the same publication. It can be easily modified for weight of sample used where other raw materials such as H.V.P., M.S.G. and YE, for example, are tested for use in canned and packet soups.

Determination of Chloride Content
Volhard Method

Principle:
An excess of silver nitrate solution is added to the chloride solution. The excess of silver ions is then back titrated with an ammonium thiocyanate solution. Indicator: Ferric alum solution.

Reagents:
Nitric acid (1:1)
N/10 $AgNO_3$ solution
$AgNO_3$ c.p. 16.9888 gr
(previously dried for 1 hour at 100° C) made up to 1 litre with distilled water. Note: c.p. in these methods means chemically pure for analysis.
N/10 NH_4SCN solution:
NH_4SCN c.p. 7.6113 gr
(previously dried for 1 hour at 100° C) made up to 1 litre with distilled water. In practice a slightly higher weight is taken, and the solution is adjusted by dilution to correspond to a N/10 $AgNO_3$ solution.
Ether or nitrobenzene.

Ferric alum solution: The indicator used is a solution of ferric alum saturated (about 40%) in the cold, which is prepared with crystallized chloride-free $Fe_2(SO_4)_3 \cdot (NH_4) \cdot SO_4 \cdot 24H_2O$. The brownish coloration of the solution is eliminated by adding pure nitric acid dropwise.

Procedure:

The ash obtained from 20 ml of a meat extract solution (10 gr/200 ml) is treated with aliquots of hot distilled water acidified with a few drops of nitric acid, until the solution measures about 100 ml.
The separate washings are successively filtered into an Erlenmeyer flask.
After the addition of 5 ml ferric alum solution, 10 ml $N/10$ $AgNO_3$ and 5–10 ml ether, or 1 ml nitrobenzene, the solution is titrated with ammonium thiocyanate solution until the red colour no longer disappears on stirring.

Calculation:

$$\frac{5.85\ (V_2-V_3)}{P} \times 100 = \%\ NaCl$$

P = mg meat extract ashed.
V_2 = ml $N/10$ $AgNO_3$ added.
V_3 = ml NH_4SCN required for back titration.

Limits of error: $\pm$ 0.2%.

Supplies of mutton extract appear to be extremely scarce at present, but whalemeat extract is readily available. The TCC for the latter is lower than that of beef extract, but it has the advantage of economy for certain products. As noted in Chapter IV, declaration of the type of meat extract used may be legislated for in the near future in the United Kingdom.

Meat extract can be obtained as a powder, prepared by the vacuum oven drying method or by the AFD process. It is more common, however, to dry the extract with other materials prior to incorporation in soup mixes.

Meat Extract Substitutes

Owing to the continued high price of beef extract, due principally to the demand for fresh instead of processed meat, much effort has been made in the search for substitutes. This work has produced a number of so-called 'meat extract substitutes' (MES) manufactured by firms in the United States and United Kingdom, although the use of H.V.P. and YE has for many many years provided an economic way of extending meat extract to give a balanced 'meaty' flavour in soups and other savoury convenience foodstuffs. Thus, these substitutes are actually variations on a theme and merely provide a conveniently packaged single item product. Whilst these substitutes may be of use to certain manufacturers, the larger soup canners and soup mix packers will probably continue to purchase the individual items and to blend these in the finished product. One must never forget that there is a good deal of professional skill required in the formulation of a soup (or any other savoury foodstuff) and that the food technologist plays a major role in this vital work.

The commercially produced MES products are many and varied. One, a U.S. material, consists of H.V.P. with added 5'-ribonucleotides. This powder is then used with another H.V.P. on a 3:1 basis to 'replace' beef extract on a 3:2 basis. The analysis of this powder is:

Moisture (per cent)	4·0
Salt (per cent)	41·4
Total Nitrogen (per cent)	5·3
M.S.G (per cent)	6·5
pH Value	5·0

Another U.S. product is a blend of H.V.P., sugars, fat, M.S.G., amino acids and 5'-ribonucleotides. This replacement level for beef extract is purported to be 3:4.

A Japanese company has recommended the use of their 50/50 blend of 5'-ribonucleotides for replacing half of the beef extract in a dry soup mix. Their formula for the replacement is:

	Per cent
Yeast Extract	49
Glucose	47
Caramel	2
5'-ribonucleotides	2
	——
	100
	——

It is probably true to say that there is no truly effective substitute for a *good quality* beef extract. The current (1969) activity in marketing 'complete' substitutes, instead of the separate components, is due simply to the present relatively high cost of beef extract. The picture is complicated by the food standards regulations of certain countries where creatine/creatinine content must be declared on certain meat soup mix packets.

5. Fats and Oils

As the selection, storage and use of fats and oils are less of a problem to the soup canner than to the soup mix manufacturer, this section will deal primarily with the latter's interests.

Up to the time of actual incorporation of the fat into the soup the technical aspects are identical, but the soup canner has rarely any problems with fats and oils once the product has been satisfactorily canned.

Chicken fat is an essential component of chicken noodle soup mixes and canned chicken soups of all kinds. Careful rendering of selected body fat of hens and chickens produces an oil of golden yellow colour with a characteristic flavour and aroma, free from all traces of scorching and off-flavours. The fat is heated to 180°–212° F. and held at this temperature for 15 minutes. After centrifuging, screening and cooling, it is filled into polythene-lined cartons or steel drums before storage at low temperature. Quick-freezing of the cartons is a superior method of storage and handling of this product, which should conform to the following standard:

Moisture	Not more than 0·25 per cent.
Free Fatty Acids (as oleic acid)	Not more than 0·6 per cent
Iodine Value	75–90
Peroxide Value	Not more than 4 millimoles/Kg.

A simple stability test is to heat a 10 g. sample in a 10 cm. Petri dish at 50° C. for 48 hours, and then repeat the tests for peroxide and free fatty acids. These should increase only slightly, with no alteration in organoleptic properties.

The selection of the fat component of a soup mix is important since factors such as mouth-feel, flavour and shelf-life are influenced by the type of fat used.

Animal fats, such as beef fat (*'premier jus'*) and lard, are sometimes used for meat soups and soup cubes where they give additional flavour. Specially processed vegetable oils and fats are more commonly used in the industry, however, since they can be 'tailored' to possess specific properties for the particular soup mix in mind.

Vegetable oils are hardened by partial hydrogenation of the unsaturated fatty acid components; thus the melting point is increased, the consistency and texture altered. The use of permitted antioxidants gives improved stability of the fat in the stored soup mix. The melted fat or oil may be added to the mix by a spray system at the intermediate or final blending stage of production. Specially developed powdered fats are available for direct incorporation.

Although it is the practice to rely on reputable oil and fat processors to supply correct material it should be borne in mind that storage of these items is important. Whether the oil is supplied in bulk tanker deliveries or in drums or carton lots, constant vigilance is required to ensure that the material is in good condition for manufacturing use. To this end tests should be made on the fat or oil as received and at frequent intervals during storage. The notes below are offered to assist in this connection.

Acid Value

This is the amount in mg. of potassium hydroxide for the neutralization of the free fatty acids of 1 g. of fat or oil. Low acid values indicate purity but these will increase on storage as deterioration occurs. The characteristic unpleasant 'soapy' flavour of soup mixes after over-long storage is often due to the fat-splitting activities of lipases which release free fatty acids. The acid value is usually expressed as a percentage of the major fatty acid component in the oil or fat, e.g., for groundnut and cottonseed oils oleic acid, for palm kernel oil lauric acid.

A weighed quantity of the oil, say 5–10 g., is shaken with 100 ml. of boiling neutral alcohol. After addition of a few drops of phenolphthalein solution as indicator, N/10 sodium hydroxide solution is titrated to a pink colour. 1 ml. of N/10 alkali is equivalent to 0·0282 g. of oleic acid or 0·0200 g. of lauric acid. A fresh oil will have a figure of 0·05 per cent or so; this will rise

P

under adverse storage conditions to 1 per cent or more, when it will be considered unsuitable for use.

Peroxide Value

This value indicates the peroxides in the oil or fat expressed as milli-equivalents of peroxide oxygen per kilogram. The Lea value is expressed as millimoles of peroxide oxygen per kilogram—therefore the Lea value is half the peroxide value.

Oxygen absorption of oils and fats proceeds numerically as a small steady increase during the induction phase until there is a sharp increase as indicated by the peroxide value. It is often considered that this period indicates the stability of the fat, but very often there is no correlation between this and the one determined by tasting tests. Accelerated storage tests sometimes differ from keeping tests where the soup mix is stored under 'normal' conditions. The theory is that the production of typical off-flavours of rancidity will coincide with the end of the induction or lag phase and that prediction of this may be easily obtained by experiment. Used intelligently it is probably a useful guide only.

The Lea peroxide oxygen test may be summarized as follows: About 1 g. of the fat or oil is placed in a boiling tube. 1–2 g. of potassium iodide are added with 19 ml. of a mixture of 2 volumes of glacial acetic acid and 1 volume of chloroform. Nitrogen is passed through the mixture so that all the air is removed. The liquid is then heated so that the chloroform vapour displaces the nitrogen and the now closed tube is shaken, cooled and the contents titrated in 5 per cent potassium iodide solution with N/500 sodium thiosulphate solution in the presence of a starch indicator. The test requires repeated manipulations before the necessary skill is acquired to obtain reliable results. Readers are referred to the British Standard Specification B.S.S. 'Fats & Oils' on the subject for further details.

6. Sugars

Sugar is another basic ingredient in canned and packet soups. In the form of granulated cane or beet sugar (sucrose) it is used for imparting the necessary hint of sweetness to many canned soups, as will be seen from the formulae given in Chapter IV. For large users sugar is supplied in bulk dry sugar installations or in liquid form as a water solution. Glucose syrup is also used as a low-cost sweetening ingredient. For soup mixes, sugar is normally supplied as a finely milled product for ease in blending, while glucose, lactose and corn syrup solids are supplied in powder form for special sweetening effects.

Sweetness tends to suppress acidity in low pH soups, another useful function of this basic food item.

7. **Dairy and Egg Products**

Fresh whole milk and cream are used in the manufacture of canned soups, the handling, storage and use of which accord with principles of modern dairy technology. In the manufacture of dry soup mixes a powdered form of milk is required, a number of milk powder types being available to the packer. Skim milk powder represents an inexpensive milk solids-not-fat source which is very useful in giving body to soup formulations. Cream powder is manufactured in certain countries and this item can be used for special cream style soup mixes. Whey powder is another useful ingredient which can be added to soup mixes, giving interesting texture effects at very low cost.

The latest development in the field is the manufacture of so-called 'instant' milk powder. This is a skim milk product made by the agglomerizing technique, a special form of spray drying. In this process particles are formed whose physical structure gives speedy dispersion and solubility in water without the usual 'balling-up' problem. Instant milk granules are of great potential interest to the instant soup manufacturer, and retail sales of this product are growing.

Although whole fresh eggs can be used for canned soup manufacture, the most convenient products to handle are the dried egg ones. Good storage life in dry form is a factor which makes these materials of prime interest to the soup manufacturer. Dried whole egg, dried egg yolk and dried egg albumen are available, these products being made to very strict standards of bacteriological control. A fairly new development (1965) in the United Kingdom was the commercial production of AFD-processed egg.

Cheese is sometimes used in soup manufacture. For use in soup mixes, it is available as a stable spray-dried or roller-dried powder. Many kinds are on the market and, like other ingredients, they can be custom-blended to provide exactly the right properties of texture, flavour and aroma for the formulation in mind.

CHAPTER XI

DRY SOUP MIXES

D RY soup mixes are now an established item on the British and world food markets, but there are very great variations in the amounts sold in different countries. In the United Kingdom the annual sales of packet soups will probably reach £10 million for 1970. Although sales increase annually, the increase is not as great as the figure for canned soups. In the United States soup mixes have a relatively low share of the total soup market whereas in many European countries packet soups dominate the market. These variations can be partly explained by consumer eating habits and by spending patterns related to the standards of living.

Dry soup mixes have very low unit volumes when compared with canned soups. This factor, combined with good storage life and low price, has led to a large market in institutional and catering soup mixes. They are also of great value for stock piling for 'disaster feeding' and as part of combat rations for the Armed Forces.

We may consider dry soup mixes as specialized composite dehydrated food items since they are compounded mainly of dehydrated foodstuffs and require a relatively short period of reconstitution with boiling water before consumption. Soups, made domestically, require a large amount of preparatory work so that the dry mix can save a good deal of time and effort. Part of the success of the soup mix as a product may be traced to satisfaction that some housewives get by the reconstitution or 'cooking' stage of preparation. This is further augmented if the housewife adds extra meat or vegetables to the mix, thereby using it as a base and in the process creating her own soup.

Apart from the dry soup mixes sold for retail and catering uses, which is the main concern of this chapter, a number of other products are available which may be considered.

(a) *Soup Bases*

These are usually marketed in the form of granulated powders and they represent the soup mix without the addition of dehydrated meat or vegetables. Particularly useful for institutional purposes, they also serve as a handy retail item as a base for a 'home-made' soup.

(b) *Soup Sticks*

These are a new development in the United States and consist of a concentrated soup base packaged in stick form by a foil wrap. Each stick makes $1\frac{1}{2}$ gallons (U.S.) and this is further marked off on the wrapper to give a calibrated portion for 1 pint of soup. The multiple pack of four sticks thus gives 6 gallons of a soup base, which can be served straight as a bouillon or broth or, with added meat and vegetables, as a thicker soup.

(c) *Soup Bars*

Soup bars are produced in Norway by using chocolate moulding and packaging machinery to produce a soup mix in chocolate bar form. The soups are made with a high fat content, giving good compression qualities, the resulting reconstituted soups having a high calorific value. The individual squares of soup bar can be used separately to give a small serving of soup. This form of soup would appear to have good possibilities for rations for the Armed Forces.

(d) *Soup Blocks or Cubes*

Under this heading we may include the inexpensive compressed blocks of dry soup mixes which are made by blending, drying and compressing the granular finished product from H.V.P., YE, starch, salt, powdered dehydrated vegetables, tomato paste, fat and spices. Originally produced as complete soup mixes they have been replaced as such by the dry soup mixes proper, the latter containing discrete pieces of dehydrated meat and vegetables. Consequently their main use nowadays appears to be confined to usage as soup bases to which the housewife adds her own meat and vegetables.

We may also consider the wide range of stock cubes now available. These are designed for use as basic stock for chicken and meat soups of all kinds and as clear soups on their own; this market for stock cubes appears to be an expanding one. Stock cubes may be manufactured from a wide variety of materials. For chicken stock cubes these would include: salt, chicken fat and dried meat, M.S.G., fat, beef extract, onion

(*By courtesy The Nestle Group*)

Two of the battery of autoclaves installed for pre-cooking of flour under pressure, before incorporation in Maggi soup mixes at the Aylesbury factory of the Nestle Group, where some 18 varieties for individual consumer and the caterer are made.

powder, YE, H.V.P., spices and caramel colouring. For beef stock cubes the materials include: salt, M.S.G., fat, beef extract, onion powder, spices, herbs and caramel colouring. Special blending and packaging techniques are necessary to produce the familiar foil-wrapped cubes, which are added to hot water to produce a tasty base or stock for the housewife to prepare her own rich soup. The key to successful manufacture of this type of product is the texture of the mix, which must have the correct moisture content for compression during packaging and for a good shelf life.

(By courtesy The Nestle Group)

Plant for the pre-cooking of meat to be used in Maggi soup mixes at the Aylesbury factory of the Nestle Group.

Similar in certain aspects to the stock cube is the gravy cube or mix. Although gravy products are produced specifically for adding to roasted meat and poultry juices they can, of course, be used as soup bases as above. It is not considered pertinent however to consider in detail gravy cubes and mixes in this book.

(e) *Bouillon Pastes*

Although H.V.P. may be used alone as a base for the preparation of bouillon, the latter may be prepared by using a paste made up as below. The ingredients are mixed thoroughly as gentle heat is applied. The paste may be packed into lacquered cans for catering and institutional purposes.

BOUILLON PASTE

	Per cent
YE Paste	35·0
Beef Extract	25·0
H.V.P. Paste	10·0
Water	8·0
Salt	7·0
Caramel	3·5
Sugar	3·5
Soya Flour	3·5
Malt Extract	3·5
Onion Powder	0·7
Ground Celery Seed	0·3
	100·0

(f) *Instant Soup Mixes*

We may define these as products which reconstitute very quickly (up to a minute or so) on addition of hot or boiling water. They do not appear to exist as such on the U.K. retail market but they are finding an increasing outlet in vending machines. Instant soup mixes are highly specialized products since they cannot contain any discrete pieces of dehydrated meat or vegetables which take up to 15 minutes or so for full reconstitution. They must contain a starch product which is 'instant' in character, i.e., which will give maximum 'body' to the soup in a short time. If they are to be used for vending machines they should flow easily so that no clogging of the feed mechanism occurs.

(By courtesy Batchelors Foods Ltd.)

Showing the interior of a Morton mixer used for mixing soup mix ingredients.

An example of an instant tomato soup is given below. This is presented as an idea for developing further since it is granular in character and is more suited in this form for retail and catering use.

INSTANT TOMATO SOUP MIX

	Per cent
'Instantjel' PA/12	26·20
Tomato Powder	37·06
Instant Skim Milk Powder	11·70
Sugar (finely milled)	9·70
Salt (fine crystal)	5·67
H.V.P. Powder	3·23
M.S.G. (fine crystal)	3·23
Onion Powder	2·41
'saromex' Pepper 'S'	0·16
'saromex' Cinnamon 'S'	0·16
'saromex' Basil 'S'	0·16
'saromex' Marjoram 'S'	0·16
'saromex' Oregano 'S'	0·16
	100·00

After weighing out, the ingredients are thoroughly blended in a suitable mixer. For retail use, 60 g. are filled into laminated soup pockets. This quantity, plus one pint of hot or boiling water, produces a reconstituted soup in about one minute.

Anti-caking agents such as 'CALFOS' (edible bone phosphate), calcium phosphate or stearate may be added to the blend to promote free-running properties in the mix.

A new idea from the United States is the instant soup mix in a drinking cup. This ultimate in instant soups packages the soup mix between the paper cup bottom and a foil lid. The cups are nested and packaged into units. All the user has to do is to add hot water to the contents after removing the foil lid. This idea appears to have good marketing possibilities.

In 1967 one of the largest food companies in the United States test marketed a range of six instant soups: chunk chicken,

chicken noodle, onion, mushroom, pea, and tomato. They were packaged in four single serving envelopes to each box and the contents of a pouch were simply placed in a bowl, boiling water added, and the ingredients reconstituted into a full bodied soup.

In 1969 a leading British soup mix manufacturer changed virtually its whole range of retail soup mixes so as to give a soup ready for use in five minutes instead of the normal 10–20 minutes simmering time. This appears to have been achieved more by the use of size reduction of discrete pieces of dried

(*By courtesy The Nestle Group*)

High- speed mixer for producing soup mixes, installed at the Aylesbury factory of the Nestle Group.

vegetables and meat items than by a use of puff-dried or AFD materials.

It has long been established that small pieces of AFD vegetables and meats will reconstitute extremely rapidly, but the cost of the AFD drying is high and its use is only economically justified with special items like mushrooms and meat products. The newer forms of puff-dried vegetables are promising with regard to ease of reconstitution as well, but if carefully air-dried foods are reduced in size then a substantial reduction in reconstitution time is possible.

In 1967 one of the largest soup mix manufacturers in the United Kingdom launched a retail range of cream-style soup mixes. These, unfortunately, were not a great success and were discontinued.

Since the last edition of this book was published the fastest rate of growth within the dry soup mix industry has been that of soup mixes for catering and institutional use. Apart from specialized companies making this type of mix only, the large manufacturers of retail soup mixes have developed separate catering divisions to enter this competitive and growing field. The early bulk soup mix packs were simply multiple weight units in tins and bags. Today the trend is to pack catering soups in one and five gallon (Imperial) packs so that the contents will make precisely those quantities of reconstituted soup.

The manufacture of these catering soup mixes follows that of the retail packs up to the final packaging stages. After final blending, the soup mixes are gravity-fed to fully automatic bag packaging machines. The laminate-lined multi-ply paper bags are pre-printed and usually fitted with easy opening bag stitch devices.

Whilst the manufacturer can simply pack his retail quality soup mix for catering use, it is usual to formulate special mixes for the trade. Soup mix bags of different varieties are sometimes packaged together in order to meet the demand for the most popular soups in catering and institutional establishments and also to provide a change of soup for different days of the week.

As with other food items, soup mixes require considerable care and development before they reach the market. The idea of a new soup mix would be based on marketing surveys to discover precisely what soup mixes are sold, what canned soups are on the market and what potential there might be for new varieties. The development of the soup mix would involve considerable experimental work with testing of new recipes and packages at all stages. Research testing panels are used for determining primary acceptability of ingredients and the effects

(By courtesy The Nestle Group)

Sieving of finished Maggi soup at the Aylesbury factory of the Nestle Group.

of variables such as conditions of storage, whereas consumer testing panels are made use of when the product has reached an advanced stage before test launching in selected areas. Specifications should be laid down for raw material purchasing and for the ordering of printed packaging materials and cartons. Quality control and reliability testing are necessary procedures to establish, if the soup mix is part of a new range; alternatively, these procedures may require modification because of new ingredients, where the soup mix is an addition to an already established line of soup mixes.

Development testing procedures include accelerated storage tests to determine probable shelf-life, an example being exposure of the filled and sealed soup mix sachets to a temperature of 77° F. and a relative humidity of 75 per cent in an incubator for three months. This will give an idea of how the soup mix will behave after six months' storage under temperate climatic conditions. The palatability of the reconstituted soups should be accompanied by peroxide value determinations on the fat extracted from them, as well as acid value tests on the fat to determine deterioration by free fatty acid formation. During storage the permeability of the pouches should be determined by moisture pick-up tests and these may be followed by periodic weighing of the sachets or by actual moisture estimation of the soup mixes by using the tests described in Chapter X.

The following is a list of soup mixes which are available in the United Kingdom:

Asparagus	Chicken, Thick
Barley Beef	Chicken Vegetable
Beef	Chicken Vermicelli
Beef Noodle	Consommé Arctique
Beef and Tomato	Consommé Celestine
Celery	Country Chicken and Leek
Chicken	Country Vegetable
Chicken, Creamed	Curry
Chicken and Ham	Danish Dumpling
Chicken and Leek	Dietetic Soups
Chicken and Mushroom	Egg Noodle
Chicken Noodle	Farmhouse Vegetable, Thick
Chicken Rice	Fish

Florida Spring Vegetable
Game
Garden Vegetable
Golden Pea
Golden Vegetable
Goulash
Green Pea
Ham Flavoured Green Pea
Irish Green Pea
Irish Potato
Italian Rice
Kidney
Kosher Soups
Leek
Leek, Creamed
Lentil
Lyonnaise
Minestrone
Mock Turtle
Mulligatawny
Mushroom
Mushroom, Creamed
Napoli
Norwegian Fish
Onion, French Style

Onion, Thick
Oxtail
Pea
Pea with Bacon
Pea with Smoked Ham
Portugaise with Prawns
Potage Ecossais
Potage Espagnole
Potage Portugaise
Romany
Scotch Broth
Smooth Rice
Soups for Babies
Spring Vegetable
Thick Farmhouse
Tomato
Tomato, Creamed
Turtle Consommé
Vegetable with Beef, Thick
Vegetable, Clear
Vegetable, Creamed
Vegetable, Thick
Viennese Vegetable
White Beans with Smoked
　　Bacon

As may be seen from the above list, the range of soup mixes is a wide one. From a technical aspect it would appear that virtually any soup mix version of a canned soup may be manufactured. Although the sales patterns of some soup mixes follow those of the canned varieties, tomato soup for example, other types have become popular on their own account. Chicken noodle soup mix, the first soup mix to be marketed in the United Kingdom, is a good example of this. Regional preferences require to be taken into account, of course, as this factor is most important and it varies with traditional soup eating and the dietary patterns of ethnic groups in an area.

Since the last edition of this book many kinds of soup packet sizes have been introduced. Composite packs with outer cartons holding multiple small size sachets are a useful development and the display carton containing separate soup mix packets are

(By courtesy Batchelors Foods Ltd.)

Soup mix plant for weighing ingredients in electrically controlled
sequence, thus avoiding ommission of any ingredient or item. Installed
at the Ashford factory of Batchelors Foods Ltd.

Q

a strong feature of modern merchandising techniques. In fact, one can find today on supermarket shelves just about every possible size of soup pack for retail sale and the great improvements in package design produce an effective display of the brand leaders' products.

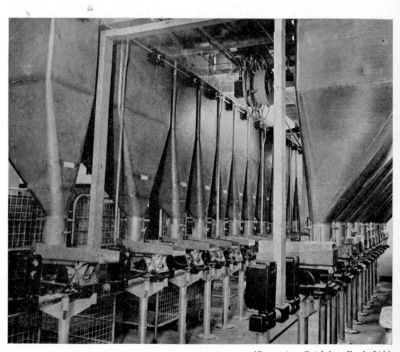

(By courtesy Batchelors Foods Ltd.)

Another view of the stainless steel hoppers and weighing heads which deliver an accurately weighed amount of each ingredient.

Needless to say, all current food legislation should be studied most carefully before manufacture of soup mixes is attempted and the summary in Chapter VIII is given as a guide for United Kingdom packers. In 1955 a British manufacturer was prosecuted because his product, a 'cream of mushroom soup', contained 0·6 per cent of fat when reconstituted. The Public Analyst stated in evidence that, in his opinion, 'cream soup' should contain not less than 3·5 per cent of fat, or not less than 2·5 per cent of butterfat. He considered that soup mixes should conform in this respect to the Code of Practice for canned soups. It would appear that this view still holds good. Perhaps it is significant that no labelled cream style soup mixes appear to be sold on the United Kingdom market although the incorporation of antioxidants in fats has been permitted for some time now.

Apart from the ingredient labelling requirement, soup mix sachets should give the net weight of the contents, the number of servings, and the directions for the preparation of the soup in reconstituted form. A correct description of the soup without misleading nutritional or dietetic claims is essential but the price is no longer printed on the soup sachet since the virtual abolition of resale price maintenance and intensive competition in supermarket trading has made this anachronistic.

The recipes given below are presented as a guide to potential soup mix manufacturers. Although they are 'working' formulae, they should be considered more as pointers to the development of soup mixes since raw material variations and the factors discussed above play a large part in the successful launching of a new product.

ASPARAGUS SOUP MIX

	Per cent
Skim Milk Powder	28·0
Wheat Starch	18·0
Cornflour	18·0
Dehydrated Asparagus (tips, butts and powder)	12·5
Salt	8·5
Vegetable Fat	8·5
Onion Powder	3·0
Sugar	2·0
H.V.P. Powder	1·0
SAROMEX Celery (on salt)	0·3
SAROMEX Pepper (on salt)	0·2
	100·0

Method

Mix the molten fat and the salt for 5 minutes in a ribbon type mixer. Add the rest of the ingredients and blend for 10 minutes more.

(By courtesy Brown & Polson Ltd.)

Automated feed for ingredients for making Knorr soup mixes at the
Paisley factory of Brown and Polson Ltd.

Packaging
    Fill 70 g. into each 4-ply laminated soup packet and heat seal.

Reconstitution
    Mix the contents of a packet with $1\frac{1}{2}$ pints of water, bring to
the boil and simmer for 15 minutes before serving.

CREAM OF CHICKEN SOUP MIX

					Per cent
Dehydrated Chicken Meat	.	.	.		28·25
*Wheat Flour	.	.	.	.	24·60
*Skim Milk Powder	.	.	.	.	22·70
*Chicken Fat	.	.	.	.	18·20
Salt .	.	.	.	.	.	3·55
M.S.G.	.	.	.	.	.	1·13
*Onion Powder	.	.	.	.	0·57
H.V.P. Powder .	.	.	.	.	0·55
Sugar	.	.	.	.	.	0·38
SAROMEX White Pepper (on salt)			.		0·04
SAROMEX Celery (on salt)			.	.	0·03
					100·00

Method
    Mix all the ingredients thoroughly. If desired, the ingredients
marked * may be pre-dried together to lower the final moisture
content.

Packaging
    Fill 91 g. of the mix into each 4-ply laminated soup packet
and seal.

Reconstitution
    Mix the contents of a packet with 1 pint of cold water, bring
to the boil and simmer for 10–15 minutes.

CHICKEN NOODLE SOUP MIX

						Per cent
Salt .	.	.	.	.	.	37·86
M.S.G. .	.	.	.	.	.	21·70
Chicken Fat	.	.	.	.	.	16·30
Dehydrated Chicken	.	.	.	.	.	14·08
Wheat Starch	.	.	.	.	.	3·26
Onion Powder .	.	.	.	.	.	2·72
Sugar	.	.	.	.	.	1·74
H.V.P. Powder .	.	.	.	.	.	1·36
Dried Parsley	.	.	.	.	.	0·54
Ground White Pepper	.	.	.	.	.	0·22
Ground Turmeric	.	.	.	.	.	0·22
						100·00

Method

Mix all the ingredients thoroughly.

Packaging

Fill 17 g. of the soup mix and 40 g. of noodles into each 4-ply laminated soup pocket and heat seal.

Reconstitution

Add the contents of a packet to 1 pint of boiling water and simmer until the noodles are tender, about 5–7 minutes.

The chicken fat may be conveniently packaged in the soup sachet by means of a gelatin capsule. Chicken fat capsules are produced by high speed automatic machinery to give a stable product which releases the chicken fat in the reconstituted soup when the gelatin capsule dissolves.

GREEN PEA SOUP MIX

	Per cent
Pea Meal	88·57
Salt	2·60
Vegetable Fat	1·89
Smoked Dried Yeast	1·89
Sugar	1·43
Onion Powder	1·42
Potato Starch	1·32
M.S.G.	0·88
	100·00

Manufacture

The pea meal is made by dissolving 28 lb. of salt and 1½ lb. of potassium carbonate in 250 gallons of boiling water and then adding 1,000 lb. of washed split peas. After cooking for 25 minutes the following are added:

Hydrogenated Cottonseed Oil	17 lb.
Locust Bean Gum	2¼ lb.
Whole Cloves	12 oz.
Whole Thyme	8½ oz.
Crushed Bay Leaves	3½ oz.

The mixture is then cooked for 10 minutes and followed by the addition of a slurry containing 36 lb. of potato starch in 60 gallons of water. A further 30 gallons of water are then added and the mixture is finally drum-dried to a moisture content of 4–5 per cent before pulverizing and using as an ingredient in the soup mix.

The salt and molten fat are mixed in a ribbon type mixer for 5 minutes followed by the rest of the ingredients with a further mixing of 15 minutes.

Packaging

Fill 113 g. into each 4-ply laminated soup pocket and heat seal.

Reconstitution

Mix the contents of one packet with 1¾ pints of water, simmer for 10 minutes and serve.

KIDNEY SOUP MIX

					Per cent
*Wheat Flour	.	.	.	.	49·10
*Salt .	.	.	.	.	16·66
*Beef Extract	.	.	.	.	8·42
Kidney Powder .	.	.	.	.	8·42
Beef Fat	.	.	.	.	4·21
Yeast Extract Powder .	.	.	.	4·21
Onion Powder	.	.	.	.	4·21
M.S.G.	.	.	.	.	2·10
H.V.P. Powder .	.	.	.	2·10
Caramel Powder	.	.	.	0·21
Ground Thyme .	.	.	.	0·14
Ground White Pepper	.	.	.	0·11
Ground Bay Leaves	.	.	.	0·11
					100·00

Method

Mix all the ingredients thoroughly. If desired, the ingredients marked * may be pre-dried together to lower the final moisture content.

Packaging

Fill 44 g. into each 4-ply laminated soup pocket and heat seal.

Reconstitution

Mix the contents of one packet with 1 pint of cold water, bring to the boil and simmer for 3–5 minutes before serving.

KOSHER SOUP MIXES

While it is not proposed to give specific formulae here, some comments about composition are appropriate.

Like certain other ethnic groups, Orthodox Jews have dietary laws which must be strictly obeyed and the same laws apply equally to the manufacturers of Kosher food products. One must always bear in mind the avoidance of pig products and that milk products and meat items must not be mixed. The ingredients for any soup mix must be obtained under strictly controlled conditions, e.g., meat and poultry products must come from animals ritually slaughtered under supervision of rabbinical authorities and vegetable products such as fats, H.V.P. and YE must be processed by authorized and inspected food plants. In Britain the rules of the Beth Din and the Kashrus Commission have to be meticulously observed, and special rules apply for foods made for Passover. For a Kosher Chicken Noodle Soup Mix the dehydrated chicken meat and fat would be produced as a distinct ingredient in special plant. The salt, M.S.G., H.V.P., starch, onion powder, sugar, herbs and spices would be from approved processes in factories to give a complete mix, after packaging, that could be regarded as Kosher. Vegetable soup mixes are not too great a problem since vegetables are normally approved for use if made under hygienic conditions, whilst the savoury flavour is provided by approved ingredients as above.

MOCK TURTLE SOUP MIX

	Per cent
*Wheat Flour	27·30
*Beef Powder	17·02
*Onion Powder	13·65
*Carrot Powder	11·40
Tomato Powder	10·80
*Salt	9·10
M.S.G.	2·85
Beef Fat	2·85
H.V.P. Powder	2·27
Yeast Extract Powder	2·27
Ground Thyme	0·15
Colouring	0·11
Ground Bay Leaves	0·07
Ground Coriander	0·06
Ground Paprika	0·05
Ground White Pepper	0·05
	100·00

Method

Mix all the ingredients thoroughly. If desired, the ingredients marked * may be pre-dried together to lower the final mixture content.

Packaging

Fill 56 g. of the mix into each 4-ply laminated soup pocket and heat seal.

Reconstitution

Mix the contents of a packet with 1 pint of cold water, bring to the boil and simmer for a few minutes before serving.

MULLIGATAWNY SOUP MIX

	Per cent
*Wheat Flour	33·70
*Beef Powder	27·00
*Salt	11·09
Tomato Powder	8·41
Sugar	6·74
Curry Powder	5·04
Onion Powder	3·57
Beef Fat	1·95
M.S.G.	0·88
Ground Paprika	0·67
Ground Turmeric	0·44
H.V.P. Powder	0·34
Caramel Powder	0·20
Ground Marjoram	0·07
Ground Clove	0·05
Ground Thyme	0·05
	100·00

Method

Mix all the ingredients thoroughly. If desired, the ingredients marked * may be pre-dried together to lower the final moisture content.

Packaging

Fill 56 g. into each 4-ply laminated soup pocket and heat seal.

Reconstitution

Mix the contents of a packet with 1 pint of cold water, bring to the boil and simmer for a few minutes before serving.

(*By courtesy Brown & Polson Ltd.*)

Automated mixing equipment for Knorr soup mixes at the Paisley factory
of Brown & Polson Ltd.

CREAM OF MUSHROOM SOUP MIX

	Per cent
Skim Milk Powder	32·65
Vegetable Fat	26·10
*Wheat Flour	26·10
*Salt	5·35
Dehydrated Mushroom Pieces . .	4·50
Dehydrated Mushroom Powder . .	2·25
M.S.G.	1·62
Onion Powder	0·81
Sugar	0·54
SAROMEX White Pepper (on salt) .	0·07
SAROMEX Clove (on salt) . . .	0·01
	100·00

Method

Mix all the ingredients thoroughly. If desired, the ingredients
marked * may be pre-dried together to lower the final moisture
content.

Packaging

Fill 87 g. of the mix into each 4-ply laminated soup pocket and seal.

Reconstitution

Mix the contents of a packet with 1 pint of cold water, bring to the boil and simmer for 10–15 minutes.

CREAM OF ONION SOUP MIX

	Per cent
Vegetable Fat	28·70
*Wheat Flour	18·61
Dried Onions	12·52
*Skim Milk Powder . . .	12·52
*Cornflour	12·52
*Salt	8·75
*Onion Powder	3·75
M.S.G.	1·25
H.V.P. Powder	1·25
Ground White Pepper . . .	0·13
	100·00

Method

Mix all the ingredients thoroughly. If desired, the ingredients marked * may be pre-dried together to lower the final moisture content.

Packaging

Fill 79 g. of the mix into each 4-ply laminated soup pocket and heat seal.

Reconstitution

Mix the contents of a packet with 1 pint of cold water, bring to the boil and simmer until the onion pieces are tender.

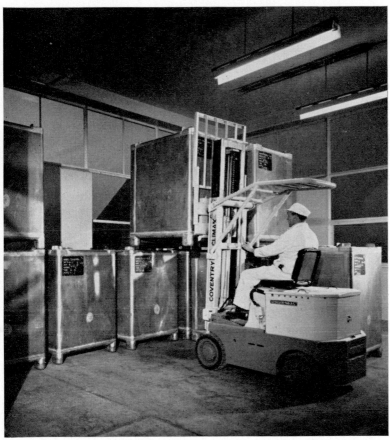

(*By courtesy The Nestle Group*

The finished soup is stored in Tote bins ready for transfer by fork-lift truck to the packaging machines when required. Tote bins are air-tight and completely proof against pilferage and attack by rodents or insects.

FRENCH ONION SOUP MIX

	Per cent
Cornflour (pre-dried)	55·36
Salt	26·50
H.V.P. Powder	11·75
M.S.G.	5·85
Colouring	0·36
Ground White Pepper . . .	0·18
	100·00

Method

Mix all the ingredients thoroughly.

Packaging

Fill 32 g. of the dried base with 20 g. of dehydrated kibbled onion pieces into each 4-ply laminated soup pocket and seal.

Reconstitution

Mix the contents of a packet with $1\frac{1}{2}$ pints of cold water, bring to the boil and simmer for 10–15 minutes.

OXTAIL SOUP MIX

	Per cent
*Wheat Flour	49·72
*Salt	18·10
*Beef Extract	8·52
*Beef Powder	4·52
Beef Fat	4·52
Yeast Extract Powder	4·52
Onion Powder	4·52
M.S.G.	2·26
H.V.P. Powder	2·26
Ground Thyme	0·23
Caramel Powder	0·23
Ground White Pepper . . .	0·12
Ground Paprika	0·12
Ground Coriander	0·12
Ground Bay	0·12
Colouring	0·12
	100·00

Method

Mix all the ingredients thoroughly. If desired, the ingredients marked * may be pre-dried together to lower the final moisture content.

Packaging

Use 4-ply laminated soup pockets; fill 44 g. of mix into each and heat seal.

Reconstitution

Mix the contents of a packet with 1 pint of cold water, bring to the boil and simmer for 3–5 minutes before serving.

POTATO SOUP MIX

	Per cent
Mashed Potato Powder (5 per cent moisture)	69·78
Salt	11·65
Vegetable Fat	5·82
Skim Milk Powder	5·82
Onion Powder	3·10
H.V.P. Powder	2·34
M.S.G.	1·17
Dehydrated Parsley	0·12
SAROMEX Pepper (on salt) . .	0·08
SAROMEX Bay (on salt) . . .	0·06
SAROMEX Celery (on salt) . .	0·06
	100·00

Method

Melt fat and mix thoroughly with the rest of the ingredients.

Packaging

Fill 84 g. into each soup pocket and heat seal.

Reconstitution

Mix the contents with $1\frac{1}{2}$ pints of cold water, bring to the boil and simmer for 2–3 minutes.

TOMATO SOUP MIX NO. I

	Per cent
Tomato Powder	51·60
Ground Biscuit Meal	16·81
Sugar	14·74
Salt	8·87
Skim Milk Powder	5·05
Vegetable Fat	1·87
Onion Powder	0·56
Spice Mix:	

	Per cent	
Garlic Powder . . .	26·37	
SAROMEX Celery (on salt) .	26·37	
Salt	27·04	
SAROMEX Parsley (on dextrose)	8·57	
SAROMEX Cinnamon (on dextrose) . . .	7·03	
SAROMEX Thyme (on salt) .	2·42	
SAROMEX Ground Cayenne (on salt)	0·88	
SAROMEX Clove (on salt) .	1·32	
	100·00	0·43
Sodium Bicarbonate		0·07
		100·00

Method

Mix the molten fat and the salt for 5 minutes in a ribbon type mixer. Add the other ingredients and finally blend for another 10 minutes.

Packaging

Fill 113 g. into each 4-ply laminated soup pocket and heat seal.

Reconstitution

Mix the contents of one packet with 1¾ pints of water, simmer for 5 minutes and serve.

TOMATO SOUP MIX NO. 2

	Per cent
Wheat Flour (pre-dried) . . .	40·22
Tomato Powder	24·70
Skim Milk Powder	9·25
Salt	9·25
Vegetable Fat	6·20
Sugar	3·10
Onion Powder	3·10
H.V.P. Powder	1·85
M.S.G.	1·85
Colouring	0·12
Ground White Pepper . . .	0·12
Ground Cinnamon	0·09
Ground Basil	0·09
Ground Marjoram	0·06
	————
	100·00
	————

Method

Melt the fat and mix first with the salt in a ribbon type mixer. Add the rest of the ingredients and blend thoroughly.

Packaging

Fill 75 g. into each 4-ply laminated soup pocket and heat seal.

Reconstitution

Mix the contents of one packet with $1\frac{1}{2}$ pints of cold water and bring to the boil before serving.

R

CREAM OF TOMATO SOUP MIX

					Per cent
Vegetable Fat .	.	.	.	.	25·500
Tomato Powder	.	.	.	.	17·921
*Wheat Flour .	.	.	.	.	16·800
*Skim Milk Powder	.	.	.	.	14·100
Sugar .	.	.	.	.	14·000
*Salt .	.	.	.	.	4·850
Onion Powder .	.	.	.	.	4·850
H.V.P. Powder	.	.	.	.	1·200
M.S.G. .	.	.	.	.	0·600
Ground Cinnamon .	.	.	.	.	0·088
Ground Marjoram .	.	.	.	.	0·040
Ground Black Pepper	.	.	.	.	0·024
Colouring .	.	.	.	.	0·016
Sodium Bicarbonate .	.	.	.	.	0·011
					──────
					100·000
					──────

Method

Mix all the ingredients thoroughly. If desired, the ingredients marked * may be pre-dried together to lower the final moisture content.

Packaging

Fill 94 g. into each 4-ply laminated soup pocket and heat seal.

Reconstitution

Mix the contents of one packet with 1 pint of cold water and bring to the boil before serving.

The following is an example of a soup mix formula where the tomato ingredient is obtained by drum drying tomato paste with wheat starch and vegetable gum. This technique has now been largely superseded by the use of good quality spray dried tomato powder; this is then used directly in the soup mix as a separate ingredient. The drum drying method was evolved in the early days of soup mix manufacture as a means of drying the heat-sensitive tomato paste and in providing this as a sheet material which could then be broken into a flake for use in the mix.

TOMATO-VEGETABLE SOUP MIX

		Per cent
Salt		9·8

Tomato-Paprika Flake:

	Per cent	
Tomato Solids	64·9	
Wheat Starch	17·7	
Paprika	12·4	
Locust Bean Gum . . .	0·9	
Calcium Oxide	0·3	
Moisture	3·8	
	100·0	9·2

		Per cent
Sugar		8·1
Fat		6·4
Potato Flour		5·0
H.V.P. Powder		3·7
Potato Starch		3·0
M.S.G.		2·8
Corn Starch		1·9

Spice Mix:

	Per cent	
Salt	59·0	
Ground Celery Leaves . .	23·8	
Ground Black Pepper . .	7·1	
Onion Powder	4·8	
Garlic Powder	2·9	
Rosemary.	2·4	
	100·0	1·5

Dried Vegetables:

	Per cent	
Carrot Flakes	45·3	
Onion Slices	22·6	
Red Bell Peppers . . .	7·6	
Green Bell Peppers . . .	7·6	
Green Cabbage . . .	11·4	
Celery Stalk Flakes . . .	5·5	
	100·0	6·4

		Per cent
Noodles		42·2
		100·0

Manufacture

The tomato-paprika flake ingredients are mixed thoroughly in a large steam-jacketed glass-lined tank fitted with an agitator. The raw materials are as follows and are given in order of addition to the tank:

Tomato Paste (11 per cent solids)	2,854 lb.
Wheat Flour	101 lb.
Locust Bean Gum	$4\frac{3}{4}$ lb.
Calcium Oxide	$1\frac{1}{4}$ lb.
Paprika Powder	69 lb.

The slurry is passed to the steam-heated drum dryer and then dried as a flake with a moisture content of not more than 4 per cent.

All the soup mix ingredients are then mixed in a ribbon type mixer. The salt and molten fat are mixed initially for 5 minutes and then with the rest of the ingredients, in order, for a further 15 minutes.

Packaging

Fill 70 g. into each 4-ply laminated soup pocket and heat seal.

Reconstitution

Mix the contents of one packet with $1\frac{3}{4}$ pints of water, simmer for 10 minutes and serve.

MANUFACTURE

It is proposed to deal with this aspect in the light of modern large-scale operations. Although large companies have dominated the retail market in the United Kingdom, smaller firms may still operate effectively by utilization of some of the techniques employed by the former and by concentration on speciality soup mix lines and on catering packs.

Preparation of Raw Materials

The reader is referred to Chapter X for further information on the production of many raw materials used in soup mix manufacture, and to the technical aspects involved.

Apart from most materials supplied or made to specification, meat appears to be the main item of in-factory preparation. This may be partly explained by reasons of economy and by non-availability of specialized products. Another reason is that the characteristic flavour of certain soup mixes is often due to the dried meat component and the production of this vital ingredient is thereby restricted to certain soup mix manufacturers.

Quick-frozen boned-out meat is usually band-sawed into pieces of convenient size which are thawed out before cooking in retorts. The liquor from this operation is centrifuged into fat and gravy; the fat is clarified for re-use while the gravy is concentrated in a film evaporator or similar machine. The meat may be minced finely before autoclaving or it may be minced with the gravy concentrate. The material is then dried by a through-draught dryer to provide the dried meat component. Some meat products, such as bacon, kidney and mutton, may be fried before vacuum drying.

Since final moisture content in the filled soup mix sachets is of paramount importance, most flours, cereals and starches must be pre-dried before use. Such products may be supplied in this form but they are at present mainly processed by soup mix manufacturers. Wheat flour is supplied at 13–14 per cent moisture content and dried down to 2–5 per cent moisture by means of steam-heated horizontal dryers or concurrent pneumatic hot air dryers. Other cereal products are treated in a similar manner whereas pea flour is cooked before use. It is cooked in horizontal autoclaves and then dried down to 5–6 per cent moisture in the same equipment before sieving and storage. Potato starch is supplied already pre-cooked and pre-dried or it may be dried down from about 18 per cent moisture to the necessary level before use. Pneumatic handling installations coupled with silo storage and cooling facilities are used with the above processing and the materials are normally screened or sieved before use. Explosion hazards must be avoided by dust extraction.

Sugar is supplied at a moisture level of about 0·05 per cent and stored in explosion-proof silos under warm conditions to avoid caking.

Dehydrated vegetables are usually passed over inspection belts where defective pieces are removed; then they are subjected to metal detection devices and magnets so that any metallic fragments are removed before the blending stage.

Blending and Mixing

The selection of blending machinery for soup mixes depends on the types of mixes used since these may vary from chicken noodle (large noodle content plus high fat/paste content) to spring vegetable (high vegetable content). As described in Chapter X, certain ingredients are specially treated prior to blending; stock, beef extract, hydrolysates and autolysates may be melted and then mixed with dry materials prior to extrusion and drying in high-vacuum ovens. After cooling, the product is reduced to size by means of pre-breakers. Special mixing machinery is required for soups with high vegetable or high fat contents.

One system of operation involves electronic sequence control. The soup mix ingredients are transferred to rows of aluminium or stainless steel hoppers arranged in two rows of twelve. They are fitted with vibrators which discharge into a central gang-way. A trolley moves along the gangway and the operator selects the formula for the mix on a control panel. The electrically driven batch hopper on the trolley is automatically filled with correct ingredients in sequence so that human error is avoided. The so-called batch skip on the hopper is next transferred to a mixer where spices and fats are added and where the mixing is carried out according to a predetermined cycle of fast and slow speeds. The now complete batch of soup mix is emptied into holding trolleys to await the filling operation.

Another system involves the use of Tote units. After mixing, the soup mix is filled into Tote bins; these bulk unit containers are between 42 and 110 cu. ft. capacity and they may be converted into discharge hoppers by means of Tote Tilt Units. The latter are stationary hopper types fitted with a screw conveyor discharge to the surge hoppers situated above the filling machines. The Tote bins are moved by conventional fork-lift or pallet trucks and the whole system is designed to afford ease of movement coupled with strict hygiene standards essential to any food handling operation. With bins of convenient size, double stacking is practised. The Tote Tilt Unit provides also a method for controlled discharge since the contents are tilted at a rate concomitant with the requirements of the filling machinery.

It should be appreciated that in all modern soup mix manufacturing plants gravity feed is practised wherever possible. This involves multi-storey building construction so that raw materials are first conveyed to the topmost floors for subsequent processing on lower floors and, usually, final packaging operations at the ground floor level. In this way an orderly controlled operation is possible and strict separation of materials may be achieved.

Mixing of 'normal' soup mixes may utilize the Lödige-Morton mixer. This type is used a great deal in Europe and it is also now in use in the United Kingdom. A 'hurling and whirling' principle of mixing is used and this handles many different types of ingredients. Streamlined ploughs are fixed to a central bar rotating inside a horizontal mixing drum. Thus the ingredients are hurled into the air where speedy and complete mixing is achieved. The drum may be jacketed for heating or cooling operations and the fat may be incorporated as a liquid, sprayed into the mix by centrifugal discs, or as a solid, where lumps are broken down by additionally fitted high-speed choppers. This versatile mixer is available in the United Kingdom in capacities up to 141 cu. ft. and all parts which come into contact with the soup mix are made of stainless steel. The output is high: 1,000 lb. batches may be mixed at the rate of 4–6 per hour.

Quality control procedures are many and varied and these differ greatly in detail from factory to factory. Basically, it is essential to control quality first by selection and processing of raw materials on the fact that one cannot make a first-class product from inferior ones. Secondly, one must operate such a system that actual *control* of quality is practised. It is quite useless to carry out detailed checks when finished goods are ready to dispatch. Samples of raw materials should always be approved by the laboratory prior to release to the factory operating floor. Samples should also be taken from mixes, prior to packaging, so that reconstitution tests may speedily confirm suitability for the filling machines.

Packaging, Filling and Packing

To ensure a long shelf life for a low moisture product such as a dry soup mix it is essential that the laminated film sachet possess a low moisture permeability. Oxygen permeability should be minimized and the pack should be mechanically strong to resist handling in distribution. Light is detrimental to many components of the soup mix so that the sachet requires to be opaque. Reverse printing of the pack is often practised, giving a good effect at point of sale; this printing is also scuff-proof. The usual soup pocket or sachet is a laminated combination of a number of films of varying properties, advantages being taken of the best feature of the individual materials. The sachet is always heat-sealed and this must remain so throughout the life of the soup mix. With soup mixes containing noodles the sachet must have special protection against 'noodle punc-

(By courtesy The Nestle Group)

A modern high-speed automatic soup mix filling machine, converting a roll of printed material into sachets, filling and sealing, Maggi soup mixes at the Aylesbury factory of the Nestle Group.

ture' since the latter will quickly lead to ingress of air to the contents. The actual selection of the laminate for the sachet will depend on a number of factors. Apart from cost one must consider the type of soup mix to be filled into it. Chicken noodle soup mix contains a viscous paste of the chicken

(By courtesy Brown & Polson Ltd.

Knorr soup mixes being packed on a modern high-speed packaging machine at the Paisley factory of Brown and Polson Ltd.

ingredient plus the noodles. These are filled in separate operations. A soup mix consisting of a granular material will require different handling from that consisting mainly of dehydrated vegetables. Hence the type of mix may often govern the choice of sachet and filler.

Materials used today for laminates include aluminium foil, polythene, rubber hydrochloride (PLIOFILM), paper, polypropylene, cellulose acetate, and polyvinylidene chloride (PVDC). The reader is referred to companies specializing in the production of laminated films for expert advice on the best product to use.

The soup pockets, pouches, packets or sachets may be preformed by machine and then filled by rotary filling machines or they may be made continuously from reel-fed printed stock. There are machines which automatically print, form and seal sachets at rates of 20,000 per hour and soup mix packaging machines which can make the sachets from printed stock and fill at about 12,000 packs per hour. Filling machinery is available for placing two types of ingredient in the soup packet and in this case double filling heads are provided. A speed of about 50 per minute is achieved with volumetric fill and heat-sealing. Statistical quality control is normally practised with automatic high-speed filling lines so that frequent weight checks may be

(*By courtesy Batchelors Foods Ltd.*)

High-speed machine for filling soup mixes into envelopes and hermetically sealing them.

plotted on charts and control of accurate contents maintained.

Catering packs of soup mixes may be 5 lb. cans or paper/ polythene bags. The latter are usually filled with soup mix to give 1 or 5 gallons of soup on reconstitution. Maximum shelf life of soup mixes can be obtained with a gas packed can. In this case the headspace of the filled can is evacuated and replaced with nitrogen. Since oxidative rancidity of the fat content of soup mixes is more liable to occur with lower moisture contents, the combination of low-oxygen headspace and very low moisture will give a very long shelf life to soup mixes even under tropical conditions. This always assumes, of course, that chemical and enzymatic changes are minimized by the correct technical procedures.

Soup mix sachets are usually hand-packed in multiples into display cartons made of chipboard and then finally into outer cases for palletization ready for despatch. Coding of soup mix sachets and containers is very important so that the date of manufacture and the batch origin may be subsequently checked. It sometimes happens that non-rotation of stock or prolonged exposure to adverse storage conditions occurs at the retail level and this usually results in consumer complaints. Therefore speedy stock turnover coupled with proper stock rotation will reduce this possibility to a minimum.

INDEX

APV —the leading name for batch **and** continuous soup processing plant

Jacketed Pans—steam heated for batch capacities up to 100 gal.

Paraflow Plate Heaters—high speed continuous heating and cooling.

Rota-Pro—scraped surface heating and cooling of viscous soups.

U.H.T. Plants—sterilisation prior to aseptic canning.

Plate Evaporators—rapid continuous stock concentration with maximum flavour retention.

Homogenisers—permanent dispersion of cream and fat content.

Pipe fittings, valves and cocks—a complete range of stainless steel ancillaries.

THE A.P.V. COMPANY LTD · CRAWLEY · SUSSEX

Telephone: Crawley 27777 · Telex: 87237
Telegrams: Anaclastic Crawley Telex

Saromex onion is enough to make any public analyst cry.

Our onion has all the tear-jerking qualities of the original package. But this isn't the big reason it can make case-hardened analysts weep.

It's simply that if all ingredients were as pure as our Saromex spices, these men would be out of a job.

Take onion powder.

It can have anything up to 50 million bacteria baddies per gramme.

Baddies that thrive on cooking.

Baddies that curtail the shelf life of a product.

Baddies that can make unwitting customers ill.

The Saromex process cuts down the chances of such things happening to you to one in five million.

The bacteria count per gramme of Saromex has a ceiling of 10.

What's more we achieve this in a way that leaves all the flavour goodies behind.

So if you want more control and fewer comebacks look into the spices we refine by the Saromex process.

Bush Boake Allen
London N1 Tel 01-253 1000
A division of Albright & Wilson Ltd

Kellie engineering makes good soups better

Kellie equipment has a good name in the food industry. We supply individual items or complete plants and, in every case, Kellie engineering ensures the very best results. Equipment used in soup manufacture includes the two items shown.
Please write for a complete list.

Stainless Steel Boiling Pan is a non-tilting type steam jacketed pan which is available in many sizes, the most popular for soup production being that with a 100 gallon working capacity.

The Kellie PF20 Rotary Piston Filler is a versatile, fully-automatic 20 station machine, easily installed in any filling line and quickly adjusted to suit any container up to 32 fluid ounces capacity. Smaller capacity machines are also available.

ROBERT KELLIE & SON LIMITED
40 EAST DOCK STREET, DUNDEE Telephone: Dundee 25522/6
Telex: Chamcom Dundee 76243 for Kellie
A member of the Vokes Group with world-wide representation

THE NATURAL CHOICE
FOR FOOD MANUFACTURERS

YESTAMIN DRIED YEASTS

YEATEX YEAST EXTRACT

CASSEROLE COMPOUND MEAT FLAVOURS

TRENT YEAST EXTRACT CO LTD

A MEMBER OF THE
BOVRIL GROUP OF COMPANIES

BURTON-ON-TRENT, STAFFS., ENGLAND   Telex 34322   Telephone 3781

Before
in the

get in touch with Spi

When you've got a name to live up to, you need to make sure the ingredients you use come from peop who value a reputation as highly as you do.

Which is a pretty strong argument for coming to Spice & Flavour Services for the spices that add ze: to your soups. With the number of famous names the food industry who entrust us with their spice and seasoning requirements, we can't afford to giv

If you'd like to know, in det
just how we could help v
your particular problem, con:

you get soup,

¿ Flavour Services

/ou anything but the best.
'here's a complete range of spices available
nder our brand name Spiceta. Produced in one of
he most up-to-date plants in the country at our
ew premises in Cam. Plus a highly experienced
eam of spice specialists who can help to
ormulate exactly the mix **you** need to keep
our nose in front.

SPICE & FLAVOUR SERVICES LTD.,
Draycott Mills, Cam, Dursley, Glos, GL11 5NA
Telephone: Dursley 2244. Telex: 43319

cpc

'Snowflake' starches for soup manufacture

a *new* range of
amylopectin starches,
modified or
unmodified,
to serve every
food processing need . . .

CPC
'Snowflake' starches for soup manufacture

Meet three soup starches from Corn Products 'Snowflake' range — a range of modified amylopectin starches specially formulated to meet changing patterns in food manufacture. Designed-in qualities include long-storage life, acid resistance, good clarity, texture and flavour, microbiological quality to meet NCA specifications — vital to the production of successful soups and baby foods. Available as standard products or tailor-made to suit special needs.

SNOWFLAKE 30201 (B9102) . . .
for thickening. An unmodified amylopectin starch for general purpose thickening. High initial viscosity and good gel clarity.

SNOWFLAKE 30210 (B9150) . . .
for long-storage life. Cross-bonded waxy starch. Slightly lower viscosity than 30201. Excellent shear-, acid- and heat-resistance. Short, soft gel, of good texture and clarity. Stable under normal storage conditions for very long periods.

SNOWFLAKE 04857 . . .
tailor-made for tomatoes. Specially formulated for specific market needs in tomato-based soups and sauces. Excellent acid-, heat- and shear-resistance. Provides *very* stable gels of short consistency and soft texture. As for stability — when autoclaved for 1-hour under test at pH of 4.3, viscosity was virtually unchanged.

For full details of the new 'Snowflake' range — write or telephone for your copy of *'Snowflake' Food Starches,* a complete full-colour guide to starches for the modern food processor.

CORN PRODUCTS
a member of CPC Europe

(In the South) Horsenden Lane South, Perivale, Middlesex. (01-998 2800)
(In the North) Trafford Park, Manchester 17, 1PA (061-TRA 2571)

HOLDENS

for can coatings